D0173850

The Mural Writer

*The unlikely story of an outcast
who fulfilled an extraordinary purpose*

LaShelle VanHouten

The Writing Show • Agoura Hills, California

Leopoldo Espinoza Madrigal

Published by The Writing Show
P.O. Box 2970
Agoura Hills, CA 91376
paula@writingshow.com
www.writingshow.com

Cover design: Jeannine Taylor
Book interior design: LaShelle VanHouten, Jeannine Taylor, and Paula Berinstein
Author photo: Heather Hammond, Capture Me Photography
Editor: Paula Berinstein

© 2014 LaShelle VanHouten, info@themuralwriter.com

All rights reserved. No part of this book may be reproduced in any form or by any means without permission in writing from the publisher, except for the inclusion of brief quotations in a review.

ISBN 978-0-986030451

Book Web site (includes all the photos),
www.themuralwriter.com
The My Father's Love Board Web site,
www.myfatherslove.info

Dedication

This book is dedicated to any person who has ever felt unloved.

To my children and granddaughter, Kaleigh, Ty and Ellianna, I hope this story will show you the real meaning of love and purpose.

To Ed's children, I pray this story will give you peace, contentment, understanding, and forgiveness.

Disclaimer

Testimonio .

This is the story of Edgar Frederick Lantzer as told to me by him. This is the way he remembered the events of his life. It is also a memoir of my experiences with Ed and the events that I witnessed. Ed told me his life story, and I put the information into scenes in a creative way to the best of my ability with the information he gave me. I wanted the reader to have the experience of stepping into Ed's shoes and to travel with him on his journey throughout his life. This book is not intended to bring hurt to anyone; it is a book about redemption and love. Most important, it is intended to bring purpose, hope, and healing for all who read it.

*EL LIBRo
ESTÁ SUSTENTADO EN . . . .*

Acknowledgments

I would like to thank all of the people that God placed in my life at just the right time for just the right purpose so that I could achieve God's will for me. You all became my relay team, handing the baton off to the next along the way.

First and foremost, thank you to my Heavenly Father for giving me the most incredible job. This has been such an amazing adventure. Most of all, thank you for loving me no matter what.

Thank you to Ed Lantzer for sharing your incredible story with me. I made a promise to you, and I hope that I fulfilled that promise in a way that is pleasing to you. Thank you for your trust, and thank you for teaching me to look at the world with my eyes wide open.

Thank you to my editor, Paula Berinstein. I could not have done this without your invaluable help. I will be forever grateful.

Thank you to my husband, Ken. Words cannot express what your love and support have meant to me. You stood by my side through this whole process. At times it was difficult, but you did not waver. I love you and am so grateful for the gift that God gave me on that September day when we met.

Thank you to my mother, Pauline Hammond. Without you, I would not have been able to reach my goals. From my very first thoughts and feelings, I recognized your love. I could feel it so strongly, radiating from you to me. You have shown me how to be a strong woman, even when things seemed dark and hopeless. Your strength and example always pulled me through.

Thank you to my children. You are the joy of my life. I love you both with all of my heart. Through ups and downs, our love has stood the test of time. You have taught me as much as I hope I've taught you.

Thank you to my stepsons, Justin and Josh. I appreciate your support more than you will ever know.

Thank you to my siblings: Christina, Tamera, Jeannine, Stephanie, Larry, and Heather. You are all so special to me in very unique ways. Each one of you taught me something so powerful that I have carried with me throughout my life. Thank you for having my back, always. Thank you for your unconditional love and support. I love you all.

Thank you to Dad, Diane, Jeff, and Birdie for all of your love and support, which have been so special and meaningful to me. I love you all.

Thank you to my stepfather, Larry Hammond. I want you to know how important the things you taught me and did for me throughout my life are to me. I am so grateful.

Thank you to Aunt Sandy and Uncle Stan. You have always been there for our family. There were times during our lives that we could not have survived without your help. I will never forget what you have done.

Thank you to Mike and Ida Fender for teaching me about God as a child. You were the first people to introduce me to Him. You unselfishly picked my siblings and me up for Sunday school each week. I have remembered that all of these years. Thank you so much.

Thank you to Larry and Debbie Brown. You taught me so much about God. You taught me so much about being a caring, faithful person. I continue to carry those lessons with me every day. Thank you!

Thank you to Anita, Dawn, and Stacy. You are my oldest and best friends. Even when we don't talk for long periods of time, when we reconnect, it is as if no time has passed. Thank you for always being my friends. Even during difficult times, you have stood by me. I cherish our friendship!

Thank you to Cherie and Melissa for your friendship. Our dinners and long talks have meant so much to me. You both keep me laughing. Thank you!

Thank you to Sharon Stockford for teaching me to be responsible and determined. You became a second mother to me as my cheerleading coach. You taught me to have the drive and passion and to go after my dreams. Thank you.

Thank you to Mrs. Poteet for not allowing me to stay mediocre. When I first sat in your high school English class at Kalkaska High School, I thought that I could just do enough to slide by. You would not allow that. You refused to let me fail. I cannot tell you how much of an impact that has had on my life. Thank you!

Thank you to Thomas and Barb Ryan for teaching me about dignity. You are the reason I went back to college in my thirties, which has led me to where I am now. Thank you for being a positive role model for me. I will remember you always.

Thank you to the My Father's Love Board Members: Paul, Dale, Woody, and Lon. We have been Ed's relay team for so long now. We have worked hard to keep Ed's panels alive. Thank you for your undying dedication to our friend. Thank you for your support during the writing of this book.

Thank you to the Kalkaska Public School staff members I have worked with over the years. I could not have asked for a better group of people to spend my days with. I hold you all in the highest regard.

Thank you to Brian Harbour for giving me a chance. When I first sat in your office pleading for a job, you did not turn me away. Even though you really didn't have room for a new teacher, you made a place for me. You gave me a shot. That moment led me to Ed and this story. Thank you, Brian!!

Thank you to Kay Sander and the Evansville group for all you did for Ed during his stay in Evansville. Thank you for all that you did for Ed's panels. Thank you for sharing your stories with me. I was so moved by each and every one of you.

Thank you to all the people I interviewed for the book. Thank you for sharing your stories.

Thank you to my students. I became your teacher, but each one of you taught me so much. My life has become so much richer because of you.

Thank you to the Charlevoix Public Library for a beautiful place to write a book. I spent a year and a half with you. I wrote the first word and the last word surrounded by your welcoming walls. Thank you for opening up your doors for me.

Thank you to the village of Kalkaska for raising Ed and me and for always being a place to call home.

Foreword

Ed Lantzer is among the most complex, irritable, compassionate, cantankerous, kind, singularly driven, and supremely talented persons I have ever met.

My introduction began innocently enough when Dale Hull, a colleague and art aficionado, said at a meeting we were both attending, "I have just seen one of the more extraordinary works of art of my lifetime, and we need to help underwrite a public display of it." Ironically, the meeting Dale and I were attending was a meeting to organize and produce the summer events connected with Petoskey, Michigan's hugely successful C.S. Lewis Festival. What none of us knew at that meeting, except Dale, was that Ed Lantzer had been profoundly influenced by the writings of C.S. Lewis. That Lewis's understanding of man's relationship with God was reflected brilliantly in Ed's artwork—120 linear feet of marquetry which had remained hidden away for years in an empty and largely ignored warehouse in Kalkaska, Michigan—a warehouse in which Ed also had been hiding away, literally.

Because of Dale's enthusiasm, the C.S. Lewis Festival underwrote the first public display of Ed's murals in Petoskey. We had anticipated that hundreds would turn out to view the murals. In fact, thousands turned out. What was to be a two-week art show turned into a two-year exhibition with Ed in place as the resident art director. So began the remarkable and continuing journey of Ed's murals.

How this artwork was found is, in itself, remarkable. How Ed Lantzer created it, and why, will keep you turning the pages in *The Mural Writer*. It is a story about lost dreams, unwitting love, unlikely friendships, and how a small group of people came together to keep Ed's dream alive.

One might think it impossible to accurately describe the many sides of this man; yet, in this thrilling account, LaShelle VanHouten does just that—with tremendous love and insight. LaShelle adeptly shifts from the objective observer to the subjective storyteller as she relates the journey from initial meeting to deep and abiding friendship.

love

A friend once said of Ed that he had a twinkle in his eye but the devil in his heart. There were many conflicts at work in his consciousness—he repeated more than once that he was told early on he did not know how to love—so that the daily challenge for Ed was how to express love. Ed was very aware that God loved him and that God's love became clear to him through art. Ed was not afraid to die, but he was very concerned about how God would view the way Ed led his life. It is a question we all have to face. Ed's hope was that when he met God, face to face, God would say to him, "Job well done."

This is a story of hope and redemption through the eyes of someone who came to know Ed Lantzer intimately and who has chosen to share his remarkable story with all of us.

David Crouse
Executive Producer, "The Magic Never Ends: The Life and Faith of C.S. Lewis"

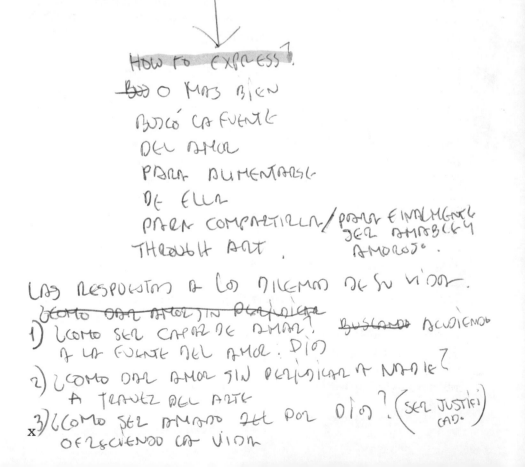

HOW TO EXPRESS?
O MAS BIEN
BUSCÓ LA FUENTE
DEL AMOR
PARA ALIMENTARSE
DE ELLA
PARA COMPARTIRLA / PARA FINALMENTE
THROUGH ART.   SER AMABLE Y
                AMOROSO.

LAS RESPUESTAS A LOS DILEMAS DE SU VIDA.

1) ¿COMO SER CAPAZ DE AMAR? BUSCANDO ACUDIENDO
   A LA FUENTE DEL AMOR: DIOS

2) ¿COMO DAR AMOR SIN PERJUDICAR A NADIE?
   A TRAVEZ DEL ARTE

3) ¿COMO SER AMADO DEL POR DIOS? (SER JUSTIFI-
   OFRECIENDO LA VIDA   CADO.)

Preface

PERJUDICAR

The intent of this book is to share the extraordinary life of artist Edgar Lantzer with you, the reader. What made him extraordinary? The answer is simple: his faith. Ed was imperfect, but his faith in God and His calling was not.

Ed had many painful memories that were not easy to share. He struggled with an inability to write or draw, he was bullied and mistreated, considered the black sheep of his family, but worst of all, he felt that he didn't know how to show love without hurting someone. Because of these struggles, his life was full of twists and turns and was more than turbulent. Yet he became an artist who chose homelessness during parts of his life so that he could answer God's call to create a large-scale mural out of wood. This mural, which is made up of thirty panels using small diamond wood pieces, was designed to move the world through God's story of love and to tell Ed's own story using hidden symbolism through sacred geometry. Ed couldn't show love, yet God selected him to tell the most beautiful love story ever told. That is extraordinary!

EXPL
RO
VER
LA
EXPLI
CACION
DE
ESTO.

When I first met Ed later in his life (he was seventy-three), he asked me to write his story. We met in April of 2005 after being introduced through my school superintendent, and from that meeting on, my students and I worked with Ed as he taught us his craft of marquetry. Each day as we worked side by side, Ed shared the stories of his life with me—his joys, struggles, and pains. Through these stories, we developed an unlikely friendship that I will forever hold dear. Ed had one request: that I write his story, but not until he was with the Father. I agreed to be the writer and I also kept my promise.

WHY?

I spent four years with Ed as an artist, friend, and biographer, and everything that I know, I gathered from him, so at times in this book there will be very detailed descriptions, and at other times, not very much. In Ed's later years, he struggled with his timeline—the dates, ages, and times that events occurred. We worked together to get this as close as possible. I remember asking Ed on many occasions how old he was during a certain event, and when he struggled, we decided the best we could do was to narrow the date down to a month, year, or even a decade. I then spent two years after Ed's death researching what I could to get the timeline accurate. This became the most difficult and time-consuming jigsaw puzzle I have ever put together.

I interviewed many people for this book. Some were eager to share their experiences with Ed. Others were not, so I let them be. For some, remembering was just too painful, which I understood and respected. As I went along, I found that some of the information from the interviews pulled me away from Ed's story, his view of how the reel of his life played out. I was so grateful to fill in many blanks after these interviews, but I also made a decision that I wouldn't let the perspective of other people's memories move me away from Ed's own. I recognized that if you ask five different people about the same event, they would probably have five different memories. As a result, I chose to focus on Ed's perspective. This is his story after all, and the way he remembered it to be.

My first decision as I prepared to write this book was how to tell Ed's story. Would it be a biography or a memoir? I quickly realized that I could not tell it in the strict, factual manner of a biography. Ed was just too emotional a person for that, so the answer was clear: it had to be a memoir, with me as the narrator. Sometimes you will hear me and other times you will not, but I am always there. Ed and I decided not to share every detail of his life in a complete timeline, but to tell the stories that had an impact on his life and its direction in a chronological order. There will be times that I skip a section of Ed's life. It is not that those events are unimportant, but they do not fit into the flow of this book. As an artist myself, I wanted to paint a picture of Ed's journey. I wanted to put you, the reader, in his shoes so that you could travel along with him, just as I did as I wrote each scene. When I reached the end of his life, I truly felt that I had lived it with him, and I believe you will too.

Writing this book was never a choice and I knew that the first day my eyes met Ed's. This is my calling from God and I answered the call with eagerness and gratefulness. This story is a beautiful portrait of an outcast in society, someone who was misunderstood by many. Ed was considered a misfit, yet he was chosen for a very special

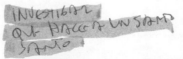

DIOS ESCRIBE DERECHO EN RENGLONES TORCIDOS.

job. In reading this book, it is possible that when you turn the last page, you will do so a changed person. That is what happened to me as I wrote this incredible story. I started this eight-year journey one person, and have become someone very different—someone with newfound faith, someone with more understanding of the world, someone who is finally content, and someone that can say truly feels and can show love, probably for the first time in my life. I did not expect this or even consider the possibility. I hope, in the end, you will feel the same way.

LaShelle VanHouten
Charlevoix, Michigan
December 21, 2013

AN AUTOBIOGRAPHY TELLS THE STORY OF A LIFE
WILE MEMOIR TELLS A STORY FROM A LIFE.

↓

RHANGELISMO CONTRA UDA DE CRISTO.
DE ED SABEMOS SV UDA
DESDE LA EXPERIENCIA

ED
ES UNA
DE TANTAS
PERSPECTIVAS
QUE SE HAN
ACERCADO AL
MISTERIO DE
CRISTO.
EL ARTE ES
SU TESTIMONIO
DE ELLO.

AL IGUAL QUE LAS MEMORIAS.
DE CRISTO QUE SON ESCRITAS
DESDE UA UDA Y LAS INTERACCIÓN
DE OTROS CON ÉL Y UAN
MAS ALLÁ DEL MOMENTO DE SU
MUERTE.
GRACIAS ALAS PALABRAS DE ED.
LAS MEMORIAS DE CRISTO Y AHORA
TAMBIEN LAS DE ED TIENEN
CONTINUIDAD. PUES SON ESCRITAS
FROM A LIFE.

Su objetivo.

1

"The very first tear he made was so deep that I thought it had gone right into my heart."

C.S. Lewis, The Chronicles of Narnia

WAS CATHOLIC?

On the day before Ed's funeral, I cradled two little pieces of wood in my palm and rubbed them as I waited for the iron to warm up. With tears streaming down my face, I opened my hand and stared at them. Each piece was cut into the shape of a diamond. They were two of millions of pieces my dear friend had created over the years so that he could write his amazing story. He didn't use a pencil, and he did not use a piece of paper, because he couldn't. Instead, he constructed his story as pictures made out of wood. That story took thirty years to tell, and it changed Ed's turbulent life. It also changed mine.

I heard the steam blowing from the iron, so I gently placed the diamond shapes on the dining room table and draped the new white-collared dress shirt over the ironing board. So many memories scurried through my mind as I moved the iron back and forth. It was as if they were traveling on a conveyor belt, and I tried to hold onto each one for fear of losing them.

I thought about the obstacles Ed had overcome so that he could stay faithful to God and the things God had asked him to do. I remembered how he had walked away from his life and chosen to be homeless so that he could answer God's call. Ed let nothing stop him from his job, from his purpose. Not the times he was pushed off his bike or called a half-wit. Not when people threw rocks or snowballs at him. Not even when someone spit on him as they passed him on the street. Many people thought my friend was worthless and a bum. For much of his life he looked the part, but he wasn't. He was one of the most remarkable people you could ever meet, as you will see.

I thought about all of our talks. Over the last five years of Ed's life, he shared his story with me. He told me all of the good and all of the bad; he did not withhold a thing. That is not an easy thing for anyone to do, but Ed had nothing to hide.

I picked up a can of Magic Sizing and sprayed. This shirt had to be perfect. A man so special to me, and for the most special occasion, would wear it. Several of my tears blended into the sizing and disappeared into the wrinkles. I had to stop for a moment. The job I had been given on this day was just too emotional and too intimate.

I thought about the soiled white dress shirt he had worn every day for the last few months. He had refused to take it off. Today he would get a brand new clean one.

I looked at the remainder of his life—besides his story, I mean—sitting in a box near his two wood pieces. I pulled out one item at a time. These were the things he had held dear. They were the only things he carried with him all of these years. There were pictures of his children, the ones he had lost. There was his senior yearbook from 1950, and all of his report cards neatly protected inside a purple velvet diploma holder. Ed had kept pictures of his mother and his wife. He had his father's Social Security card. And there was a picture of Ed sitting next to his young friend Nathan, whom he'd met just months before. He also had a bookmark and Bible verses given to him by his grandmother.

These things meant the world to Ed. He kept cards and letters from the few people in his life who had reached out to him. He had a letter his brother had written to him during World War II, and next to it was his brother's death notice. I knew that these two items brought him pain, but deep, deep down, he had still harbored a speck of love for his brother.

I unsnapped his worn brown leather wallet. As I looked through the contents, I pulled out the card given to him

2

when he had officially been declared homeless. I looked at his picture. There was a sparkle in his eyes and a wide grin on his face. This was not a typical reaction to homelessness. I also noticed many library cards, one from every town in which he had lived. Ed couldn't write, but he loved to read and study.

I put the wallet down and pulled more items from the box. He had kept a copy of *Traverse, Northern Michigan's Magazine* and a plastic bobble head of Big Boy. He also had a copy of his favorite movie, "Fiddler on the Roof." This had been my last gift to him. I cried as I realized that we would never have the chance to watch it together as we had planned. I could hear Ed singing "Sunrise, Sunset" in his perfect pitch as I pulled the last item out of the box. It was a picture of me. I had forgotten that he had that. I wept as I remembered the day he asked for it. "I want to keep this with the other pictures that mean something to me," he'd said.

One by one I put each item back into the box. *How can a life come down to just one small box?* I asked myself. But that was all that Ed had needed. I went back to the dress shirt and continued to move the iron over it until every crease was gone. I carefully put the pressed dress shirt onto a hanger and hooked it to the chair next to me. I stared at it. *This will be the last shirt that he will ever wear,* I thought. Tears covered my face as I realized that I had just completed one of the last things I could do for my friend, my unlikely friend.

I was one of many people God placed into Ed's life to help him complete his job so that he could become "The Mural Writer" for Him. There was a group of people that God sent at just the right time to help Ed in specific ways throughout his journey. We became Ed's relay team, each handing off the baton to the next when it was time, so that Ed could tell the world his story of love. The last part of my job, my purpose, is to share Ed's personal story with you. It is a story you will find incredible. It is a story that is even unbelievable at times, but true.

I turned from Ed's shirt and picked up the two pieces of wood and held them tightly in my hand again and rubbed. Those pieces have changed the lives of many people. I believe they can change yours too. Let me explain.

Ed Lantzer's first experience with wood was less than spiritual. When he was born, his family was living in a chicken coop! It was the Great Depression, and times were tough, but Ed's father, Ervin Lantzer, had managed to purchase property in the rural town of Kalkaska, Michigan, known for its wild beauty. When he acquired the empty lot, an old chicken coop came with it, so Ervin, a carpenter, used what he had and transformed the shack into the family's residence.

Before the family moved in, the chicken coop had sat abandoned for years. The only occupant was a wild animal or two. The structure was built out of old barn wood, and the grayish planks covered the perimeter in a horizontal direction. Every hole and crack in the wood showed its age. Once a tree, alive and fresh, it sat tired and worn. But the day Ervin and Ruby moved their family in, the chicken coop became a home.

By the time Ed turned four, the home no longer resembled a chicken coop except for a chicken or hog running through the space here and there. The coop had been divided up into separate living areas. The kitchen, dining, and living room flowed into each other. Ervin had built most of the furniture by hand. A small room was sectioned off for the master bedroom, and the children shared a loft that was split into two: a dormitory-style for the four girls in the front, and a small corner for Ed and his older brother, Junior, in the back. Ervin had also added a small Michigan basement to store vegetables from the garden and an addition off the back of the home that he used as a shed.

Most people would be embarrassed by these humble beginnings, but Ed didn't know the difference. To him, life seemed enchanted, at least when he was outside. He spent his young days roaming the land and going on adventures. One day, Ruby sent him out to do his morning duty. He was assigned two daily chores: to collect eggs and to pump water. As he headed toward their makeshift hen house with a battered basket in hand, he was swept away by nature. He breathed in the summer air, skipping through the tall grass whistling a tune as he swung the basket back and forth. After he had gathered the eggs and visited each

4

chicken, his next stop was the hogs. He opened the gate and entered as several of his animal friends ran towards him snorting.

"Hi, pigs. How are you today?" he said. He took turns patting each one on the top of their heads with his small fingers. One of the hogs pushed his nose into Ed's hip. "You had your breakfast," Ed giggled. "I have to go now so I can say hello to the cows. Okay? I will be back in the morning." Ed patted each hog one more time and made his way towards the pasture.

After Ed delivered his greetings, he found a spot under a large maple and sat against the trunk. He slid down onto his back into the long blades of grass and gazed into the sky. He could feel the heat of the rising sun. He could also feel energy all around. He had no idea what it was, but that energy represented warmth. It felt like a cocoon of tenderness.

"Morning, God. It's Edgar. Are you up there?" Ed squinted as the rays of the sun became stronger. "I just wanted to wish you a happy day," he said with a wide grin.

Just then a yell came from the distance. "Edgar!" Ed bolted up, grabbed the basket of eggs and started running towards the call. "Edgar! Edgar! Where are you?"

Ed's little legs ran faster. He knew he was in trouble. As he neared the coop, Ruby was standing in the doorway with a deep scowl on her face. The premature lines around her eyes and mouth told her story of struggle. She rubbed her pregnant belly as she waited for her youngest son to appear in the distance.

Ed's amber eyes matched the color of his wavy hair that was blowing against the wind. "I'm coming!" he yelled.

As he came into view, Ruby pressed her fists deep into her sides and waited. Ed knew he had been sent off for one job, and by the look on his mother's face, he realized he had taken too long, again.

When he reached the coop, he stopped, panting, and handed his mother the basket.

"We've been waiting!" Ruby said.

Ed gave her his best "sorry" look. She held the basket in one hand and opened the creaky door with the other to let him pass through. Before entering, he moved slightly to the right to let a cackling hen run outside.

"Go change that shirt before breakfast," Ruby demanded.

Ed looked down and saw mud smeared diagonally on his front. "Okay," he said as he made his way across the sandy floor of the coop.

"And watch out for those chicken droppings."

Ed looked down and stepped over the pile. He quickly ran upstairs and made his way to his bedroom. He pulled out a clean hand-me-down shirt from an old bureau and slipped it on. Then he followed the sound and smell of the sizzling eggs back down to the kitchen.

It wasn't an auspicious beginning to a life, but Ed was happy. It didn't take much to make him feel that way. He had his family, he had the animals, and he had nature.

He also had books. He learned to read at an early age, earlier than most. His parents were surprised when he first read something to them, and even more so when he began showing early signs of above-average intelligence, maybe even genius. To his family, Ed seemed wise beyond his four years. Both Ervin and Ruby recognized this and encouraged him by surrounding him with books whenever they could. They had high hopes that this would be the child to break out of their poverty-stricken life. Ed's future was looking bright, and his possibilities seemed limitless. After years of uncertainty, the Lantzer household was finally settled and life seemed to be going smoothly. But things are seldom as they seem.

On December 27, 1936, Ed's little brother, Otto Lee, was born. Ed was the second to the youngest child until Otto joined the family. His birth taught Ed the meaning of love. Ed loved his parents and he loved his other siblings, but Otto was different. He was special. Maybe it was because Ed had always felt like the baby. Or maybe it was because at four years old, this was his first experience feeling love.

Ed so enjoyed playing with Otto. One day after bringing in water for the family, Ed sprinted to his room. He climbed up on the crib bars and leaned over to pet the baby's soft hair and make goofy faces until he smiled. He spent hours just talking to him. Some days, Ed even climbed right into the crib with Otto. Nothing was more important to Ed than the time he spent with this baby boy.

But then, within a few days, Ed began to feel ill. He started to run a fever and a red rash covered his body. In no time, his mother realized that he had scarlet fever. It was sweeping through the small town of Kalkaska and many villagers were becoming ill. Ruby realized that she had to quarantine Ed from the family, and especially Otto, who was almost a month old. This was difficult for Ed, but he did as he was told and hunkered down until he was free of the symptoms.

It was a cold winter in Kalkaska. The town was always hit hard because of its location smack in the middle of the Snow Belt. The fever had taken its toll on Ed. It had reached a level so high that his parents worried about the effect on his brain. But finally the day came when Ed was released from his scarlet fever prison and allowed to go outside to play. He put on his winter clothing, covering the remaining red spots on his skin, and darted outside.

As the door slammed, the weathered wood plank siding on the chicken coop shifted. Ed ran through the snow as if he were a wild stallion finally released from captivity. *This is the best day!* he thought. He ran in circles and then fell back, spread-eagle style into the white fluff. He spent an hour in the glistening snow and then wiped the flakes off his shoulders as he trudged to the door. He kicked off his hand-me-down rubber boots, wool coat, and tattered gloves. *That's right!* he thought. *I can play with Otty!!* Young Ed skipped to Otto's room and mounted the crib bars.

"Hi, Otty Lee, how are you today?" Ed asked in a squeaky voice. Otto stared at him, watching every move Ed made. He was very curious about his older brother. "This little light of mine, I'm gonna let it shine," Ed sang as he moved his tiny pointer finger side to side. He loved to sing, and Otto watched his lips move as he did. "This little light of mine, I'm gonna let it shine." He continued until the call for dinner roared through the house. Ed hopped down and marched through the door, "Don't let Satan blow it out, No! I'm gonna let it shine." Ed followed the aroma towards the dining area. He found his chair, pushed a hen off the seat, and plopped down in anticipation.

The Lantzer household was finally getting back to normal, and each member back to their responsibilities. Several days had passed when Otto started to run a fever. Ruby held him in her arms, swaying back and forth as she tried to comfort him. The heat radiated off his small frame. "Please, God, no!" she said. Ed could see that she was very concerned because of the scarlet fever epidemic that had just toured the family home. Just shy of a month old, Otto was not as strong as the older children, so Ruby rubbed his head and body with a cool cloth night and day, hoping to break the fever.

But the fever continued, and as the days went by, Otto became sicker and sicker. The whole family worried about their new addition, including Ed. Before they knew it, Otto's influenza symptoms had turned into pneumonia. Ed knelt by his crib and quietly prayed for his little brother. "Please help him!" he pleaded. But on January 26, 1937, little Otto Lee died.

After returning home from the burial, the older children tried to help Ruby to the dining room table. Her piercing cry traveled through the coop. "No, no, no!" Ervin tried to embrace her as if he could shield her from the pain, but she pushed him away. She was inconsolable.

Ed, too, was in deep despair. His little heart felt too heavy to hold up. He paced back and forth trying to understand what was happening. *This can't be true!* he thought. He tightened his little fists and ran up to his parents.

By this time, Ruby was sitting at the table with her head buried in her arms. Her whole body moved with each sob. She looked up as Ed bounded into the room.

"I want Otty Lee back!" Ed demanded.

Ruby paused for a moment, and then her eyes penetrated through Ed. "This is your fault!" she said. "You did this! You took my baby away!"

Ed stared at her in sheer terror. *This is my fault?*

Ruby yelled, "Why? Why didn't you warm your hands before you touched him?" Ed rewound to the last day he had played with Otto. He remembered that day after he played in the snow and crawled on the crib bars. "He would still be here if you had just done that simple thing! You killed him!" Ed was motionless. "Is that how you show love?

Didn't you love Otto enough? Don't you know how to love?"
Ed listened. "No! You don't!"

Ruby fell to the floor, weeping uncontrollably. Young Ed just stood there for a moment and watched his mother mourn. His heart felt heavy for the first time in his short life. He didn't know what that feeling was until that moment. Tears rolled down his face as he slowly turned around and walked hunched over towards the loft stairway. He paused and looked towards Heaven.

"Am I bad?" He looked to the floor. "Yes, I am," he said, and slithered away.

SE FUÉ LEJOS.

NO COMO LA PIEDRA.
IMPERTURBABLE

EL AMOR
QUE MATA
¿POR QUÉ?
Dios?

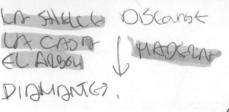

2

*"Since it is so likely that children will meet
cruel enemies, let at least have heard of
brave knights and heroic courage."*

*C.S. Lewis, On Stories and other Essays on
Literature*

The four barn wood walls became a protector for the
Lantzer family during their time of grief. The wood was like
God's arms placed around them to lovingly hold them up as
they attempted to move on. This was not an easy task.
Ruby showed little emotion, while Ervin tried to keep the
children busy.

Ed spent more and more time with his father. If they
weren't working at the local sawmill together, they were in
Ervin's workshop cutting leftover wood into small square
shapes. Ed's father was experimenting with a parquetry
technique he had learned from his father. It was a
technique that had been handed down from generation to
generation.

One day, Ed sat on a stool as he watched Ervin come
up with interesting designs.

"Why do you cut it that way?" Ed asked.

"So the pieces will fit together. Watch."

Ervin placed each piece onto a larger piece of wood. He
alternated a light piece of wood with a dark piece. Placing
row after row, he created a large square, then looked at Ed
to see how he was reacting.

"What does this look like?" he said.

Ed's face lit up. "A chess board!"

TENGO UN IMPRESION DE QUE EL LIBRO FUE MODIFICANDO DESPUÉS DE ENTREVISTARME

"Very good!"

"Can I try?"

"Sure."

Ervin handed Ed a pile of squares. Ed tried to copy his father's design. He dipped a dark square into the glue on a board, and then next to that he carefully set a light piece of wood, positioning the two pieces so they fit perfectly together. He froze for a moment and stared at the two squares, and a magical expression crossed his face. It was as though he had just opened a hidden treasure chest to reveal the shiny gold inside.

"Wow!" Ed said, and began to giggle as he reached for another dark piece to continue his pattern. He looked up at Ervin watching him with pride and said, "Hey, Dad, can I have your chess board?"

"It looks like you can make your own." Ervin smiled as he went back to work.

Ed could watch his father work with wood for hours. The tools mesmerized him. The saws and knives were strategically placed by size on the homemade workbench. After recognizing Ed's growing interest, Ervin was ready to hand the tools over to him. He felt that he was finally ready to learn more about wood and parquetry. This was the beginning of a newfound love. When Ed was in the workshop, he felt happy. There was no guilt and no pain, only peace. Ed also had a strong feeling that his father's technique would hold great importance for him someday. An innate feeling of something very meaningful to come shimmered through him.

As Ed got older, his fascination with wood increased. Ervin and Ed spent hours walking in the woods with Ervin pointing out the varieties of wood species that lived in the Northern Michigan landscape.

"Look at this one, Ed," Ervin said on a particular day when Ed was seven years old.

They walked towards a towering tree. The stout branches appeared to be reaching towards the sky.

"What is it?" Ed asked.

"This is a northern red oak. Did you know that the color of this wood changes depending on the soil it grows in?"

"Really?" Ed's eyes widened.

ROBLE

"Yes. The change is due to the composition of the soil."

"What do you mean?"

"For instance, the wood color from a tree grown in Michigan can look different than a tree grown in Tennessee." This revelation was exciting to Ed. He stored this information away for later use.

Ervin continued. "One way to recognize this tree is to look at the vein-like bark. Notice the shiny stripe down the center of the bark ridges. The northern red oak is the only tree with striping all the way down the trunk."

Ed nodded in acknowledgment and they moved on.

Ervin felt that Ed needed to know each species of tree to become a good carpenter and craftsman. He didn't have to worry. Ed was an enthusiastic student. While sitting in the classroom at school, Ed couldn't wait to get home. Instead of listening to the daily lesson, he daydreamed about what he was going to build next. As soon as the students were released, Ed ran home, did his chores, and went into the workshop.

Soon, Ed and his father started to compete. Ervin would build something and then Ed would build something, and then they would compare to see whose was better. Usually it was Ervin's, but the older Ed got, the better his woodworking became.

Cuchichea! *Pierde el hilo.*

The opposite was true for Ed's education. The older he got, the harder school became. He squeezed by during the elementary years. His report cards often had a teacher comment like "Ed whispers too much," or "Ed is bright, but has little follow-through." But as the curriculum advanced, Ed's ability to write became increasingly limited. He could read. In fact, he loved to read. Now, however, he was having trouble with the process of holding the pencil and writing, even the simplest of words. He could hold a hammer and nail, but something was wrong with the connection between the pencil and his brain.

So of course, he became frustrated. Ed was not stupid. He was extremely bright, but his problems with writing put a damper on his education. Each school year, he struggled more and more. This caused him to hate school. He dreaded every moment of it. Ervin and Ruby were starting to become concerned. *What has happened to our brilliant boy?* they wondered. *He was the child who was supposed to succeed.* But instead of succeeding, Ed was in danger of failing. Each year, the teacher warned Ed's parents that if he didn't try harder, he might not move on to the next grade. Even so, at the end of each year, they'd slip him through.

Ruby and Ervin considered the possibility that Ed had damage somewhere deep in his brain due to the scarlet fever years before. "Could this be possible?" they asked each other. "And if it is brain damage, what do we do?"

They made a decision to work with Ed. First, Ervin bought Ed a set of used encyclopedias and dictionaries. Ed read them over and over. Since he loved reading, he became obsessed with the information inside each volume. Next, since Ervin had a full schedule, Ruby spent time with Ed trying to develop his writing skills. She was the logical, mathematical type. She loved numbers and symbols, so that was where she started. Day after day, Ruby presented Ed with a list of numbers and symbols. Ed sat an hour at a time practicing. Even though he struggled, his left brain was being developed in a way that would hold great importance for the future. He just didn't know it yet.

It didn't take long for Ed's classmates to pick up on his challenges. "Hey half-wit," they would say. "What's wrong with you? Are you stupid?" And then they would laugh. Ed tried to ignore them, but gradually the bullying became a daily occurrence.

Ed developed a plan. While at school, he kept to himself. During class time, he daydreamed about being at the workshop, and during recess time, he sat under a tree and read an encyclopedia.

Ed finally made it to fifth grade, an amazing accomplishment. Then on March 2, 1943, the school burned down. There was nothing left except for the gymnasium. While school officials tried to plan reconstruction, the students were split up by grade and sent to a variety of locations to continue their education. Just six days after the fire, Ed and his classmates were sent to the Methodist Ladies Aid Hall. They were instructed to bring their own pencils, paper, and a wooden box to be used as a desk. In no time, their teacher, Anne Makel, had every one back on track.

One day during recess, Ed was reading under a large maple tree and heard, "Hey, idiot, what are you doing?" Ed looked up and there stood three boys. "We know you can't read that book because you are stupid!" Ed's jaw tightened. "Look at him. He thinks he's fooling us." All three boys roared with laughter. Ed had been taught not to fight back, but this day he could feel the hatred building. "Half-wit, half-wit," they heckled. Finally, Ed stood and scooped up a handful of stones. He wiped away the running tears from his cheeks, pulled his arm back, and launched the stones towards the boys. He missed. All three boys bolted back as they watched the stones travel through a window. The glass fell onto the grass below, and the boys jumped up and down and pointed towards Ed in amusement. "You are in so much trouble!" Just then, Ed spotted Miss Makel clomping towards him. Her hands were pressed deep into her hips.

"What did you do, Edgar?"

Ed's face turned pale. "They were bothering me. They wouldn't stop."

"That is no excuse to break this window! This isn't even our building."

"I know, but—"

"You are going to replace it, Edgar. I hope your parents have a nest egg, because this will not be cheap!"

The boys laughed as Ed stood by in disbelief. *The boys are right. I am in big trouble,* Ed thought. He knew his parents didn't have an extra dime. This was going to be Ed's responsibility. He would have to find an extra job to earn the money.

The end of the day finally arrived, and this was the first time that Ed didn't want to leave school. He walked home extra slowly. He tried to put together the right details for his parents. *Please let Dad be home,* he thought. He knew that Ruby would not be as sympathetic. Ed had never felt love from his mother. He knew that she still blamed him for Otto Lee's death and probably always would.

As Ed quietly opened the screen door and tiptoed into the coop, he remembered her many harsh comments since that tragic day. "You don't know how to love!" "Just get out of here. You are always in my way!" "Why do you mess

Soy especial (soy) un conjunto de eventos de un evento in/9to que te alejan de un to que eres : |soy especial ante Dios |

everything up? You are always causing trouble!" He was sure that this time would be no different.

Ed peeked into the low-lit room, and there stood Ruby, waiting. "Where have you been, boy?" she said. She crossed her arms. "What have you done now?" Ed opened his mouth and tightened his throat as he stumbled over his prepared explanation.

Ed had been running his own paper route since he was eight years old, but this money was being used to help support the family. So each day after school, Ed walked over to the local sawmill, where he had worked with his dad, to earn money to replace the window. Ed delivered *The Leader and Kalkaskian* newspaper before school and worked at the mill afterwards. His duties at the mill were to pick up scrap wood and sweep up the sawdust. Finally he earned enough money to pay for the window. He was relieved to have this pressure gone, but unfortunately, the pressure he felt due to the bullying continued. Actually, it got worse.

As Ed entered the schoolhouse each day, he heard snickers from several of the boys. He knew the sneers were aimed at him, but he did his best to ignore them. It was difficult on his walk to the sawmill, or on the way home. While he made his way after the last bell of the day, he tiptoed past trees because he had no idea who was waiting for him behind one or two of them. Sometimes he would make it safely to his destination, but most of the time he was not so lucky. He could count on two methods of attack: either rocks were launched his way, or the boys would jump out and spit in his face. Ed tried to decide which method he preferred, but the contest was too close to call. Ed did tell me that he had one or two friends who were nice to him, but they risked being teased themselves if they defended him, so they kept quiet.

By now, Ed was retreating more and more into his own little world and focusing on the feeling that he had something important to do with his life. It is difficult to pinpoint the exact day he first felt this way, but when I asked him when it started, he said, "I always felt it. It was a strong feeling deep within me. I often didn't feel special to the world around me, but I felt special to God. I just

Solo mi hermana mi madre y mi padre han defendido o intervenido en momentos de injusticia.

15

innately knew that He had a special job for me to do, but it took me many years to figure out what it was."

At this point in Ed's life, two things in his world made him happy: working with his father in the workshop and the paper route. The paper route became a big part of his retreat from the harassment. He serviced the whole town of Kalkaska. On delivery day, he picked up the newspapers, brought them home to fold each one, ate breakfast, and was out the door by five-thirty in the morning.

At first, he walked the route, but after a time, Ervin bought him a faded candy-apple red vintage bicycle and built him a wagon to carry the papers. Ervin and Ed spent time remodeling and reinforcing the cruiser, and when the bicycle was ready, Ed excitedly folded the papers, loaded the wagon, and soared down the road in style. Every day became an adventure. House after house, he leaned back, grabbed a paper, and lobbed it as far as he could. The paper usually made it onto the porch. If not the porch, at least the paper hit the sidewalk.

Day after day, Ed rode through the streets of Kalkaska. He loved the feel of the breeze in his face as he pedaled. The villagers could often hear him coming because he sang the whole way. An older resident or two watched for him along the way and waved. "Morning Edgar!" they'd call. Ed smiled and waved back as he coasted by.

Singing was pure joy for Ed. When he sang, the whole world went away. Ed sang the classics and opera. He had perfect pitch. No one else existed at this moment—that is, until collection day.

Ed eagerly looked forward to Saturdays, when he collected. This was the time he could talk with the elders of the community. They ranged from a retired hardware store owner to a magician. They were so kind to him, and the magician taught him a new card trick every visit.

Ed's favorite stop was at the house of a woman in her eighties. She had retired as a head nurse from Chicago and relocated north to Kalkaska. Ed didn't have to knock on her door because she was always waiting in the doorway with a plate of peanut butter cookies or chocolate cake.

"There you are, Edgar. Come on in," she would say. She'd hold the screen door with her hip as Ed entered. "Do you want milk with your cookies today?"

"Yes, ma'am."

On one particular day, the woman escorted Ed to her Victorian-style dining table. Ed noticed the scrolls and curves in the rosewood as he carefully sat down on the floral tapestry upholstered chair. She exited to retrieve a glass of milk while Ed attacked his first cookie.

"Here you go, Edgar," she said. She placed the glass in front of him, and his dirty hands cupped it as he rinsed down the remaining crumbs.

Ed wiped the corner of his mouth with his sleeve and said, "So, where did we leave off?"

They picked up the conversation as if there had been no time in between visits. "You were telling me about the certificate you earned from Sunday school," she said.

"Oh yeah, I've never had anything like that before. It has gold trim, and Miss Banks signed it."

"Well, you should be proud, Edgar. That is quite an accomplishment!"

"Thank you," Ed said with pride.

They talked about many topics during their time together. Her artwork and her various collections were on the top of the list, but most important were their talks about life. The woman still had a very sharp mind, and Ed loved how she challenged his thinking. Time always slipped away quickly, and before they knew it, an hour had passed. On this day, Ed sprang to his feet and gave her a hug and then dashed to the door. She followed as she wrapped a couple of cookies into a napkin and handed them to Ed. He slid them into his pocket. He had no intention of eating them. He always found someone else along the route who was hungry, so he passed them along.

"See you soon!" he said as the screen bounced behind him.

"Goodbye, Edgar," she said. She stood on the inside of the doorway and smiled as she watched him pedal away.

Each collection day seemed to take longer and longer. Ed didn't want to let any of the old people down, and he knew how much they enjoyed his visits. He risked trouble from Ruby when he returned home, but that was worth the joy he brought to each senior on the route. Ed realized that these people just wanted someone to talk to. They were lonely. They wanted to share their life stories: where they came from, their career, children and marriages. They told Ed about the loved ones they'd lost and how they coped. He knew that the best gift he could give them was to listen; that was all, just listen. They also listened to Ed when he talked about his hopes and dreams for the future. He often described his latest wood project while they imagined the creation with delight. They encouraged Ed to continue his woodwork and explained that a skill like that could take him far.

Finally, on one particular day after hours of chitchat and collecting newspaper money, Ed steered towards home. He started to get nervous as he realized how long he had been gone, again. He left as the sun was coming up, and now it was going down. As the coop appeared in the distance, Ed sighed and rehearsed another prepared explanation for Ruby.

3

"We laugh at honor and are shocked to find traitors in our midst."

C.S. Lewis, The Abolition of Man

As always, Ed was reprimanded for his lateness. He promised to try harder, but failed each time. Ruby finally recognized that she was wasting her strength on this issue and backed off. She had enough on her plate raising six children. Junior was the oldest, and he was preparing to enlist in the army. He was eighteen years old and World War II was in full swing, so Junior walked away from his auto mechanic job to answer the call of duty.

Ed had just turned eleven, and he looked up to his older brother as a hero. Ed had recently endured excessive bullying and the loss of his school to fire, and now he feared for his brother's safety. The years between Junior and Ed were many, but because they were the only boys in the family and they shared a corner in the loft, they had many long talks over the years.

The main topic was girls. The first time Ed heard the word "girls," he said, "Yuck!" Junior chuckled. "Oh, don't worry, little brother. Someday you will understand what I am telling you." Ed rolled his eyes as he continued to listen. But it didn't take long for Ed to appreciate that this was the best topic ever. Ed loved the girls! He liked the way they moved, the way they talked, the way they smelled, and the way their long hair blew in the breeze.

After Junior left, Ed missed their talks about girls. The only communication they had during the war was a letter here and there. At first, the letters came frequently, but after a year, they dwindled. When he couldn't stand it anymore, Ed wrote Junior. This was not an easy task because of his struggles with writing. He worked night after night to construct a readable letter. Soon it was in the mail. He waited patiently for a response. Each day after Ed completed his duties, he ran to the house to see if he had a letter, and time after time, he was disappointed.

Finally, in mid-August of 1944, there it was. Ed grabbed the letter off the dining room table and zipped to the loft. He eagerly tore it open.

August 12, 1944

Dear Brother,

Will answer your letter I received last night and shore was glad to hear from you and to know that every thing is all right with you and you are making out so good to. But I am feeling very good to day but I am a little tired this morning. Well just keep right working and you will be doing alright.

How is you and your girlfriend coming along? I bet that you are having a lot of fun to. I just wish that I was there. I know that you and wood have a lot of fun and how. Well what grade are you in this fall? I bet you made it and had a lot of fun also. Well Bud, I guess that is all, so will close and hope to hear from you soon again. So till next time, so long.

Your brother

Ed cautiously folded the letter as if it were a rare jewel. He looked around the corner loft and located a hiding spot. He placed the letter under a loose wooden plank in the floor. There weren't many people in Ed's life that he could trust, but his brother was one.

After Junior had served as a combat engineer, World War II finally came to an end. Junior's service also ended and he returned home to the chicken coop. Ed was beside himself with joy. The family came together to prepare a warm welcome home for Junior. Ruby breathed a sigh of relief knowing that she would not lose another son. Ervin did more work on the chicken coop to give his soldier a hero's welcome. And Ed, he counted down the minutes.

Finally, the dust whirled in the wind and Ed noticed a vehicle steering towards the coop. "Junior is here!!" Ed announced as he sprinted outside. A black Ford Deluxe Coupe halted. The passenger door opened, blocking the whitewall tires, and Ed leaped into his brother's arms. Junior spun Ed around and then set him down as he accepted his mother's embrace. Ruby held her son tight. She feared that if she let go, he would disappear again. Ervin held out his right hand as Junior grasped and squeezed. The Lantzer family was whole again. One by one, they entered the chicken coop and began the next chapter in their lives.

The adjustment back to civilian life was not easy for Junior. During the war, he was responsible for keeping the army troops moving. He helped construct bridges and roads and kept the path to the enemy clear of obstructions and entanglements at all costs. Now he found it difficult to keep his own life free of entanglements. These occurred mostly in his mind. He fought to rid himself of the memories of war. The sights he had endured: blood, death, and evil. How can a person come back to a normal life after that? Can life ever be the same again?

Junior struggled with these thoughts daily, and his mental state began to deteriorate. Ed noticed the changes. He knew this was not the same brother he had said goodbye to just a couple of years before. Their long talks were gone. No more advice and no more discussions about girls. They again shared the corner loft, but they were now strangers.

Winter returned to Kalkaska, and it came in with a roar. The picturesque countryside was blanketed with snow. Death was everywhere: the northern red oak, the black-eyed Susans, and the countless blades of grass withered. The Lantzer family prepared as best they could and nestled in for the long haul. One December night was especially cold. Each member of the family was tucked in tight under their well-worn covers. Ed, now thirteen years old, and Junior shared a cot. There wasn't enough money or space for two beds in the corner loft, so as they had many nights before, they dusted off the snow spread across the left corner of their quilt and squeezed in together. Ed was grateful to have the extra body heat from his brother on this bitter night. Before long, he was fast asleep.

21

Suddenly, Ed's eyes flew open. There was a large hand pressed over his mouth. "Quiet. Don't make a sound," Ed was ordered. He tried to squirm back and forth, but his assailant used his other arm like a hook and pinned him down. Fear traveled from head to toe. "Whuu yuu doo," Ed tried to mumble. The hand pressed harder. Then, the arm unhooked as it ripped off Ed's bedclothes. A deep voice said, "If you want to live, don't make a peep." Ed's right and then left hand pushed back and forth as he attempted to fight. The perpetrator's body weight became too heavy, and finally Ed closed his eyes tight and whimpered. He realized there was no way to stop what was about to happen.

When it was over, Ed hesitantly opened his eyes again. Junior stood at the end of the cot. "If you tell a soul, I will kill you!" he said. Ed trembled as he nodded. Junior disappeared into the night, and Ed replayed the torture over and over in his head until light finally broke through the cracks of the aged barn wood.

In the morning, life below the loft went on as usual. Ed heard footsteps, voices, and pots and pans banging. He sat on the edge of the bed trying to get the strength to move. "Why? Why?" he pleaded upwards. *How can my life ever be the same?* he thought. The smell of ham and eggs floated through the air. *How can my family act so normal? Don't they know my life has been changed forever?*

Ed positioned his face in his hands and rocked back and forth. *What do I do?* He trembled. Then he remembered Junior's threat: *I will kill you if you tell!* His choices were limited. He needed either to pretend that nothing had happened, or tell. Ed was not ready to make a decision like this, so he stood up, took a deep breath, dried his face, and headed down to the kitchen.

Ed's mother and father dove into the morning meal. Ed cautiously looked around the room. Junior was not there. He sighed with relief as he made his way to his chair.

"You are a little late this morning son, aren't you?" asked Ervin.

Ed stood at the back of his chair and nodded. He looked past his father, fearing that if he made eye contact, Ervin would know something was wrong.

Ruby glared at Ed. "What's wrong with you?"

"Nothing, I was just tired."

Ruby groaned and returned to her meal. Ed sat down and contemplated how he could possibly take one bite. He had a knot the size of a grapefruit in his stomach, and food was the last thing he wanted. Almost by its own will, his fork deposited a small portion of runny egg into his mouth. He cringed and swallowed, then managed to consume the remaining food on his plate.

"Let's go, son. It's time to work," Ervin said.

Ruby began clearing the table, and Ed followed his father outside.

As the days went by, the effect of his brother's assault overwhelmed Ed. Guilt consumed him. *Why did he hurt me? Did I do something wrong? Is it my fault?* he asked himself. The incident played through his mind over and over, but he couldn't think of a reason his brother would hurt him like that.

Ed stayed as busy as he could. With his paper route, school, and chores, there was little time to think about the assault, but he carried a lump of sadness within him everywhere he went. He made sure to mask his sadness from others as best he could. He was grateful to be busy. He was also grateful that his brother had disappeared from the family farm. Ed had not seen him since the attack, and he mentioned nothing of his disappearance. He hoped that Junior's absence would continue.

One day, Ed overheard his parents talking about his brother's new job. "This is a great move for Junior," Ruby said.

"I agree. The Pennsylvania Railroad has been around for years. I think he will do just fine," Ervin said.

"I know shoveling coal isn't easy work, but who knows what it could lead to in a large company like that? I am so proud of our boy!" she said.

Ervin smiled and nodded in agreement. Ed paused as he analyzed the information he had just heard. *Junior is gone and I am safe,* he thought, relieved. But then anger overcame him. He thought about how his parents adored his older brother, especially Ruby. Ed couldn't remember the last time he had felt that kind of love from his mother. He flashed back. *Oh yeah, before Otto Lee's death.* That was the last time Ruby had showed Ed any kindness. She consistently showed Junior how much she loved him, but not Ed, and that was baffling.

Ed thought about the day that both he and Junior were outside fetching water so Ruby could wash the dinner dishes. Ed had entered first with his bucket.

"Here you go, Mom," he had said. "Where do you want it?"

Ruby sternly pointed towards a wash bin with an expression of annoyance. Ed did as he was directed. As he poured his bucket into the bin, Junior entered the coop with his bucket. Ed turned just as he saw Ruby's face light up.

"Thank you, son. Let me get that for you," she said.

Ruby took the water from Junior. Ed stood there stunned. He always knew how his mother felt, but this was the first time he had really seen the difference in the way she treated the two boys. She didn't even have to say a word. It was the way she looked at Ed's older brother, always with affection. When she looked at Ed, he saw disappointment in her eyes.

The memory enraged him, and before Ed knew it, he was charging into the kitchen. "Junior attacked me!" he yelled.

Both Ervin and Ruby jumped at the unexpected entrance. "What are you talking about?" Ervin asked.

"He hurt me, Dad. While I was sleeping."

Ruby froze as Ed continued with the gory details. When Ed had finished, Ruby opened her mouth, and a lion's roar blew through the core of Ed's being. The remaining pieces of his heart fell as he listened.

"You are a liar!! He would never do something like that!" she screamed. Ruby's arms flailed. "What's wrong with you?"

Ervin tried to grab her to settle her down. "That's enough Ruby," he said.

"We have raised a liar!!!" she continued. "Junior is a hero! You?" she pointed, "are wicked!"

Ed knew at that moment that he was right. She would always blame him for Otto's death. There was no way to fix it and no way to change it. Ruby stomped out of the room.

"Edgar, don't you ever say another word about this. Do you hear me?" Ervin said. Ed looked at his father and answered without a word. "Now get back to work."

Depleted and dejected, Ed did as he was told. After this, he often felt like the black sheep of the family. He tried to convince himself that it wasn't true, but now, for the first time, he knew it was.

4

"God, who foresaw your tribulation, has specially armed you to go through it, not without pain but without stain."

C.S. Lewis, Collected Letters of C S. Lewis

By the time he was fourteen years old, Ed no longer had any interest in going to school. He was now in ninth grade and there were so many other things he preferred to do to satisfy his mind. His thoughts were raging and he didn't quite know what to do with them.

Ed had wisdom far beyond his years. He was very observant. Because of the trauma he had endured starting at a young age, he found himself watching human behavior. As a result, he became consumed with philosophical and psychological questions. What is the meaning of life? Why is society a certain way? Why do people act as they do? What is my purpose? Why am I here?

Ed knew he was the black sheep of his family, but he also knew that he had a special job to do during his time on Earth. He felt it so strongly. The Lord had a plan for him, but he was still searching to figure out what it was. He didn't understand why some people treated him so poorly, yet he still felt special. His father made him feel special, and the Lord made him feel special. So he treasured them, and decided to continue searching for the job that the Lord had so lovingly planned for him.

Ed's reading flourished, but his writing shriveled. The effects of the brain damage and the torture he endured at home began to intertwine. Writing had always been difficult for him, but now he was tired of trying. At this point, he decided to focus his time on woodworking and reading, but writing had to go. He didn't need it. Now, instead of battling with his teachers, he skipped school as often as he could. By the end of the school year, Ed had missed so many days that his teacher, Miss Banks, sent a note to Ervin and Ruby. "Edgar is cheating himself if he doesn't take time next year to go to school and master all that he can," it said.

Ed's parents were furious. "Edgar, why don't you want to learn?" Ervin asked.

"Dad, I learn every day. I just don't need school to do it."

"Son, you do need school. I need you to step up and try harder. Can you do that for me?"

"Yes, Father," Ed replied. By now, all of the older Lantzer children were out of the house and Ed's sister Mary had just married. She moved south to Battle Creek, Michigan with her new husband, Arthur. Ervin and Ruby decided to send Ed down to stay with them for the summer. They hoped that this time would give him a chance to rearrange his priorities. It would also give Ruby a reprieve.

Once Ed was settled in the "Cereal City," Arthur and Mary helped him get a summer job at the Kellogg Company. Before long, his bosses made him an assistant to one of the foremen. Ed felt good about what he was accomplishing. This was the first time he had been away from home, and being a part of a company that made Corn Flakes, Rice Krispies, and Raisin Bran cereal was intriguing, even if it was only temporary.

He was also grateful for the opportunity to earn some extra money. He knew that his parents didn't have much, and as he grew, he needed new clothes. The ones he owned no longer fit, and he was starting to become a young man. He was also starting to really have an eye for the young women. Since he had made a deal with his father to try harder in school, when autumn arrived, he wanted at least to look his best.

Fort Custer Training Center was four miles west of Battle Creek, and a couple of years after World War II ended, the army training post was still active. The Veterans Administration hospital was also in use. Injured soldiers occupied every cot, and the staff was in need of volunteers.

Ed decided to get involved with the wounded during his spare time. He saw what the war had done to his brother, and even though Junior had caused Ed so much pain, Ed felt a calling to help these brave soldiers. Maybe it was his way to make sense of his brother's gruesome attack, but one thing Ed knew for sure, he had no choice. This step was part of God's plan for him. He had to make a difference for these brave men, even if it was in a small way.

The nursing staff assigned Ed several menial tasks, like changing bed linens and escorting patients. Soon, Ed had free run of the hospital. He became interested in the patients who had served in the Pacific. He wanted to know what it felt like to be in their boots. What was war like? What were their missions like? Were they scared? Ed asked these questions as he sat by their beds. Some of the patients refused to talk and some couldn't, but Ed found men who were eager to share.

One evening as Ed was pushing a young father in a wheelchair, the man asked him, "How old are you, kid?"

"Fifteen."

"My, that seems just like yesterday."

"How old are you, sir, if you don't mind me asking?"

"I just turned twenty-seven. Do you know what the hardest part is?"

"No, sir."

"I no longer feel like a man."

Ed seemed confused. "What do you mean?"

"A Japanese soldier shot me in the groin!"

Ed winced. "What?"

"Yes, and now I am no longer a man."

The soldier hesitated, and Ed felt his hopelessness. He could not imagine what this man was going through. *How will he ever have a normal life again*? Ed wondered.

The man continued, "My wife has been strong, but how can she endure this forever? I fear I will lose her."

Ed knelt in front of the wheelchair and repositioned the white cover over his right big toe. "It will be okay, sir," he said. "I am sure she loves you no matter what. Have faith. The Lord will take care of you."

Ed paused as he thought about what he had just said: *Don't worry about it, the Lord will take care of it.* Vivid rays of white and golden light arced from side to side in Ed's mind. *Could this be true? No matter how hard things are, will faith get you through it?* He flashed back to his mother insisting that he had killed Otto Lee, his schoolmates heckling him every day, and his brother abusing him. *Now I understand,* he thought. *God doesn't guarantee that we will feel no pain or hurt, but he does promise that through faith, he will guide us through.* Ed smiled at this new revelation. *The Lord will take care of me. I just have to have faith!* Ed repeated the words to himself. He then silently sent a message above: *I do have faith, Father.* Ed could almost feel a gentle pat on his shoulder, as if it were the energy of God's loving hand sending him assurance.

The sound of the soldier's voice brought Ed back. "You are right, kid. How old did you say you were again?" he said jokingly.

Ed laughed as they reached their destination. He gently helped the soldier out of the wheelchair and into his bed. He tucked the man in and said, "I'll be back tomorrow. Would you like some company?"

"I look forward to it," the soldier said.

Ed pulled the wheelchair in reverse and then swung it around. "Tomorrow then," he said as he tipped his head forward and waltzed away.

After each shift at the Kellogg Company, Ed pleaded with Arthur to give him a ride to the hospital. And each day, he sat with the wounded and listened to their stories. They spoke of the buddies they had lost in battle and how they had fought through the trenches. Ed felt the courage and love they had for their country. The war had brought some of the patients to a state of insanity. Ed had to be careful because sometimes they would lose track of reality and think they were still in battle. Ed was mistaken for the enemy more than once.

But one day, a patient who was considered "crazy" sat up in bed and put his right hand across his heart. Ed stopped to see if he was okay. The man started singing. "Oh, say can you see by the dawn's early light..." Ed made the same gesture and joined in with his perfect pitch. "What so proudly we hailed at the twilight's last gleaming?" More patients followed suit as they continued. Finally, "O'er the land of the free and the home of the brave!" There were hoots and hollers and then the man slid back down and went to sleep. Ed continued on with his task as he thought about how these men had proudly served our country. They had sacrificed and yet still felt undying patriotism. By the end of the summer, Ed had brightened many dreary days for these soldiers, but in the end he left with a newfound wisdom. He learned life-changing lessons. As he traveled north to Kalkaska, he knew that he was on the right track. His purpose was becoming clearer and his faith stronger.

5

*"The door on which we have been knocking
all our lives will open at last."*

C.S. Lewis, *The Weight of Glory*

When Ed returned to Kalkaska, he was ready to follow through on his promise to his father. The first day of school was only days away and he was actually excited. He had a feeling that this was going to be a good year. *If those soldiers can endure, so can I*, he thought. He put on his new white-collared dress shirt, navy tie, and the beige pants he'd bought with part of the money he'd earned. He then fastened each end of his navy and gold suspenders to his waist. Last, he rubbed Brylcreem through his wavy hair, parted it on the left side, and combed it back. Ed looked in his handheld mirror. "Debonair, I'd say! Watch out, ladies. Here I come!"

He was right: the first day proved to be a good start. Shortly after entering the building, Ed noticed a redheaded beauty. He nudged a classmate beside him.

"Who is that?" he asked.

"That's Jean. She moved here a year ago. Where have you been?"

"I guess in the wrong place," Ed said.

Every school day, Ed roamed the halls in between classes to get a glimpse of his new crush. Once he saw her, he could go on with the rest of the day satisfied.

Winter returned and Ed was working in the shop with Ervin. They were preparing a collection of parquetry pieces to sell in the front window of the local hardware store. Ervin was working on a mosaic tabletop, and Ed was building a wooden frame for a jewelry box.

Ed looked up as he heard a vehicle pull into the driveway. He stood and looked out the window. Ed's cousin stepped out of the driver's seat and headed towards the shop.

"Hey, bud, what are you doing?" his cousin asked.

"Just putting this box together. What are you guys doing?" Ed looked out the window again and noticed four heads inside the car.

"Well, listen. We are headed to Grayling to go skiing. Would you like to come?"

Ed looked surprised. "Who's coming?"

"My girlfriend, Jack and his girlfriend, and then there is Jean."

Ed lit up. "Jean?"

"Yeah, I don't want her to feel out of place, so I thought you could come along and keep her company."

Ed turned to Ervin in anticipation. Ervin grinned. "Sure, take the day and go."

Ed beamed. He couldn't believe the young lady he had been observing for weeks was now in his driveway. The best part was, he was going to keep her company.

Ed followed his cousin to the car as his heart jumped around his chest. He opened the rear door and there she was with her red hair, bright eyes, and even brighter smile.

"Hi, Jean," Ed said as he slid in beside her.

This skiing event was the beginning of Ed and Jean's courtship. They began dating that night and continued through their senior year. Life was finally going Ed's way. He had a girlfriend he adored, and he was going to school regularly. He joined the debate, glee, and Latin clubs and started studying some of philosophy greats like Homer, Plato, and Socrates. He even adopted the name "Homer."

Ed decided that he wanted to be a lawyer. He was an effective oral speaker and he had no trouble winning any debate. His mind was brilliant and others found it difficult to outthink him. He started visiting the courthouse and watching the trials. He observed the lawyers, how they spoke and how they gestured. He developed a special interest in real estate law. This world was exciting to Ed. He started to feel that maybe this was something he could do. Maybe this was his calling.

Then the school woodshop teacher, Mr. Guy, and the school board came calling. Ed was behind in credits, and his hopes of graduating were looking slim.

"Hey, Ed. I have a proposition for you," said his teacher.

"Yes, Mr. Guy?"

"If you accept my idea, you can call me Lester," he smiled

"Wow, okay. What is it?"

"We have just moved an old church into town, and we are transforming it into classrooms."

"Really?"

"Yes. We are calling it the Holly School. This is where we'll be teaching the manual arts program," Mr. Guy said. Ed was now interested. "At the end of last school year, the tools, machinery, and materials were moved from the old school basement to the Holly School. The problem is that they were just left scattered everywhere."

"That sounds like a mess."

"Yes it is! I need your help, Ed."

"What do you want me to do?"

"Can you help me set up the new shop? I know you have a lot of experience, and I am hoping you can help me design a floor plan that will be efficient."

"Yes, sir. I would be happy to!"

"Call me Lester. But that's not all."

"Huh?" Ed seemed surprised.

"I also need your help teaching the class." Ed was stunned. Him? The boy everyone made fun of? "I know how talented you are with wood. I talked to our school board president, and he has agreed to give you the credit you are short of so you can graduate on time. That is, if you agree to help."

"Oh my goodness, Mr. Guy—I mean Lester. I would be honored!" Ed said.

"Okay." Lester held out his hand. "Deal then?"

Ed grasped it tight. "Deal!"

Ed couldn't believe his luck. He could finally see the end. He just had to spend his senior year teaching something he loved, and then school would be a thing of the past. His future was in sight, and it was looking bright.

Ed was nervous on his first day of woodshop as he assisted Mr. Guy. He was unsure whether his classmates would take him seriously in his new role. The bullying Ed had faced throughout his childhood was difficult, but he hoped that his classmates would see that he had something to offer. When Ed put two pieces of wood together, something magical happened. People noticed and started to pay attention to him. He hoped that his peers would do the same.

Ed's first lesson was to give the class a tour of the equipment. Ed and Mr. Guy had spent a great deal of time setting up the shop, and they were both proud of the outcome. Now it was time to see if the layout was successful.

"Come on in, class," said Mr. Guy. One by one, they filled the room. It was going to be a tight fit since the Holly School was much smaller than the old basement, but they had used each inch of the room wisely. "Class, Edgar will be helping me this year." Not surprisingly, there were grumbles around the room. "As many of you know, Ed has been working with wood since he was a child. I believe he will be a wonderful asset to your learning." Lester looked at Ed. "Will you give them a tour?"

Ed nodded and directed the class's attention to the first machine. "If you look around the room, you will see we have a nice variety of tools and machines to work with this year. Here we have a table saw. This is a ten-inch Delta Unisaw. It is three horsepower and has a 220-volt single phase motor." The boys seemed interested as they each took a turn inspecting the saw. "Now look over here." Ed escorted them to the next station. "We have a variety of other saws. There is a band saw, a radial arm saw, and a scroll saw." The class continued to listen intently. "Take a look at this band saw. This is one of the most versatile tools in the shop. With this saw, you can cut curves and organic shapes."

"Neat," said one of the boys.

"Notice the upper and lower wheel. Look at the continuous band of blade that travels around the two. The blade rotates in a clockwise direction so that cutting will be uninterrupted." Ed was feeling more confident as he continued the tour. "Let's look at the sanders next," he said as he moved across the room.

When the tour was complete Ed asked, "Are there any questions?" Ten hands flew in the air. Ed grinned as he turned his attention to the first question.

Throughout the school year, the woodshop was filled with noisy excitement. At any given time you could hear the saws buzzing, the drills squealing, and the hammers tapping. Ed loved it! He found the sounds exhilarating and the smell of wood refreshing. He was always on hand for anyone who needed his aid.

Midway through the semester, Ed noticed a student trying to run the belt sander. He placed his small oak tabletop under the belt, which was held by two six-inch-diameter pulleys at each end of the table. He turned on the switch. Then he waited patiently with a perplexed look on his face as he watched the belt travel.

Ed watched him for a minute, laughed to himself, and then walked over to him. "You look puzzled," he said.

The student scratched his sandy hair. "Yeah. I can't figure out why the belt isn't touching my project."

Ed stood next to him for a minute, not wanting to embarrass him. "Hmmm." Ed scratched his head too. "Hey, I know. Let's try this." Ed pushed the belt down. "Come help me."

The student imitated Ed, and his large frame shook as he laughed. "We got it!"

"Do you feel those sparks through your fingertips and the soles of your shoes?"

"I sure do. It tickles!" he said.

Ed bellowed. "Yes, it does. When you feel those sparks, just remember you are creating friction with the pressure pad, which will give you a beautifully finished piece of oak."

The student's wide smile spread across his face. "Well, all right then. You're okay, man!"

"Thanks," Ed replied with satisfaction. He couldn't believe what his classmate had just said. *I'm okay!* This was not something Ed heard often. It may have been a brief compliment, but it was meaningful to Ed. He was finally beginning to believe that he was okay.

Near the end of the school year, the wood projects began to build up. There were various sizes of bookcases, tables, and picture frames. Ed observed as his students and classmates felt a sense of pride in their creations. Ed also felt a sense of pride. The end of the school year was closing in and Ed knew that he had conquered a major obstacle in his life. He was ready to start looking ahead.

Ed with his high school Latin club.

Ed with the debate club.

Edgar Lantzer
"Blush is handsome, but
  often inconvenient."
Latin 2-3-4
Glee Club 3-4
Annual Staff 4
Chorus 3
Baseball 1-2
Basketball 1-3

Ed's senior picture.

Ed (in suspenders) teaches his high school shop class.

6

"To be Christian means to forgive the inexcusable, because God has forgiven the inexcusable in you."

C.S. Lewis, Essay on Forgiveness

There was still one obstacle in his way though: his brother. Ed had not spoken to Junior since that horrific night, and he used every defense mechanism he could to keep the thought of it at bay. He was always busy, whether it was work, woodworking, school, reading, or Jean. He left little time to allow the memory to interfere.

This worked for a while. He almost had himself believing that the attack hadn't happened. *Maybe if I ignore it long enough, it will disappear from reality*, he thought. But that didn't work.

Then he tried to validate his masculinity. He became stronger and stronger. One day Ed and his father went outside to find firewood. They picked up logs, lumber, and railroad ties. The railroad ties were extremely heavy, so they split them down. Ed said, "I can lift a whole one."

"That isn't a good idea, son," Ervin said.

Ed lifted one anyway, grunting like an ox. He lost his footing and came crashing down, hitting his head on a rail. The pain was intense, but so was the feeling that he knew what he had to do. He had to confront his brother. It was the only way to put the whole thing behind him. No amount of pretending would stop the hold this memory had on Ed, and it was time to cut it loose.

Ed found out that the train Junior was working on would be making a stop at the Kalkaska depot the following week. He knew this was his opportunity. It wasn't going to be easy, but he had no choice.

One morning, he woke up before dawn and was out the door before the first rooster crowed. He made his way to the depot and sat on a large stump to wait. It was a brisk morning. His nostrils stuck and his breath was visible after each exhale. Ed was unsure what to do or say, but he decided to just let it flow.

Suddenly, he heard the train blowing in the distance. He shot off the stump and eagerly gazed south down the tracks. First he saw a light and then the train's silhouette. Several people were waiting outside the depot doors with their luggage. Finally, the train came to a stop. Ed stayed slightly out of sight for a moment as the depot came alive. People began piling off the train going in every direction, either doing their duty or reuniting with a loved one.

Just as the sun rose above the horizon and peeked through the trees, Ed spotted his brother. Junior was standing on the last step of the train exit. His left foot landed on the ground and his right followed. He looked straight ahead for a moment, paused, and turned north. His startled eyes connected with Ed's. They both froze. The last time Ed had seen his brother, Ed was a weak adolescent. Now he was a robust young man.

Junior moved tentatively towards Ed. Ed planted his feet, clenched his teeth, and clasped both fists into a ball as he waited.

"Hello, Edgar. How are you doing?" Junior asked.

"How am I doing?" Ed laughed mockingly. "How do you think I am doing?" The steam whirled out of Ed's nostrils.

"Uh . . ."

"No, wait. Let me tell you how I am doing. Do you know what you did to me? You bastard! Do you? You not only hurt me, you changed me as a person! Do you know that? I am not the person I was supposed to be because of you!"

"I,I,I—" Junior stumbled.

"I thought you loved me. I looked up to you!" Tears streamed down Ed's face. "But you were nothing but a phony! Every person in our family loves you, but you are a fake! You are a betrayer!! Judas, that's who you are!!! No one sees the truth but me. They see you as a hero, but to me you are a wolf in sheep's clothing!!!"

Ed pulled his clenched right fist back as if to wind up, and then BAM! It landed in the pit of Junior's stomach. The left fist followed. Ed continued back and forth until his brother tried to fight back. Ed was too strong and too fast. Then Junior tackled Ed to the ground and the two of them rolled. Alarmed passengers and train employees watched in horror as the dust drifted around the ball of arms and legs kicking and punching. They finally halted. Ed pinned Junior down.

"See how it feels to be helpless?" Ed pressed his arm deep into his brother's throat. "Well, I will tell you what. I am no longer helpless! I am strong! The thought of what you did to me will no longer torment me in the middle of the night, or during the day for that matter. From this day forward, I will leave the pain with you. You can carry the weight of this alone." Ed stood up and threw a handful of dirt in his brother's face. "It's all on you now!"

Ed brushed off his hands, did an about-face, tipped good day to the onlookers, and sauntered towards home. With each step, he felt lighter and lighter. The heaviness and darkness that had lived inside him was floating away.

By the time he reached the coop door, he felt light as a feather. The familiar screech of the door welcomed him. He walked in, turned around, and pulled the door shut. At the same time he knew he was also shutting the door on this painful memory. He was cutting it loose forever.

The next day, the world seemed to be a different place. With the weight of the torment he had carried around for years now gone, Ed was ready to start a new life. He had a plan, but before he could act on it, he had to take care of one more thing: graduation. After all of the years of tolerating school, it had finally come to an end. Ed entered the school on his last day and walked out when the final bell rang with enough credits to receive a diploma. What an accomplishment! As he walked home for the last time, the thoughts of his future endeavors danced through his head. He couldn't wait to get on with his purpose. He was still unsure what that entailed, but he did know one thing: it involved Jean.

"This world is a great sculptor's shop. We are the statues and there's a rumor going around the shop that some of us are someday going to come to life."

C.S. Lewis, *Mere Christianity*

Ed walked right into the workshop when he returned home. Ervin was sitting at his workbench organizing his tools.

"Hi, Dad," he said. Ervin looked up. "Guess what I have."

Ed beamed as he held his hands behind his back. Ervin grabbed a nearby can and spit the tobacco from his bulging bottom lip into it. Ed watched as he flashed back to childhood memories of his father chewing. Ervin rarely spit, so when the kids would ask him a question, he grunted for yes or no and the kids had to figure out which was which.

Ed snapped back as Ervin spit the remaining chunks into the can and said, "Let's see, could it be a diploma?"

Ed smiled. "Nope."

Ervin looked puzzled. "Uh, you stumped me, son. What could it be?" Ed's right hand traveled around his side and then propelled out in front of him. Ervin's heart skipped a beat. "What is that?"

"This is my future, Dad." Flashes from the ring resting on his palm shot out in every direction as the light hit it. "I am going to ask Jean to marry me."

"What? Are you sure?" said Ervin.

"Absolutely! This is the one thing I am sure of. I love her, Dad."

"Well then, I guess you better get on with it," Ervin said as he grinned from ear to ear. "When are you going to ask her?"

"Tonight."

"I am happy for you, son." Ervin snapped his fingers. "Hold on. I have a surprise for you too."

He shuffled over to a mahogany hope chest sitting in the corner of the shop, pulled out a package wrapped in newspaper, and put it behind his back. "Pick a hand." Ed chuckled and pointed to the right. Ervin moved the package from the left to the right. "Bingo!" Ervin handed his son the gift. Ed shredded the newspaper in a matter of seconds to reveal black leather and gold lettering. When he saw it, he stood motionless.

"Oh, Father, I can't believe this! Is this really mine?" Each scrolled letter creating the words "Holy Bible" lit up alongside Jean's soon-to-be engagement ring. Ed put the Bible to his nose and inhaled the scent of the leather, then put the book to his heart. "Thank you, Father. I will treasure this always."

"Edgar, I know it hasn't been easy for you so far," said Ervin. "Now that you are beginning adulthood, let this Bible be your guide. Through these words, you will find the truth. Don't let anyone steer you away from God's word. His words are the only way. Do you understand?"

"Yes, Father. I do."

Ervin embraced his son. "I am proud of you, Edgar!"

"Thank you, Dad."

Ervin sat down at his workstation and looked up. "Have a seat, son. I have something else I want to talk to you about."

"Okay." Ed pulled up a stool across from his father. "Your table top is looking very nice, Dad."

"Thank you, Edgar. That is actually what I want to talk to you about."

"What do you mean?" Ed was confused.

"Well, you have been working with me in this workshop since you were old enough to hold a hammer, right?"

"Right."

"What have I taught you?"

"You taught me everything, Dad."

"Like? Give me some examples."

"Well, I know most species of wood, not only from Northern Michigan, but from around the world. You taught me how to look beyond the tree and focus on the grain and the colors. You showed me the importance of color harmony, how each species of wood looks next to another. I can use a wide variety of tools and build anything I envision in my mind. Most importantly, Dad, you taught me the craft of parquetry."

"Okay. Now, what is my favorite angle to use in my woodwork?"

"That's easy. Your work is done in either a ninety-degree or forty-five-degree angle," Ed said with confidence.

"That's right. I have perfected my craft, and you have also become a master. It's now time for you to find your own angle."

"What do you mean?" Ed said, alarmed.

"I want you to stretch your abilities. Move beyond what we have done here together. You are young, and you have so many years ahead of you. It is time to find your own angle and your own way."

Ed felt challenged. "But how do I find my own angle? Where do I start?"

"You want to know where to start?" Ervin pointed to Ed's Bible. "You will find your answers there."

Ed was confused as he flipped through the pages. *The answers are in here?*

"Son, the most important thing I want you to remember as you search is that the angle you choose must have meaning. It must have meaning to you." Ed stared at his father for a moment. "Do you understand?"

Ed trusted his father's advice, but he also recognized that his father was releasing him. It was time for Ervin to let him soar.

"Okay, Dad. I understand," he said. Ed rose from his stool.

"Good luck, son, and good luck tonight."

"Thank you, Father." Ervin and Ed shook hands and embraced one more time. Ed picked up Jean's ring and his new Bible and held them both tight. "Well, Father, this is it. I have a beautiful redhead to call on."

Jean accepted Ed's proposal and they were married on August 20, 1950 at the Kalkaska Church of Christ. Ed was now a husband, and shortly after the wedding, he found out he was also to become a father. Ed and Jean were thrilled with the news. They had plans to have a large family; their goal was twelve children. The first child was on the way and the new Lantzer family began making preparations.

Ed was beside himself with joy. He worked two and three jobs to earn enough money to take care of his new responsibilities. One of them was with the Kalkaska Road Commission. By now his father was working there, and Ervin helped Ed get the job. Ed beamed everywhere he went. The anticipation of being a father was almost too much to bear. Ed secretly felt that this child might help him finally heal from the loss of his young brother, Otto Lee. He missed him so much, even though it had been years since his death. Throughout Ed's life, his mother reminded him of this loss. She also reminded him that he could not love. Ed struggled with this burden and silently suffered great pain as a result. Now, he was going to help bring a new baby into the world and he would prove that he was capable of love. He would prove Ruby wrong.

La Iglesia Catolica
puede reconocer a
un Santo Protestante

45

8

"The death of a loved one is an amputation."

C.S. Lewis, A Grief Observed

Ervin's gift to Ed gave him much comfort throughout the nine months. He read his Bible front to back and inside out. Each time he read it, he felt more at ease, and his understanding of the scriptures gave him peace as his journey into the adult world revved into high gear. Ed also became more involved in church. He started teaching a Sunday school class and became a choir leader. Ed truly felt grown up and knew for certain that he was ready to be a father.

Finally the big day arrived. The new little Lantzer began the journey into this world. It started with the usual labor pains and the breaking of the water.

"Ed, it's time," Jean said.

Ed's whole being lit up with excitement. "Okay. Let's go."

Ed grabbed the prepared caramel leather suitcase and tucked it under his left arm. He wrapped his right arm around Jean's shoulder as he escorted his wife into the car he had borrowed from his father. Ed backed up and then hit the gas pedal. A cloud of dust followed as they barreled down the driveway and headed towards Cadillac, which was a forty-eight minute drive from Kalkaska.

Their doctor was based out of Mercy Hospital in Cadillac, and since Ed and Jean did not have a phone, they could not warn him that they were coming. As each contraction came, Jean held her breath and tightened up.

"Are you okay?" Ed asked.

"Yes," Jean said as the pain subsided.

Ed felt like he was driving in slow motion. Getting Jean to the hospital was his mission and it wasn't happening fast enough, so he decided to speed up. "Oooh," Jean grumbled at the start of another pain. Ed nervously looked her way as he realized they were now coming closer together.

"Don't hold your breath. Try to breathe in and out slowly," Ed said

"I'll try."

Jean did as Ed suggested and sighed with relief as another contraction receded. Finally, the Mercy Hospital sign was in sight. Ed pulled into the parking lot at high speed and came to a stop in front of the door. He left his car door wide open as he ran around the vehicle to help his wife into the hospital.

"My wife is in labor," Ed said to the nurse rushing towards them.

He was comforted to know they had made it to the hospital in plenty of time and their baby would soon arrive to greet them.

"Who is your doctor, sir?" asked the nurse. Ed gave them the name. The nurse had a look of concern on her face and said, "Uh, sir, I am sorry, but your doctor is in Texas. He won't be back until tomorrow."

"What?" Ed said, beginning to panic. Jean grabbed Ed's wrist as another contraction began.

"We don't have anyone else here that can deliver your baby."

"What do we do?"

"The closest hospital from here is in Traverse City," said the nurse.

The fear on Jean's face told Ed that he had no time to spare. "Okay, thank you," he said as he swiftly escorted Jean back to the car and raced off to the next hospital. Traverse City was an hour away and Jean's contractions were coming more often and lasting longer.

"Owwww!" Jean shrilled with the next pain.

"It's okay, darling. I will get you there." Ed drove faster and faster.

"Oh, no! Here comes another one!" Jean cried.

"What? You just had one!" Terror swept through Ed. He knew they were in trouble. "Hang on, Jean. Hang on!!" Ed said as he passed the car in front of them.

At thirty minutes into the drive Jean started screaming. "It's coming! It's coming!!"

"What?!!" Ed shouted.

Jean's screams continued. Ed was now traveling as fast as the car would go. "Help me! Help me!!" Jean pleaded.

"We will be there soon. Just hold on, okay?" Ed felt helpless as he passed car after car.

Just then, a look of horror came across Jean's face. "It's here! I can feel the head!" The baby was ready to arrive. "What do I do?" Jean shrieked.

"Just hold it in. We are almost there!"

Jean began pushing the head back in. The baby continued to emerge. The remaining ride to the hospital was filled with piercing cries as Jean persistently thrust her child back to safety. As Ed turned the last corner, the second hospital became visible. He bolted to the entrance. This time he didn't turn off the ignition. Instead, he ran to his wife, picked her up, and carried her into the hospital.

"Help!!!" Ed yelled.

Two doctors came running towards them. "What is going on?"

"She's having a baby!!"

"Who's her doctor?"

"He's in Texas!"

The two doctors took over from there and wheeled Jean to the delivery room. Ed paced back and forth outside the door as he waited for some news. Finally, one of the doctors appeared.

"Mr. Lantzer, both your wife and your child are in distress. The umbilical cord is wrapped around the baby's neck. We are trying to untangle it, but we are struggling. I need to know, if it comes down to saving your wife or your baby, who do we save?"

Ed was stunned. How was he supposed to make a decision like that? Tears rolled down his face as he put his head down.

"My wife," he said. There was no question, but Ed was crushed.

"Okay," the doctor said as he ran back into the delivery room.

A short time later, Ed saw the same doctor walking towards the delivery room doors through the window. He met the man just outside the doors.

"How are they?" Ed asked impatiently.

"Mr. Lantzer, both your wife and daughter are alive."

"Daughter?!" Ed asked grinning from ear to ear.

"Yes, a daughter. But there were complications." Ed looked concerned. "Your daughter became entangled in the umbilical cord while your wife tried to keep her from being delivered in the car."

"So what does that mean?"

"She was not getting enough oxygen during the birthing process. Mr. Lantzer, I am not sure if she is going to make it."

"Where is she? I want to see her!"

"Follow me." The doctor ushered Ed to a small nursery. Inside were cribs and incubators. "There," the doctor pointed.

Ed walked over to his daughter. She was inside an incubator with breathing tubes secured through her tiny nostrils. Ed just stared at her. He inspected every part of her body, from her fingers to her toes. *She is beautiful!* Ed thought. He began to cry. At this moment, Ed felt a new kind of love. His heart melted and the only thing he wanted to do was hold her. He put his hand through the portholes and caressed her arm. A nurse approached him.

"Mr. Lantzer, your wife is ready to see you."

"Okay. Thank you, ma'am." Ed took one last look at his precious daughter and followed the nurse to Jean's room.

Jean looked worn as he entered. "How is she?" she asked.

"She looks good." Ed didn't want to scare her. Jean gave him a questioning look. "Don't worry, everything will be okay." Ed pulled up a chair by her bedside and held Jean's hand while they waited together for more news.

A short while later, the doctor entered Jean's room. Ed bolted up. "Have a seat, Ed," the doctor said in a grim tone. Jean and Ed stared at him in anticipation. "I am sorry to have to tell you this, but your daughter just passed away."

"What?!" Ed and Jean both screamed.

"I am so sorry. We did everything we could to save her."

Ed tried to comfort Jean, but she was hysterical.

"I need to see her," Ed said.

"Okay. I will come and get you when we are ready."

"No. I mean now!" Ed dodged passed the doctor and raced down the hall.

"Mr. Lantzer!" the doctor yelled as he tried to catch up to Ed.

Ed made it to the nursery, and there was his beautiful daughter, lifeless. He bawled so hard the walls trembled. The nurses and the doctor stepped back and watched in horror. Ed picked up his little girl and held her.

"My beloved" he whispered. "Jean Evon, you are 'My Beloved' forever. Everything I do from this point forward will be for you. I will live for you."

Ed pressed his face into his daughter's small body as he wept. He then sat in a nearby rocking chair and held her close to his heart, rocking back and forth, unable to let her go.

The undertaker arrived and entered the nursery. "Mr. Lantzer, I am here to take your daughter," he said.

"Absolutely not!" Ed said.

"I know this is difficult, but this is procedure. I must take her with me."

"You are not taking her anywhere!" Ed cried.

"Sir, please."

Finally, Ed stood up and gently wrapped his daughter in a white blanket. "I will take her. Just show me where to go."

The undertaker looked at the doctor, and the doctor nodded. Holding his baby securely, Ed followed the undertaker down a hall and faded into the dark.

After the burial, Ed and Jean struggled to continue. Ed felt Jean's anger towards him. He sensed that she believed the baby's death was his fault, and he agreed with her. He beat himself up day and night thinking about the things he should have done. *There is something I should have been able to do*, he thought. *Something I missed. If I only knew, I could have saved her. I could have tied my belt around Jean's legs to stop the baby coming. I'm just pathetic!*

Instead of healing from the death of Otto Lee, Ed was now reeling from the loss of another child: his beloved daughter. *Maybe Mother is right. Maybe I don't know how to love without hurting someone*, he thought.

9

"God intends to give us what we need, not what we now think we want."

C.S. Lewis, The Problem of Pain

After the death of the firstborn Lantzer child, Ed spent day and night soul searching. The distance between Ed and Jean grew. He needed to figure out a way to make his marriage work and not hurt one more person.

He made a decision. He would work and take care of his family responsibilities, but it would be without emotion, without love. He would no longer let his compassion get in the way. He just couldn't risk it. He realized that he couldn't stop feeling love for people, but he would keep it private from now on. However, there were two places where he felt safe, two places where he could unlock his heart and let his emotions flow: in his workshop and in his Bible. Ed began spending a lot of time in both places, and soon they would intermingle.

One evening, Ed was alone in his workshop reading the scriptures. They always gave him a sense of calm and a feeling that everything would be all right. After a tough day, he knew God's Word would comfort him. Ed had read the entire Bible before, but on this night he decided to skip around, reading a random passage here and there. Each passage lifted Ed's spirit. He was now ready to get to work in the shop. He set the Bible aside and started piling up some scrap wood pieces that were scattered around.

Suddenly Ed shot up and yelled, "I got it!" He paused as ideas began spinning around his brain. He thought about some of the passages he had read. "Father is God, Jesus is God, and the Holy Spirit is God," Ed recited. He paced around the room. "There is only one God." Ed thought about what his father had told him: *You will find your answers in the Bible.* He then flashed back to his childhood when his mother had worked with him using numbers and symbolism. She had talked about sacred geometry and the meanings that numbers held. She especially stressed the importance of the number three. "This is a sacred number, Edgar and it relates to the Trinity," she'd said. "The Father, the Son, and the Holy Spirit." At the time, this had little meaning to Ed, but now it made all the sense in the world. Now he understood.

His father's words, *The angle you choose must have meaning*, whizzed around in his head. He sat down at his workbench and grabbed a straight edge and a pencil. He began playing with a variety of angles. He connected the three lines to create an assortment of triangles, at thirty degrees and sixty degrees. Finally, he grinned, "This is it!" He connected two triangles together as he thought about his mother saying, "Each triangle represents a male and a female. If you put them together, they become one."

Ed stood back and analyzed his markings. In the center of a piece of wood, he had created two glorious diamonds. This was his new angle: a diamond created at either a thirty-degree or a sixty-degree angle. Ed could hear Ervin's voice again. *It is time for you to find your own angle and your own way.* Ed nodded. "I've found my own angle. Now it is time to find my own way."

Ed began working with his new angle. He played around with different ideas and different saws to get the diamond shape he was looking for. He felt he was ready to start working with new designs. He sat at his workbench for hours forming a variety of tessellations. He found that he could put cubes and stars next to each other to create an interesting optical illusion. Depending on what he focused on, either a cube or a star popped out.

Ed's time was now devoted to work, teaching Sunday school classes, and studying his new angle. He prayed daily for God to show him how to use his gifts. He wanted to make sure he was heading in the right direction. The feeling that there was something important to do with his life was still strong.

Then Ed was given an opportunity to pursue one of his interests and potentially his calling. He was offered a chance to go to Great Lakes Bible College to become a pastor. After spending countless hours reading the Bible and studying Hebrew and Greek, Ed felt that he was ready to take the next step. In the fall of 1951, Jean stayed back at the family home while Ed traveled two hours south to Vestaburg, Michigan.

Great Lakes Bible College had been open for only two years, and many churches around the state of Michigan had committed to support the college. The Church of Christ was one of them. So with the encouragement of Ed's church, he enrolled. Since the college was so new, they didn't have a campus of their own. Classes were temporarily offered in a log cabin on Rock Lake near Vestaburg. Ed was so happy to start a new life and potentially a new career, but he knew he had one problem: his struggles with writing.

Ed enrolled on October 18, 1951. He started off with four classes: orientation and doctrine, English I, Acts, and pastoral leadership. He knew that English was going to be a challenge, but with his vivid memory, he hoped to somehow make it through.

The semester started off successfully. Ed was relieved that he was not asked to take any tests. Instead, his skills as an effective speaker and his knowledge of the Bible served him well. As time went by, Ed became more and more confident. He often knew what the professors were going to say before they spoke. He was brilliant.

Each student in the program had to do an internship. Ed was given a busted church in Hillsdale, which was another two hours south. Every week he went to classes, and every Sunday he drove to Hillsdale to preach. He also took a part-time job at a nearby trailer company and sent the money he earned to Jean. He went home to see Jean as often as he could, but with his crazy schedule, it was difficult. Finally, the end of the first year was approaching and Ed went to his doctrine class.

"Have a seat everyone," said the professor. Ed made his way to his table and noticed a sheet of paper in front of him. "Okay, class, today we will be having an exam." Ed's eyes widened. "When I tell you to begin, turn your paper over." Ed was now in a state of panic. *I cannot do this!* he thought. "Okay, class, you may begin."

Ed turned over the paper and just stared at it. He knew the answer to each question, but it would take him too long to write them all out. There was no way he could finish in time. Ed grabbed his test and made his way to the teacher's desk.

"Sir, I refuse to take this test."

"What?" the professor said.

"I am not taking this test," Ed repeated.

"I don't understand. Why won't you take the test?"

Ed looked around the room to see if anyone was listening and then looked back at his professor. "I can't write," he explained sheepishly.

The professor looked up in surprise. "What do you mean you can't write?"

"I just can't do it!" Ed thought this was a better explanation than going into all of the details of the damage from his scarlet fever. "Can't I just tell you the answers?"

"Mr. Lantzer, we can't have a preacher that can't write."

"I thought you guys knew I couldn't write." Ed was grasping at straws.

"No. This is the first I have heard of it. I am sorry, but you need to have a seat and take this test or we are going to have a problem."

"Yes, sir." Ed walked back to his desk and sat down. He put the test in front of him and glared at the first question. He exhaled and then picked up the paper, crumpled it, and threw it on the floor.

"Mr. Lantzer?" said the professor.

Ed ignored the call, slid out from his desk, and at the end of his first year, walked out the door of his classroom and of Great Lakes Bible College. He had earned enough credits to complete both semesters, but he realized this was as far as he could go. He now knew for certain that this was not to be his calling.

Ed worked at the trailer company later that day. It was twenty minutes from the college. When he arrived, he marched right into Mr. Redmond's office and said, "Good afternoon, sir."

"Afternoon, Ed. How can I help you?"

"Any chance you could put me on a full-time shift?"

"Actually, Ed, I could really use you more. When can you start?"

"How about now?" Ed smiled.

"Okay, now it is."

Since there was no work in Kalkaska, Ed felt that this was a smart move. The Redmond Trailer Company had been in business since the 1930s, and Ed knew that his woodworking and building skills would be an asset to the company. The firm had taken over a pickle factory in Alma, Michigan and had begun making longer trailers than any other company. This set them apart. After World War II, when they'd made trailers for the government, a boom had hit when the soldiers began coming home. Redmond offered an affordable solution to housing, and their sales skyrocketed as a result. By 1953, the Redmonds changed the name of the company to New Moon Homes after the New Moon Trailer line became popular.

Ed was now a full-time employee, and after his first year, he was made interior foreman. He did all the setup of machinery and took over the jobs that others felt were impossible.

One afternoon, Mr. Redmond called Ed into his office. "Ed, we just got an offer from Hollywood. They want to do a motion picture based on the book *The Long, Long Trailer* by Clinton Twiss, and they want us to build it."

"Hollywood, huh? That sounds exciting."

"Yes, it does. From what I understand, Desi Arnaz and Lucille Ball will be starring in the movie. Desi supposedly fought hard for this project. He felt it would be a success even though the production company had doubts. He even bet $25,000 that it will earn more at the box office than the new movie 'Father of the Bride.'"

"He must really believe in this then," Ed said.

"Yes. And they chose us to create the main character— aside from Lucy and Desi, that is." Mr. Redmond assumed a serious look. "Ed, I need you to take this on. I need you to oversee the project, and I especially need your expertise to help build the trailer. Can you do that?"

"You can count on me, sir. I won't let you down."

"Thank you, Ed."

"Thank you, Mr. Redmond, for believing in me."

After the design was agreed upon, Ed and his employees spent the next six months building the long, long trailer. They couldn't build just one; they had to build three in case something happened to the first one during production.

Ed first built the interior without the side walls, and then he built each room. The cabinetry was Ed's design, and it became his masterpiece. The wood of the cabinets had to match perfectly in each trailer. Once the interior was complete, it was time to build the frame. Ed demonstrated how to build it and weld it together. The shop had to be modified because the trailer was so long that they couldn't turn it around. Finally, the long, long trailer was complete and ready for the journey to Hollywood.

"Ed, this is spectacular!" said Mr. Redmond. "You and your men did an amazing job! You did me proud."

"Thank you, Mr. Redmond." Ed beamed with pride.

"Well, I just pulled a special permit and I plan to transport the trailers personally."

"When do you leave?"

"We leave tomorrow morning."

Mr. Redmond began the trip when the sun rose, and Ed and his men started the cleanup. As Ed began to make piles of all the leftover material, he stopped in his tracks and paused for a moment.

"Come on over here," Ed directed his men. "I have an idea. Since we have all of this material that we didn't use, what do you think about building a long, long trailer for Mr. Redmond?"

"Let's do it!" the men said eagerly.

"Since Mr. Redmond will be gone for a while, we have the time." Ed said.

The team worked diligently to imitate the three movie star trailers. By the time Mr. Redmond returned to the plant, it was complete. Christmastime was also around the corner, so it would be the perfect gift.

When Mr. Redmond walked in after his trip, the whole shop was waiting. They were gathered around the trailer with the anticipation of children.

"What is this?" Mr. Redmond asked.

Ed stepped forward. "This is for you, Mr. Redmond. Merry Christmas."

"Merry Christmas!" the whole group said in unison.

Mr. Redmond became emotional as he inspected the work of art. "How did you guys do this in such a short time?"

"I don't know," Ed shrugged.

"Well, I can't thank you enough. This is the most thoughtful thing anyone has ever done for me. Thank you!" Mr. Redmond fought to keep his composure.

"You're welcome, sir. It was our honor."

Each member of New Moon Homes shook Mr. Redmond's hand and then went back to work, feeling like they had made a difference. Ed smiled knowing they had, and to him, that made it all worthwhile.

10

*"You must ask for God's help . . . after each
failure, ask forgiveness, pick yourself up,
and try again."*

C.S. Lewis, *Mere Christianity*

The movie opened in New York City on December 31, 1953
and around the country on February 18, 1954 to rave
reviews. Desi Arnaz won his bet, and Ed got something
much more: a sense of accomplishment.

Ed also received his own gift in 1953: a daughter. Jean
gave birth to a beautiful baby girl, and Ed was relieved that
she was healthy. Ed and Jean named her Donna. Ed
decided that he wanted to name each child based on what
they meant to him. Donna stood for "My Madonna." Ed felt
that she was his first love. Finally he had a living daughter
to love. But he had to be careful. He remembered his
promise to himself. He would no longer show emotion
because he did not want to hurt anyone. He especially did
not want to hurt this precious child. Donna was alive, she
was healthy, and Ed was not going to let anything happen
to her. So he silently loved her the best way he could.

The Lantzer family continued to grow. In 1955, Ed and
Jean had a son, and by 1965, they had eight children: six
girls and two boys. The household was now full of life and
responsibility. It was also full of tension. Ed and Jean were
fighting constantly and the anger continued to build. Their
relationship had not been the same since that fateful day in
the spring of 1951 when they lost their first-born. Ed felt

that Jean held him responsible and was not able to let it go, and Jean felt Ed's absence, physically and emotionally.

With the growing tension and larger family, Ed needed to make a change. He needed to bring in more money to support his children, and he needed to break away from the stress. Kalkaska was located in a rural part of Northern Michigan. As a result, it had little industry, so the state of Oregon answered his plea. Ed and his brother-in-law were offered temporary jobs to help build a school. It was a way to make more money fast, so Ed wasted no time in accepting. He kissed his family goodbye, and then he and his brother-in-law headed west.

Ed and his brother-in-law made it to Portland, Oregon safe and sound. They found an inexpensive motel in Tigard, just fourteen minutes away. His brother-in-law waited in the car while Ed checked in. Behind the desk in the office stood an older gentleman with graying hair and black horn-rimmed glasses.

"How much for a room by the week?" Ed asked.

"How many weeks will you need it?" the man asked.

"Well, I'm not sure. We're in town for work."

"Okay, I can give you a deal on the room at the end of the building for thirty-five dollars."

"Does it have two beds?" The man nodded. "Okay, that'll work."

"Just fill in your information here and I will get you set up." The motel manager opened up a frayed guest book and pushed it towards Ed. Ed signed his name and handed the gentleman the money. "You need to pay on Sundays by noon. My name is Vic if you need anything during your stay."

"Thanks, Vic," said Ed.

Ed took the key and went to retrieve their luggage. The two men were soon settled and prepared for the long stay. The next morning, they walked right onto the construction site and began working.

Ed felt so good. Oregon country was beautiful. He felt alert and uninhibited. There was nothing he couldn't do. He was skilled and strong and certain he could lend his expertise to this school project. The men felt grateful to have a job. Since work in Kalkaska was limited, many men from the community had to leave their families to find work. Ed planned on making the most of this opportunity and would let no obstacle get in his way.

Three weeks into the project, Ed noticed his brother-in-law coming back to the motel later and later. Each night, he reeked of alcohol.

"If you don't knock it off, I am taking you home to your wife," Ed said.

"What's your problem? I'm not doing anything wrong."

"Yes, you are. And if you don't stop, I will stop you myself and take you home."

The behavior didn't stop. The drinking increased, and so did the dates with strange women. Ed had had enough and insisted that they pack up their stuff and head back to Kalkaska. His brother-in-law knew he had no choice. Ed would waste no time informing his sister of his escapades, and he was not willing to risk losing his wife over this. So after just a few weeks on the job, they packed up the vehicle and headed home.

Ed's plan was to escort his brother-in-law to his front door, spend time with his family, and then take his old, dilapidated truck back to Oregon. His job was waiting and he had little time to spare. After three days home and a few days back on the road, Ed made it to Portland ready to work. He rolled into the motel at dusk, so he decided to get a decent night's sleep. The next morning, he stopped into the motel office to let Vic know he was back and then returned to work. He pulled up to the construction site and noticed little activity. He located his manager and asked, "What's going on? Where is everyone?"

"I hate to tell you this, Ed, but we ran out of money. They're shutting us down."

"What?"

"Sorry, Ed. We appreciate all your work, but this is the end of the line."

Ed walked away in shock. *What do I do now?* he thought. But immediately, he knew. He had no choice. He had to go back home. He had just enough money to get back, and he couldn't waste another dime on his motel. So with his tail between his legs, he went to retrieve his unpacked suitcase.

Before he left, he stopped into the office. "I just wanted to say bye, Vic. Thank you for everything."

"You're leaving already?"

"Yeah. My job is gone, so I am going back to my family."

"Well, if you ever come back, you'll always have a room here, Ed. Take care of yourself." Vic patted Ed on the shoulder.

"I will, Vic. You too."

Vic followed Ed to his truck and waved goodbye as he pulled out of the dusty driveway. Ed returned the wave and headed back to Michigan.

Ed was home only a short time when problems arose. The fights with Jean picked right back up where they had left off. Ed wanted nothing more than to take care of his responsibilities. He wanted to provide for his family. But no matter what he did, he felt it was not good enough, and he began to feel like a failure. As a result, his temper started to flare. Since he had to protect his family from his love, providing for them was all that he had, and now he couldn't even do that.

Ed's in-laws were not fond of him. They had never felt he was good enough for their daughter. When Jean had first introduced Ed, they feared she was making a mistake, and when Ed and Jean decided to marry, they *knew* she was. In their eyes, Ed was not capable of giving her the life she deserved. They felt that he had little to offer her. Their dreams were higher for Jean. They wanted more for her than a boy who had grown up in a chicken coop. But Jean insisted she was in love and that was that.

Now they were furious with Ed. They believed he was not taking care of his family properly. They stepped in when Ed was at bible school and working downstate. They helped Jean take care of the children's needs and those of the household. Now they were ready to step in again. Soon, Ed's father-in-law paid him a visit in his workshop.

"How are you doing, Ed?" he said.

"Just fine sir, thank you." Ed cringed.

"So, what is your plan next, Ed? What is your next move?"

"I plan to get a job and take care of my family."

"Really, Ed? Take care of your family? And how do you propose to do that?" Jean's father said sarcastically.

"The way I always have." Ed was now steaming.

"Well, Ed, you know what I think you should do?" Ed gave him a quizzical glance. "I think you should just get out of here. You have nothing to offer your family. You are worthless! Just leave and let my wife and me take care of them." Ed glared at his father-in-law in disgust. "You are no good, Ed. Just leave. That is the best thing you could do for your kids: just leave!!"

Ed could feel the heat building, and it began escaping out each pore of his body. He was literally biting his tongue so that he wouldn't say or do something he would regret. He knew that if he started, he wouldn't be able to stop. He could potentially hurt this man if he cracked open the floodgates even a millimeter. So he remained silent.

"Here, Ed. Take this and move on."

Ed's father-in-law threw four twenty-dollar bills at him and departed. Ed sat down on his stool. His mind started racing. *What do I do? Is he right? Am I worthless?* The one thing Ed knew for sure was that he didn't want to hurt his family. He wanted to do the right thing.

He knelt on the floor and put his hands together. "Father, please help me. Show me the way. What do you want me to do, Lord? What do you have in store for me at this point in my life? I want to do the right thing. Show me what that is."

Ed placed his two hands on the cold cement floor and began to cry. He felt so alone, and the workshop felt so still, except for the particles of sawdust that took flight with each breath he exhaled. Ed crawled over to his workbench and leaned against the leg. He took in one deep breath after another to slow down his heartbeat. *What should I do? Do I stay or do I go? If I go, where do I go?* Ed wrapped his arms around his legs and clasped his hands together in front of his knees. *Oregon? I do love it there, and it feels like God's country. Vic said I always have a room there.* Ed sighed. *I wonder if I can find work.* Then the thoughts started to flow as if he were channeling something from outside himself, but still in his voice. He stiffened.

Go, Ed. You know what you have to do. Go.

Ed faced the sky. "Is that you, God?" Ed whispered. Nothing came, but he knew. Ed pulled himself up, wiped the sawdust off his pants, and prepared to pack.

11

*"One road leads home and a thousand roads
lead into the wilderness."*

C.S. Lewis, The Pilgrim's Regress

Ed loaded up his old truck with as many tools from his shop as he could fit. He then dug out a space for his suitcase and himself and drove out of Kalkaska once again. The truck was so full that he could barely move, but he ignored that, and with faith and the eighty dollars in his pocket, he turned the wheel towards Oregon.

Ed had carved a path in the road by now, so he relaxed and settled in for the long journey. He deliberated over his plan. *I will find a new job and a new home for my family.* Finding a job was first on his agenda, but getting his family away from his in-laws was his main objective. There was no way Ed would let them take his children away from him, and he would take care of them one way or another.

He worried about his old truck making it to Oregon again. It was worn and he was not sure how much life it had left. As Ed drove through state after state, he felt relieved. The truck had not burned a drop of oil and the motor was purring like a kitten. This was unusual. "Thank you, Father," he said with gratitude.

Ed recalled the beauty of Oregon: the mystical mountains, the pristine rivers, and the lush vegetation. *Maybe I can buy a place by the Columbia River*, he thought. *Wouldn't that be nice?* He could picture his family there and imagined his children running free in this land of glory with smiles on their faces. *Once I buy a place, I will go back for them*, he promised himself.

Just then, as he was entering the desert, his smile turned to panic. A pile of rocks was scattered in the road, and he instinctively jerked his steering wheel to the right to miss them. He lost control and swerved back and forth until he ended up halfway in a field and halfway on the shoulder. Ed trembled as he tried to calm his nerves. He opened his door and stepped out, one foot at a time, as the dust slowly dissipated. He walked around the truck to analyze the damage. Everything seemed okay until he reached his back tire.

As he stood next to the passenger side, he stared at the missing chunk of rubber in disbelief. "Oh no, no, no!" he yelled. He was gripped with fear. He knew he had barely enough money to make it to Oregon, and now he had a bad tire. He had no way of fixing it and no money to get it fixed. Helplessness followed the fear. Ed kicked the ground in anger and got back in his truck. He put his forehead on the steering wheel and banged it once, then twice, then began to weep. There was no answer. No solution. Ed was stuck, and for the first time in his life, he had nowhere to turn and no one to help him.

Ed continued to cry. As he sat on the east side of the Cascade Mountains, he wondered how God could bring him this close to his destination to fail him now. "If you wanted to kill me, why bring me out here? I don't understand!" he yelled.

Ed pounded his hands on the top of the steering wheel. *What in the world do I do now?* he thought. *I'm almost out of money and now my tire!!* He threw himself back against his seat. *I could try to walk and find a phone. But I have no one to call. I can't just sit here and do nothing. Maybe I should just try to drive. But I don't know if I can make it an inch now with a damaged tire.*

Ed pulled out his weathered brown leather wallet and counted his money. *Ten, twenty, one, two, three. Twenty-three dollars?* "Not good!" Ed hollered. *Well, how do you know you can't make it on a quarter, Ed?* "I'm broke. A quarter is not going to get me anywhere!" Ed half yelled and half cried. *Just start the motor and go. Let's see how far we can go on what's left.*

Ed just sat there in silence for a moment. "Okay." He took in a deep breath and then his entire body relaxed. *Faith. I have to have faith.* He turned the key and the motor roared. With a newfound confidence, he pushed the gas pedal and reconnected with his path in the road.

Ed heard thump, thump, thump, as he neared the Cascade Mountains. This thumping sound penetrated the interior of the truck and reminded Ed of a beat to a song as he traveled up the mountains and then back down. When he finally saw the Portland sign, he barely let himself breathe. He still had nine miles to go to reach his motel. It was going to be close. The gas gauge was now below the red line and the tire was becoming weaker.

Finally, five days after leaving Kalkaska, Ed pulled into his Tigard motel. He now breathed with the full capacity of his lungs. "Thank you, Lord. You turned the impossible into the possible. Thank you for loving me!" Ed now knew for certain that God loved him unconditionally, and he felt bad for questioning Him. He had put His protective shield around Ed and escorted him to safety. After defying the odds, Ed knew God's love would be enough for him to continue on this new journey.

Ed parked his old truck in front of the motel office and got out to knock on the door. It was very early on Sunday morning and he hoped the owner was awake. Just then, the door opened and the familiar older gentleman appeared.

"Hi, Vic," Ed said.

"You've come back. I didn't expect to see you again," Vic responded cheerfully.

"Vic, I don't have a job, and the truck is now burning more oil than it is gas." Ed looked at the back of the truck. "And worst of all, I blew a chunk out of my tire."

"Go on. Go up there and go to sleep. You've been on the road too long. We'll worry about all of this later," Vic said.

"Thank you, Vic!" Ed was overwhelmed with relief.

He followed Vic to the front desk. Vic handed him the room key and Ed made his way back to the same room as before. When his head hit the pillow, he spent a minute thinking about scouring the town for a job in the morning, and then he fell fast asleep.

Spring was in the air when Ed woke. The aroma of the Columbia lilies penetrated his nostrils as he made his way to the motel office. He walked into the lobby and poured himself a cup of the complimentary coffee.

"Morning, Ed. How did you sleep?" Vic asked as he entered the room.

"Very sound. It was the best sleep I've had in a while."

"So tell me, Ed, what is your plan?"

"Well, I am going to start looking for a job. Do you know of any openings, Vic?"

"I have a buddy that might have something. I don't want to say too much until I check with him. In the meantime, I could use your help around here."

"Really?" Ed lit up.

"Yes. There are things that need fixing up around this old place. Would you be willing to help out around here for your rent and a little pocket money?"

"Oh, that would be wonderful, Vic! Thank you so much!" Ed shook Vic's hand. "Where do you want me to start?"

"How about with the rain gutters?"

"You got it." Ed downed the rest of his coffee.

"Oh yeah, when you get a chance go look out back. I have some old tires out there. You just might find one to fit that old truck of yours."

"Thank you, Vic," Ed said with great relief as he went outside to inspect the gutters.

Ed spent the next couple of days working from dusk to dawn on the motel. Vic was grateful to see the place coming alive again. There were new light bulbs in every room, and the once loose rain gutters had been tightened. The motel was also cleaner than it had been in years.

One Sunday afternoon, Ed was pulling weeds in the flowerbeds when a metallic powder blue Oldsmobile pulled into the parking lot. He watched as a stocky man stepped out and went into the office. Minutes later, Vic was heading towards him.

"Ed, Ed!" Vic said enthusiastically.

"Yes?" Ed answered with some apprehension.

"I have someone I want you to meet. Come on inside." Ed pulled himself up from the ground and followed Vic. When they entered the building, the same man Ed watched getting out of his car was sitting in a chair. "Ed, this is my friend I was telling you about."

"Your friend?"

"Remember, the one that might have work for you. He is the district manager for the local union."

"Oh, yes. Hi, I'm Ed." Ed walked over to the man and held out his hand.

"I'm Joe. Glad to meet you." Joe stood up and accepted Ed's hand. "Listen Ed, Vic has told me about you, and he has a lot of confidence in you." Ed and Vic exchanged glances as they both grinned. "I want you to go down to the union hall," Joe continued.

"But I don't belong to the union."

"I want you down to the union hall in the morning," Joe insisted. "I am going to come over to your table, and I am going to say a word. The rest is up to you to figure out what I mean."

"Okay," Ed said, rather confused.

"I can't say any more than that because you are not a union man. I don't want any trouble in the union hall. Do you get it?"

"Oh, I got it. I can't thank you enough, Joe."

"Don't thank me. I can only give you a clue. The rest is up to you."

"I understand." Ed walked over to Vic. "Thanks, Vic. I owe you one."

"No you don't. We're even with all that you've done around here."

Ed left the two men and went back outside to the flowerbeds. *Yep. Faith, you have to have faith.* Ed's grin grew wider as he began pulling weeds again.

The next morning Ed followed his orders. He was at the union hall at eight o'clock sharp. There were men of all shapes and sizes there. He made his way to a table and sat down. He hoped that he wouldn't stand out. He didn't want anyone to question why he was there and who he was.

Soon he saw Joe across the room. He watched him as he conversed with one union worker after another. *There are so many people here*, Ed thought as he waited for his clue. Finally, Joe walked by Ed's table and said, "Deer

Island" under his breath and continued on. *Deer Island? What is that? Is it a place?* Ed was puzzled.

Just as he had slipped into the union hall a few moments before, he just as smoothly slipped out. He opened the old truck door and slid onto the discolored seat. "Deer Island, huh?" Ed pulled out his Oregon map from the glove box and scanned it from top to bottom and side to side. *There it is!* He folded the map back up, threw it on the seat, and began driving north. He had no idea what was in Deer Island, but he was eager to find out. At this point, he would do anything to find a job and hopefully reunite with his family.

The water of the Columbia River shimmered as it kept him company along the route to his destination. As soon as he saw a sign that said "St. Helens," he knew he was close. Finally, the Deer Island marker came into view and Ed became anxious. *What do I do now?* he thought. He moved at a snail's pace while analyzing both sides of the road. "Okay, Lord, I need your help again. Where am I going? Show me the way."

Ed came to an intersection and turned right. He followed the road until he came upon a large structure. There were men bustling here and there. The structure appeared to be some sort of a warehouse under construction. *Is this it? Well, I guess it is time to find out.* He put together a game plan as he exited his truck and made his way into the crowd of hardhats and tool belts.

Ed walked up to two construction workers sitting on a stack of cinder blocks. It was lunch break and both men had an open lunchbox and thermos strategically placed beside them. They still wore their grimy hardhats, and their soiled hands held half-eaten sandwiches.

"Hey, guys, what are you building here?" Ed asked as he approached.

The men stopped chewing and analyzed Ed for a split second. One of them answered, "We are building a storage warehouse."

"What kind of warehouse?" he asked.

"For paper. It will be used to store paper they're making at the mills. When it's finished, it will be a mile long."

"No kidding," Ed said. "Do you know if they are hiring?"

The men shrugged and looked at each other quizzically. One of them said, "I don't know, but the general contractor is around here somewhere. He's the man to ask."

"Do you have any idea where he might be?"

"Look for the guy with a red and black flannel shirt. You can't miss him."

"Thank you," Ed said.

The men went back to eating, and Ed began his search for the flannel shirt. He walked around the site for a while. *This is incredible!* Ed thought. The scale of the project and the atmosphere gave him a boost of adrenaline.

Finally he spotted the contractor. The red and black stood out among the web of steel I-beams. Ed looked up. *Okay Father, are you with me?* He moved toward the man in charge and waited. The general contractor had a blueprint spread out on a table made out of two sawhorses and a piece of plywood. After a few seconds, he rolled up the print and put it under his arm.

"Excuse me, sir," Ed said.

The man looked Ed's way. "Yes?"

"I'm a carpenter with years of experience. I just came to town from Michigan to look for work. Do you have any positions available?"

"What's your name?"

"Ed Lantzer."

"Ed, tell me about your experience."

"My father taught me how to build when I was a child. I can build anything. If you just give me a chance, you won't be disappointed."

The contractor rubbed his chin. "You know what? This is your lucky day. I actually have a position that just opened up. It's yours if you want it."

"I can't thank you enough, sir!"

"Come back in the morning and we'll get you started."

"I'll be here!"

Ed's new boss went on his way, and Ed pranced to his truck. "Oh, Lord, you continue to amaze me!" he said as he began the journey back to Tigard.

The paper warehouse was a large project, and men came from neighboring states to work on the temporary job. Ed arrived for his first day of work with his weathered tool belt strapped around his waist, eager to start. He made his way through a group of fifty or so carpenters until he spotted the general contractor.

"Morning, sir. Where would you like me to start?"

"Good morning, Ed. First, I want to set you up with a partner."

"Okay."

"We have a buddy system here. The carpenters are paired up and work together throughout the project." He signaled one of the carpenters. "Ed, this is Gene. He will be your partner."

"Nice to meet you, Gene," said Ed.

"Likewise, Ed." They shook hands.

"Okay, Gene will show you what to do today," Ed's boss said over his shoulder as he walked away.

"Thank you, sir," Ed said, and then followed Gene deep into the construction site until they came to a stop.

"We are probably only a week away from completing the outer framework of the building," said Gene.

"I can see that," Ed said as he looked up. "How long have you guys been working on this?"

"I've been here for four weeks."

"Where are you from?"

"Northern California. How about you?"

"I came in from Michigan."

Gene gave Ed a look of surprise. "Wow. You are quite a ways from home."

"Yeah, I know," Ed said as he bent over to help Gene move an I-beam.

The personal conversation ended as Gene and Ed dug in and began their first of many days working together. It didn't take long for them to become friends. Each day, they learned more about each other's lives, and soon it was as if they had known each other for years. They found out that they had many things in common, including love for their families and love for God. During the next six weeks, they had many deep conversations about both. They were both in search of a new job and a new home. They hoped to transport their families from the rural communities, where work was hard to come by, to a new part of North America. Oregon seemed to be the answer. They made a pact to help each other make this happen

Finally, the warehouse was nearing completion. Each time Ed sent money home to his family, he was reminded of how much he missed his children. At first he was so busy getting acquainted with the job that he had little time to think at all. Now he thought about them day and night. He had been gone for nearly six weeks, and a longing to see his family began to creep into his every thought.

One evening after a tiring day, Ed entered his motel room and lay down on his bed. He positioned himself on top of the bedspread and stared at the ceiling. *I wonder what my children are doing right now. Oh, how I miss them.* Ed sniffled. He began to have a tug of war in his mind. *I think I want to go home. But I can't go home. What about my father-in-law? I have to see my family. They need me! I need them! But what do I do for work? How do I prove that I am a worthy father and husband?* The thoughts continued to battle until he drifted into unconsciousness.

The next morning, Ed woke and darted out of bed. *I know what I have to do*, he thought. He rubbed the wrinkles out of yesterday's work clothes, grabbed his belongings, and headed out the door. He knew he was making the right decision. The only task left was telling Gene. He replayed the pact they had made in his head as he drove towards Deer Island. *I hope Gene is not too disappointed*, he thought. *I have no choice, though. This job will be over soon, and I can't wait to find another.*

Ed pulled into the parking lot and noticed Gene getting out of his truck. Ed took a deep breath and met him at his vehicle.

"Morning," Ed said.

"Morning, Ed. How was your night?"

"Not too bad." Ed paused. "I made a decision. I have to go home," he said remorsefully.

"Isn't that funny? I made the same decision."

"You did?" Ed said with relief.

"Yes. I am going back to California because that is where I feel I am needed."

"I am needed at home too." Ed and Gene shook hands. "Thanks for everything, Gene. You're a good man."

"You too, Ed."

The men entered the construction zone side by side and worked their last day together. At the end of the day, they walked back to the parking lot. Ed knew it was going to be tough to say goodbye to his friend. They had been inseparable for six weeks, and now they would probably never see each other again.

Gene turned towards Ed and shook his hand one last time. "Take care of yourself, Ed."

"I will, Gene. You too," said Ed.

Minutes later, they were both in their packed vehicles driving in different directions, Gene to California and Ed to Michigan. They had been gone from their families too long. Ed and Gene both wanted a new life and a new home for their families, but in the end, they realized that they already had a home, and it was waiting for them.

12

*"When we lose one blessing, another is
often most unexpectedly given in its place."*

*C.S. Lewis, Yours, Jack: Spiritual Direction
from C.S. Lewis*

Ed pulled into Kalkaska forty-eight hours after leaving
Oregon. He was so anxious to see his family that his only
stops along the way were to pump gas. The old truck fought
hard to transport its owner home, but the motor held on
tight, and by the end of the trip it had only burned a drop
of oil. Ed was relieved. He knew it was unlikely that the old
truck could make a trip like that again. After pulling into
his driveway, he stepped out and patted the hood with
gratitude.

Ed stood outside for a moment as he watched his
children through the window. *They have grown so much,* he
thought as he was overcome by joy. He now knew how
difficult it was to be away from his family. From this day
forward, he would do what he could to be near them. His
protective shield would remain up for his children's sake.
He reminded himself of his pact, "I will not hurt the ones I
love again," but he would be present. "Thank you, Father,"
he said as he made his way to the door and entered his
home.

By now, Jean was used to Ed working elsewhere. It was
something they had both become accustomed to. It wasn't
easy to adjust to Ed's homecoming, but after a short period
of time they were reacquainted. Ed found a job at Alden
Marketing and Supply working in the lumberyard. He felt

right at home surrounded by a variety of softwoods and hardwoods. Some of these woods, such as oak, maple, and cherry, had become his companions over the years. Now they were present daily. Ed loved the smell of the fresh pine and cedar as he traveled from aisle to aisle. Life couldn't be any better. He was reunited with his family, and he had a job he enjoyed.

Spending so many hours in the lumberyard began to inspire Ed. As he helped residential builders find the materials they needed for each project, he had an idea. *Maybe I can build a house. How hard can it be? If they can make a living at it, so can I.* Ed couldn't get this idea out of his head. He thought about it while at work and at home, night and day. If he could build a house and sell it, the profit would help support his family.

He would also prove to his in-laws once and for all that he could take care of them. It was not that he felt he owed this to them, especially his father-in-law. He had practically run Ed out of town, and it was going to be difficult for Ed to forget that. Ed knew that his father-in-law's dislike for him was still present and it was unlikely that would change. The best thing he could do for both of their sakes was avoid him. But if Ed could earn enough money to support his family, there would be no reason for his father-in-law's intrusion. *Yes! I could work at the lumberyard during the day and build the house in the evening and on weekends. It will be perfect!*

But there were two obstacles in Ed's way: the money for materials and the land where he would build the house. There actually was a third obstacle too, but Ed didn't view it that way. He had never built a house before. He had tried to build one prior to marrying Jean to give her as a wedding gift, but he had failed to complete it. At that time, he was barely eighteen years old. Now he was thirty-five, and he had much more experience behind his tool belt. He had no fear. He knew he could do this.

In mid-October of 1967, Ed went to visit his father. By now, Ervin and Ruby not only owned the property where the chicken coop stood, but they had bought the adjoining land named the Old Court Square by the older villagers. The first courthouse of Kalkaska County had made the property home in 1877. The wood-framed building had only cost $1075.50 to build, and after ten years of use, a more elaborate courthouse had been constructed in the village. Now the courthouse was a distant memory, and any traces of the building were long gone.

Ervin was repairing an old barn wood fence when Ed pulled into the driveway. Ed spotted his father and strolled towards him.

"Hey, Dad. How are you?" he said.

"I am well, Ed. It's good to see you."

"You too." Ed sat down on one of the fence posts. "Dad, I have this idea that I just can't stop thinking about." Ervin stopped hammering and observed Ed's excitement. "I want to become a builder."

"A builder?"

"I want to build a house and sell it. You know, for money."

"Okay." Ervin continued to listen.

"I know my experience with building houses is limited, but I can do this. I know I can."

"I have all the confidence in the world in you, son," said Ervin. "I know what you can do with your hands. But where will you build it?"

"I don't know yet. I still have to figure that out." Ed scowled. Silence filled the air for several minutes as they contemplated Ed's options.

"I tell you what, son," Ervin said at last. "I will give you a quarter of the Old Court Square. You go show me that you can build a house."

"Are you serious?"

"I am serious. I have faith in you. The property is yours."

"Thank you! I can't believe you would do that for me!"

"I would do anything for you, Ed. You know that." Ed grinned. "You have the land. Now where are you going to get the materials?"

"Well, I don't have the money for the materials, but I do have an idea."

"What do you mean?"

"Russ Wheeler." Ervin looked at Ed in confusion. "Don't worry. I will explain later. Just trust me."

"I trust you, son."

And with that, Ed departed.

Russ Wheeler had started Alden Marketing and Supply just after World War II. He set up his warehouse along the banks of Torch Lake in Alden, Michigan. Torch Lake, with its magical cyan water, was known as one of the most beautiful lakes in the world. People flocked to the area to get a glimpse of the enchanted water. Soon after the war, the visitors began purchasing lakefront property to build their dream homes. Russ was equipped to supply all of their building needs. Now Ed was his employee, and he hoped that Russ would help him with his building needs too.

Ed thought about how to approach Russ. Russ was a kind man, and Ed felt a connection with him. He hoped that he could set up some sort of payment plan. *I know money is tight, but if I take a little bit off the top of my paycheck each week, maybe we won't miss it*, he thought. He knew it would be difficult since there was little money to spare, but he also knew the sacrifice could pay off in the end. *Maybe I could work a little overtime too. That might be the answer! There has to be a way to make this work.*

Ed arrived early on a blustery morning. Northern Michigan was preparing to say goodbye to crisp autumn and hello to old man winter. It certainly wasn't the best time of year to begin a building project, but Ed didn't want to wait. He couldn't wait. His children's future depended on the project.

As soon as Ed entered the warehouse, he sought out Russ. "Hey, Russ, do you have a minute?"

"Sure Ed, what's up?"

"I have a favor to ask you."

"Okay, shoot."

"Is it possible to set up a payment plan for building materials?"

"What do you mean by a payment plan?"

"Russ, I want to build a house. I have the property, and I know if I build the house, I can sell it. I just don't have the money for the materials up front." Russ listened with an inscrutable expression on his face. "Can I make a weekly payment towards the materials? And if you'd allow me, I could also work an extra hour each week."

"Oh, I see," said Russ.

Ed waited for a response. He had no expectations. *I know this is a ridiculous request*, he thought. He scolded himself as he prepared for the expected no.

After a brief pause, Russ said, "I will make you a deal. I have known you for a while now, and I know your abilities. I want you to go out into my warehouse and pick out everything you need to build your house, a two bedroom. I don't want you to come in and write it up or anything. You keep track of your own books and your own time. When you sell it, then we will even up."

Ed was speechless. It took him a bit to take in what Russ had just offered him. He couldn't believe the kindness of this man. "Are you sure?"

"Positive. Now get to work," Russ said with a smile.

"You got it, boss."

Ed had overcome both obstacles, and now it was time to put his plan into motion. At the end of the day, he clocked out and went directly to the Old Court Square. He walked the invisible perimeter of his new project. He had the blueprint in his head. He knew exactly what he wanted to do. He designed each room as he put one foot in front of the other. He calculated the dimensions and stored them away. *Tomorrow. I will begin tomorrow.* When he felt confident that his plans were in order, Ed jumped back into his old truck, and he and his building materials made their way home.

The next morning, Ed woke bright and early. It was Saturday, and he knew it was the perfect day to start. *I can spend all day*, he thought as he leaped out of bed and sprang to the window. He opened the curtains, and to his surprise a blanket of fresh white snow greeted him. It was the first snow of the season. *Oh boy! Not good!* He considered the problem for a split second. He had hoped the snow would wait for him to get the frame up, but that was not to be. *That's okay. We can still do this*, he thought.

He grabbed a quick bite to eat and downed a cup of black coffee. He then slid a rusty shovel in the back of his truck and drove to the property with excitement. He shoveled enough of the snow to lay the brick, footers, and steel. In no time, he had the frame assembled.

Day after day, he worked hard. He felt invincible. As he picked up a piece of wood, he taught himself to build. Each time he was ready for a new phase of the project, he paused and breathed in deeply. He intuitively knew what to do next. He could feel it. It was as if the materials were talking to him, instructing his every move.

After months of dedication, Ed completed his first house. The house sold before it was finished. He knew that this was his next calling. He was meant to be a builder. He proudly entered Russ Wheeler's office and threw a wad of money onto his desk.

"There you go, Russ." Ed beamed.

"What? Already? Good for you, Ed."

"Thanks, Russ. I couldn't have done this without you. I will be forever grateful," Ed said.

"I never had a doubt. I knew you would pay me back, and I knew you would be successful. Congratulations!"

"Thank you, Russ!"

Ed left that day with a new sense of pride. He was certain that he could earn enough money building houses. It was a way not only to make his dreams come true, but the dreams of others, by creating a place where families could live generation after generation.

Ed knew that something wonderful happened when he and wood got together. Just like years before when he was building with his father, people noticed him. It was the only time he did feel noticed. It was the only time he felt like an acceptable human being. He had spent so many years overcoming the laughs and snickers of classmates. He had fought to overcome the tortures of his childhood. Now he knew he was no longer the town idiot. People were finally looking at him in a brighter light. When Ed put his hands on wood, he was redeemed. He became whole. Most important, he became worthy.

Ed spent the next several years building house after house. His carpentry skills served him well and before long, he could build a house like no other in town. He even built a home for his family. A large tree stood in the middle of the property where he wanted the house to stand. Instead of removing the tree, he decided to build the house around it. When the house was complete, the tree stood tall in the middle of the home. It became the support of the structure and the family. Over the years, the children carved their names and messages into the tree. It represented strength, family, and life.

When Ed and Jean's older children were not in school, they became Ed's assistants. Each day, they took their neatly packed lunches and went off to work with their father. Ed was finally making a living doing something he loved, and having his children by his side made it even better.

13

*"Each day we are becoming a creature of
splendid glory or one of unthinkable horror."*

C.S. Lewis, *Mere Christianity*

By the early 1970s, Kalkaska County had experienced an awakening. After a substantial amount of oil and natural gas was discovered beneath the scenic land, the once small rural town went from having little industry to being the center of a major economic boom. As a result, flocks of new families began moving into the community. Many of the villagers were not prepared for the sudden explosion and had to make accommodations. Local businesses went from struggling to make ends meet to an immediate turnaround.

The Kalkaska public schools were no exception. Prior to the discovery, the town had housed two schools. Since new families were taking up residence at an exponential rate, the number of children enrolling in classes skyrocketed. The two schools were no longer large enough to hold them, so after much deliberation, school officials had no choice but to turn to split sessions. The community was divided into two. Half of the children went to school in the morning and the other half in the afternoon. A plan to build new schools was quickly put on the table. Kalkaska citizens pulled together to make the transition as smooth as possible, and in a very short time, the once sleepy town, now labeled the fastest growing town in America, was wide awake.

Ed's building business also took off. Russ Wheeler and Ed became a team and continued to build houses together.

Russ supplied the materials and Ed supplied the labor. Ed was now building houses full-time and buying up older homes to fix up. Before long, the local bank was calling on Ed to take over their foreclosed homes. They made a deal with him. He would fix them up and sell them, and after the sale he could keep the larger portion of the profit. Ed knew that his early interest in real estate law was coming in handy.

Ed and Jean were grateful for their good fortune, and they knew who was responsible: the good Lord above. They thanked Him daily, whether it was at the start of the day, before a meal, or prior to going to sleep. Church became a top priority in the Lantzer family. They continued to attend Kalkaska Church of Christ regularly. God was the head of their household, and other families in the community admired their faith. It seemed as if after all of the struggles, Ed's life was finally happy. Everything was finally going his way. He had overcome so many obstacles and now he had everything he wanted: his family, a successful business, and God's unconditional love. What could possibly go wrong? You would think that the next sentence would say, "Happily ever after" and "The End." But unfortunately, that is not what happened.

Instead of "The End," it was the beginning of a very dark time in the Lantzer household. Ed's career was growing, but so was the tension in his marriage. At the beginning of their union, Ed knew he wanted a large family. He loved children. He hoped for a dozen, but decided to leave it up to God. According to Ed, they would have as many children as the Father would allow. Ed didn't believe in birth control. He believed they would naturally have the number of children meant for them.

Jean felt differently. Taking care of the children they had was a full-time job. She also worked cleaning for other people, as well as cooking meals for some of the elderly in the community. Her plate was full, and she knew that she had no strength to have another child. She just couldn't do it.

In the end, Jean won. This destroyed Ed. He felt his right to have more children had been taken from him, and this battle became the main source of their arguments. Ed could not get over it. Every time he thought about the fact that his ability to have more children had been taken away, he became angrier, you could say to the point that his family worried about his emotional state. They also worried about his sanity.

The fighting between Ed and Jean became bitter. Ed stayed as busy as he could with his business, but it was not enough to eliminate the arguments. The fighting continued, and so did the stress. The Lantzer children were trapped in the middle. The house often felt like a war zone to them, and one of the few reprieves they had was from their church family. The children attended a weekly youth group program, and they eagerly looked forward to the time away from their stressful lives.

Ed found his reprieve in a different place: a bottle of bourbon. He had not been a drinker before; he believed that that was not proper Christian behavior. But after years of frustration, he found that a drink here and there helped to soothe his anxiety. After a fight, he would go to his workshop and take a sip. This calmed him down and allowed him to let go of his anger.

As time went on, a sip or two was not enough. Soon he could empty a whole bottle. Between this and his anger, it was becoming difficult for Ed to stay in control. It took very little to set him off. One night, he came home from work, and within minutes, a fight erupted. Ed and Jean yelled back and forth. The shouting match escalated until Ed heard the words he hoped never to hear again: "You don't know how to love! And you especially don't know how to love your children!" Ed stood motionless. *But I love my children! How can she say that?* Ed could feel the heat rising from his toes. He flashed back to his childhood. Ruby's words rushed around in his head: "You can't love, you can't love, you can't love!" The heat traveled through his neck and cheeks and out his ears. Before he knew what he was doing, he had spit in Jean's face. Rage filled the core of his being and he lost all control.

"What do you mean I can't love? You don't know anything!"

"The one thing I do know is that I want a divorce!" Jean shouted.

He spit at her again. "There will be no divorce!" Ed screamed.

Ed tried to get himself together, but he couldn't. His rage was too powerful. For the first time, he was truly afraid of himself. He was afraid of the bubbling fire burning deep within. He knew he had a temper, but what he was feeling now was beyond that. He knew that if he didn't leave he could really hurt Jean. He didn't want that, so he made his way out of the house and to the comfort of his bottle. He tipped his head back and gulped a mouthful. His esophagus burned as the Jim Beam slid down his throat. Ed took another swig. Soon, the fight was a long lost memory.

After Ed left for his workshop, Jean gathered up the children and had them pack a bag so she could get them out of the house until Ed calmed down. This became the first of many times that the pastor of their church and his wife came to the rescue of Jean and the Lantzer children. When they returned home, it was not for long, and Ed continued to drink more and more. As a result, the fights became more intense. Their pastor began receiving calls at all hours of the day and night. Jean's frantic plea, "Help, he's out of control again," was all they needed to hear, and both the pastor and his wife were on their way to referee and escort the children to safety until the next morning.

In the children's eyes, Ed was becoming a monster. All his years of tribulation were coming to a head, and the words "You don't know how to love" were cracking open the protective seal he had guarded for so long. Ed was now out of control and he knew it. He didn't know during his tirades, but in the aftermath, he did.

One time after his family had again been escorted out of the home, Ed entered his workshop, yanked out his stool, and sat down. The half-empty bottle of Jim Beam was inviting him to indulge. The temptation was difficult to resist, but with intense strength he backhanded the bottle off his desk. It sailed through the air like a missile until it made contact with the teeth of a saw blade and shattered in every direction.

"Father, I am a failure! I have failed you!" Ed's cry rolled like thunder. "I have destroyed my marriage, I have destroyed my family, and I have destroyed my life!" he screamed. "I don't know what to do. I am not worthy to be on this earth any longer."

Thoughts of ways to exit the world filled his mind. *Knife, gun, or rope? It would be so easy to just end it. Everyone would be happier if I was gone.* Ed stood up and paced back and forth. His heart pounded against his chest. "Should I do it?" Ed tried to picture the world without him, his children growing up, having a career and children of their own. He could even visualize what they might become: ministers, educators, and town officials. *My children are so very intelligent,* Ed thought. *They could become anything they wanted.*

He pictured the citizens of Kalkaska going on with their everyday lives as if nothing had changed, each villager passing by the large brook trout fountain that sat in the center of town on their way to their daily routines. The fisherman's shrine received many visitors during the annual National Trout Festival, which was held every spring to kick off the opening day of fishing season, but the rest of the year it sat, as if watching over the town like an ancient gargoyle. An occasional passerby would stop for a picture in front of the trout, but other than that it just sat, alone. *I feel like that trout,* Ed thought. *Sometimes people make a spectacle of me, but most of the time I feel alone.* "Oh Father, what is happening to me? What am I becoming? Who am I becoming?"

Being a "biblical" father and husband was the most important thing to Ed, but as that dream slipped further and further away, so did he. He continued to pace as he came closer to a decision. "Will it be life or death?" Death seemed to be winning. No one would miss him. After all of the years of turmoil and unworthiness, he would finally have peace. No more pain and no more anger.

Just then, a feeling swooshed through his chest. *God will miss me,* he thought. Ed knew God had a plan for him. If he ended his life, his job would be over before it had begun. Visions of the times that had led up to this moment flitted through his head, all of the moments that were preparing him for God's plan. "I can't quit!" Ed said as he pounded his fist on the workbench.

His raging heartbeat slowed as he became still. The room was so quiet that he could literally hear the pounding in his chest beat lower and lower, as if a musician were gliding back down from the peak of a scale. Ed now knew what he had to do. He walked to the door, turned around for one last look, and exited.

14

*"God allows us to experience the low points
of life in order to teach us lessons that we
could learn in no other way."*

C.S. Lewis, The Problem of Pain

Rumors started swarming around Kalkaska that Ed had "gone mad." When the townspeople spotted him walking towards them, they grabbed their children by the hand and pulled them the other way. "He will hurt you, so just stay away from him," they warned. Ed noticed. He heard statements like "He's crazy!" or "He's a Jesus freak gone mad!" He felt like an alien living among the normal. He was teetering on the edge of sanity and was fighting with all he had to stay on the sane side.

Ed remembered meeting the director of the mental institution in Traverse City, Michigan years before. He didn't make it clear to me how they met, but I do know that he was very fond of him. Ed remembered him to be a kind man, and he felt that he was the one person who could give him answers. Ed needed help, or at least a reprieve from the pain, so one day he decided to make contact with him. He picked up the ebony telephone receiver and placed it between his left ear and shoulder. He then turned the rotary dial clockwise until each digit of the phone number had its turn, and between each turn of the wheel he almost put the receiver down. The first ring came (put it down?), and then a second (put it down?). On the third ring he had success.

"Hello, can I help you?" Ed recognized the director's voice.

"Hello, sir. This is Edgar Lantzer."

The doctor paused for a moment. "Edgar?" Ed was one of those people who once you met him, you never forgot. Maybe it was his short stature and prominent nose, or maybe it was his robust voice and personality. Whatever it was, he remained with people. "From Kalkaska?" the director continued.

"Yes."

"How are you, Ed?"

"Not so good, Doctor."

"I'm sorry to hear that. Is there something I can do to help?"

Even though Ed had only briefly met this man, he instantly felt comfortable with him. He knew that this doctor was the only person who could help him right now.

"Well, I'm losing everything, Doc. My marriage is falling apart, my children hate me, and I'm losing control."

"What do you mean you're losing control?"

"I just feel so angry all the time. I've been drinking and lashing out at my family." Ed choked up. "I don't know what is happening to me."

"I am sorry to hear this, Ed," said the doctor.

"That's not all. Everyone is saying that I'm crazy. I'm not crazy, Doc!"

"Ed, can you come in to see me? We need to talk in person. I think I can help you make sense of all this."

Ed nodded to himself. "Okay." After months of drinking binges and out-of-control behavior, he was about to make one of the toughest decisions of his life.

When Ed arrived at the facility, many changes were occurring on the grounds of the sprawling 400-plus-acre compound. The main building, called Building 50, was built in the Victorian-Italianate style in 1885 and was the first structure on the property. As time went by, many more buildings and cottages for patients were constructed due to the rapid need for mental health facilities. One reason for the increase was the rise in contagious and unknown diseases. Since knowledge of these diseases was limited at the time, patients who had them were put into mental facilities. Many gay children were also sent away to this facility due to ignorance and prejudice. But now, in the late sixties and early seventies, most of the cottages and portions of Building 50 were being closed. The mental health system was drastically changing. The "beauty is therapy" approach, which was the belief that beauty in nature can have a healing influence on patients, was being replaced by psychotropic drugs, which were developed in the 1950s. The once overcrowded wards were now being closed because fewer patients required in-patient treatment. But Ed knew deep down that he needed to be there.

As the wheels on Ed's old truck rolled down the driveway of the hospital grounds, he noticed the landscape. The sprawling lawn looked so vibrant. The colors popped like a Van Gogh painting. He could visualize the swirls of emerald greens and chrome yellows in "The Starry Night." Tree species from around the world stood proud in every direction. He gasped in awe. He had the feeling that the branches were wrapping around his shoulders as if to say "Welcome. You have come to the right place."

For the first time in a very long time, Ed felt a sense of relief. *This is where I need to be right now*, he thought. This probably wasn't the case for most of the patients entering this facility, but Ed felt like it was an answer to his spiraling decline. He needed someone to talk to, someone to oversee his actions and keep him from making more mistakes.

As he moved closer to the entrance, he noticed various breeds of flowers and what appeared to be a pond off to the left. He parked and stepped out of his old truck. He planted his feet in front of Building 50's enormous facade. "Wow!" was all he could say. He gazed upward and analyzed the castle-like spires that adorned intricate towers. The building spanned four blocks! He felt as if he were standing in front of a castle built centuries ago.

The center of Building 50 had been torn down because the main staircase was a fire hazard. A new center had been built in its place. However, it was not in the same style. It was a modern design and looked like a misfit stuck in the middle of elegance, much like many of the misfits who had called this place home over the last century.

Ed entered the center and was guided to the director's office. He heard distant screams as he knocked on the door. The screams were almost haunting. *Who is that?* Ed wondered. *I hope they are okay.* He approached the door and knocked.

"Come on in, Ed," said the director as he pulled the door open. Ed walked in and sat down in an oak chair near the desk. "Okay Ed, tell me more about what is going on."

Ed hesitated. He looked at the floor while the director studied him. Ed met the man's stare with guilt in his eyes. "Doc, I thought about ending my life."

The director didn't even flinch. He had become immune to these words over the years. "Can you tell me why?" he said gently.

Ed explained that he was being judged by some townspeople and struggling to cope with the whispers. He told the director about the pain he had caused his family and the drinking binges that added to his destructive behavior. He bowed his head in shame and said, "I feel like a balloon that has been filled with so much rage over the years. It started when I was just a boy, and it just kept expanding and expanding until finally, recently, it just burst."

"Are you suicidal right now?" the doctor asked.

"No. I realized that I have too much to do to check out now," Ed said.

"Okay, good. Ed, my suggestion to you is to sign yourself into our hospital. This will give us time to discuss these issues more, and it will get you away from your stressful life for a while. Think of it as a vacation." The director waited for an answer. "Remember, it is voluntary, so you can leave at any time."

Ed didn't have to think long. "Okay, Doc. I will do it."

"Follow me and I will get you set up."

They stood up simultaneously. The director led Ed out the door and down the hall. Ed glanced upward, thinking, *Father, stay with me, okay?* Ed's answer came through a flutter through his heart. This reminded him of God's unending presence. When they had stopped in front of the admission desk, Ed picked up a Bic pen, pulled off the black cap, took a deep breath, and scribbled his childlike signature on the bottom line of the form.

Over the next few days, Ed nestled into his temporary home. His room was barren. It consisted of a metal twin bed covered with a vintage army blanket and a dresser. Ed was okay with that; he didn't need much to be content. There was one window in the room that overlooked the beauty below. *How odd. These two spaces are completely opposite*, he thought. *It looks like a scene from a fairy tale outside and death row in here.*

Ed shrugged as he made his bed military style, which he was ordered to do by the staff. After his blanket was neatly folded at each corner, he walked back to the window and gazed at the trees. "Black willows, red elm, weeping maples," Ed said. "So many trees." He reminisced about the many walks he had taken with his father in the woods as Ervin labeled each tree species for Ed. He felt a wave of emotion thinking about a time when life was just beginning and there was so much hope and promise. "What happened?" Ed asked.

Then he heard BAM! BAM! BAM! The pounding on the door brought him back to reality. "Time to line up for breakfast!" Ed bolted to attention and hurried to the hallway to find his spot in the single-file line.

During Ed's stay at the Traverse City State Hospital he became a number. It was a highly regimented community, much like a prison. Patients were told when they could eat, when to take medication, and when to sleep. They could earn a grounds pass with good behavior. The better the behavior, the farther they could roam. Ed received a grounds pass with full privileges. Maybe it was because he had voluntarily signed himself in, or maybe because he was "friends" with the director. Whatever the reason, Ed was grateful. Most patients learned the hard way that if you just follow the rules, you receive more privileges. If you don't, you risk isolation or even worse, electroshock treatment. This approach was accepted in the seventies, and since Ed was not treated in this manner, he didn't think to question it.

On his second day, after Ed met with a therapist and had downed the last of his instant mashed potatoes at lunch, he decided to take advantage of his grounds pass.

There were so many things to see at the mental health compound, but he had his eyes set on one thing: the trees. He turned the ornate door handle and walked down the steps as he tucked his pass into his front pocket. He closed his eyes and breathed in deeply, then slowly exhaled. The air was fresh, and it filled him with exhilaration. It had been a long time since he had felt so peaceful. Yes, he was "confined" in a mental institution, but it was through his own will. He could leave any time, and that kept him at ease.

Ed quickly realized that the hospital had good nurses and bad nurses, good doctors and bad doctors, good treatments and torturous treatments. The mental health system was in a state of confusion at this time. A century before, doctors and hospital administrators had started off with good intentions, but over time, they had lost their way. Some patients found the help they needed, while others found torture, and in some cases, death.

Ed looked at his stay here differently from the other patients and their families. I guess it was a matter of perspective. He looked at the hospital as a place to learn about himself, a place to learn about life, and a place to heal. He also looked at it as temporary. The one thing he did know was that his friend, the director, was one of the good guys, at least for Ed. Talking to him always helped. If that was the case, how could he be anything but a good guy?

Ed spent the next hour wandering. *So much land to cover and so many trees to investigate,* he thought. He knew many tree species, but he realized that on this property, there were trees from places around the world that he had never seen or heard of before. The first superintendent of the institution, Dr. James Decker Munson, had lovingly planted each of the one hundred species after bringing them back from his travels around the country and abroad. He was passionate about these trees, and now Ed was too.

Ed pulled a notepad the size of his palm and a stubby pencil from his back pocket. Each tree had a metal tag that listed the breed. Ed struggled to write, but he could copy the words from the tags. His writing looked like a small child's or a very elderly person's, but Ed didn't care as long as he could read it. He journeyed from tree to tree writing down each name. Before moving on to the next, he studied each detail and character. "English hawthorn, horse chestnut, Colorado blue spruce, Russian olive, sweet gum, sycamore maple," Ed recited aloud as he moved in the direction of the next species.

After an hour of this, he had almost filled his notebook. He halted at one of the black willows and sat against it for a moment so he could read over the list one more time. Then he sat still, listening to the sparrows singing and watching a monarch dancing from one blade of grass to another. *I could use exotic wood in my work!* he thought suddenly. Ed was so inspired that images were flying at him. *Just imagine what I can do with such varieties of color.* Ed faded out of the here and now and into the future. Nothing existed around him except for his ideas. He thought about all of the possibilities that this new concept could bring. After what seemed like an instant and an hour at the same time, he snapped back to reality. He pulled himself up, wiped off the stray weeds from his slacks, and headed back to Building 50.

During the next couple of weeks, Ed received what he considered to be the "best education of his life." He went on daily walks with the director as he made his rounds. They talked about what brought some of the patients there, why they behaved a certain way, and how that all related to life. Ed tucked away each lesson deep in his mind for later use. He knew the information could be helpful in the future, but he was unsure how.

Ed also spent time in the day room with a variety of male patients. Some had been there several months and some forty-five years or more. Many patients were incapable of communicating with Ed, but he befriended many who could. One afternoon Ed and an older man were playing cribbage. The man wore a dingy beige cardigan that draped around his shoulders and rested in his lap. He had probably brought it with him decades before, and it had probably fit him then. His face and hands revealed his years of confinement. *Was his skin smooth and fresh when he first entered Building 50?* Ed wondered. Now it appeared wrinkled and bulging with blue veins around his diminishing frame. With his long skeleton-like fingers and jagged fingernails, he pulled out a pack of Lucky Strikes. He cupped the red and gold package under the table as he quickly pulled out a cigarette and then buried the pack beneath his sweater.

"Don't tell anyone," he whispered conspiratorially.

"What?" Ed whispered back.

"I said, don't tell anyone about my cigarettes."

"I don't understand."

"If any of these jackasses in here find out I have a full pack of cigs, they'll be all over me."

Ed nodded. The man tapped the butt of the cigarette on the table and placed it between his lips as he lit up. Ed watched the smoke spiral upwards to join the haze that hovered just above their heads.

Ed scanned the room. In one corner sat two men fighting over the console television.

"I want to watch 'Let's Make a Deal,'" one man said.

"No, 'Get Smart' is on!" said the other.

They went back and forth. Another man sat off to the side just staring at the television. He was oblivious to the bickering beside him. In another corner there was a small group playing gin rummy. Ed wondered what their stories were. *Did they have a normal life before? Did they have wives, children, careers?*

"Are you ready?" said the cigarette man.

Ed's attention bounced back to the cribbage board. "Yep, let's go."

The man slid the red pegs over to Ed, while he kept the blue ones for himself. "Hey, have you been in the tunnels yet?" the man asked after the game was underway.

"No, I haven't," said Ed. "Where are they?"

"They go from building to building. They used to use them to transport patients. One tunnel comes out in downtown Traverse City."

"Have you been in them?" Ed asked.

"Many times. They say if you listen close, you can hear the cries from the spirits of past patients." Ed's eyes widened as he flashed back to the cries he had heard when he first entered Building 50. *Were they patients or ghosts?* Ed wondered. "There have been thousands of deaths in this place. It won't be long before I will be another one."

Ed watched the man for a moment. *How sad. This is his life. This will always be his life. I have a chance to do anything I want, but he doesn't.*

Ed's heart broke for his new friend. He pulled out a red peg from the wooden board and moved it forward. *I think it's time for me to go home*, he thought. He knew he was ready. He had received everything this place had to give him, and now he was ready to take his new knowledge home.

After telling the director of his decision, Ed walked with him one last time. They visited each room, and then the doctor led Ed outside.

"Ed, I need to tell you something before you leave," he said.

"Yes, Doc?"

"Out of concern for your well-being, your wife tried to keep you committed."

"What?!" Ed yelled. The director could almost hear Ed's anger sizzle.

"But she didn't succeed. You are still free to leave."

"I don't understand. Why would she do that to me?"

"She is worried about you, Ed. She wants you to get help."

"I don't need help!" Ed's voice had risen nearly an octave.

His face burned as he fought to control his emotions. *I got the help I needed. Can't she see that?* He paced back and forth gulping air and then blowing the steam out of his body. He slowed down and tried to make sense of Jean's actions. *I know I scared her. I also scared my kids*, he thought. Ed was furious, but he also felt guilt. He did understand what he had put Jean through, the physical and verbal abuse. The time he had spent in the hospital helped him to see and face that. Ed shook his head. *How can I erase all of that? How can I make up for all that I have done?*

"One more thing, Ed," said the doctor. "She filed for divorce."

Ed was now speechless. He walked over to a nearby bench and sat down. He bent over and put his face in his hands. Jean had threatened divorce before, but he never thought she would go through with it, especially not now, after he'd fixed himself. *After all of the years together, it's over*, he thought.

Memories flooded his brain like a tidal wave. The time they had gone on a family trip, singing in the car. His children working by his side as they built houses in the community. The giggles around the tree in the center of their home as they carved their names. The director watched as Ed scrolled through the movie of his life. *I know the answer to my questions. I can't make up for it all. It's too late. That's right. I can't show love. See, I always hurt the ones I love if I do.* Ed remembered the pact he had made with himself years before. *Don't show love, Ed. It will only cause pain.*

"Are you going to be okay?" the director asked.

"Yes, I will be fine, Doc," Ed said. Whatever hadn't been fixed in the hospital he'd take care of himself. He still had his mission, and he'd fill his life with that. As long as he didn't get close to people again, everything would be fine.

"Okay, I will be inside preparing your discharge papers. When you're ready, come on in."

"Thank you, sir. Thank you for everything."

They shook hands and the director departed. Ed was unsure of his next move. His marriage was over and he had nowhere to go. He would be homeless for the first time. He then noticed something carved into the exterior brick wall a few feet away. It reminded him of the old tree in the family home. He wandered over and read the engraving. His eyes followed along the indentation of each letter. He thought about what it said for a moment and then he read it again. "Make weary in well doing and fear ye no evil, for God said eat, drink and make merry, and God said let nothing suffer, for tomorrow you may at least die."

Ed sat in silence thinking about the words. *Let nothing suffer for tomorrow you may at least die.* He knew what he had to do. It was clear that Jean couldn't take any more. It was time to let them go, Jean and the kids. It wouldn't be easy, but it was the only way.

15

*"No man knows how bad he is till he has
tried very hard to be good."*

C.S. Lewis, *Mere Christianity*

Since Ed no longer had a home, after his release he decided to seek solace in the one person who would accept him without judgment: his father. Ervin gave Ed a home while he prepared for the upcoming divorce. On July 8, 1970, almost twenty years after she and Ed were married, Jean officially filed for divorce. She also filed a temporary restraining order against Ed. The papers were served and the date was set.

Something happens to people when they go to battle. They leave no stone unturned in the effort to win. Jean decided to fight for full custody of the children, and she would do whatever it took to shield them. She no longer felt that Ed was capable of fulfilling his parental responsibilities. Her goal was to protect her children, and in her eyes, the only way to do that was to terminate Ed's rights.

When Ed first realized that Jean was fighting for full custody, he was angry and hurt. He knew that he needed to give his family space to heal, and the day he left the hospital, he had every intention of doing that. But the thought of losing them forever was too much. He wasn't ready or willing to let his children go permanently. Shortly after being served the papers, Ed marched into his lawyer's office.

"Did you see these?" Ed waved the papers back and forth. "What can I do about this?" The lawyer was silent. "They are going to take my family and everything else!"

"Ed, I'm not your lawyer anymore. I'm Jean's," he said. Ed was more than startled. "And everything you tell me, I will use against you."

Ed stared at his onetime lawyer in disbelief. He couldn't believe what he was hearing. *How can you turn on me like that? I trusted you,* Ed thought. Without another word he turned around, crinkled the papers, and walked out the door.

Life felt like it was spinning out of control for both Ed and Jean. Their separation and pending divorce may have stopped the fighting between them for now, but other issues were magnified. One issue was money to support the Lantzers' eight children. By this time, the children ranged in age from five to seventeen. Jean's income was barely fifteen dollars a week. They did have various property and rental houses that Ed had accumulated from his building business, but they were tied up until the divorce was final. As a result, their church family stepped up to help support them.

Ed and Jean were also ordered to begin marriage counseling. They had tried getting professional help prior to the separation, but to no avail. On the first visit, the new counselor suggested that part of the problem was a lack of steady income. Ed had been self-employed since starting his building business. He had experienced some success, but just like with many self-employed people, his cash flow was unpredictable. With all of the family stress, Ed's business had slowed and money was tight. Ed listened very carefully as he heard this suggestion. *Does this mean if I find a steady job, I could save my marriage?* He knew what he had to do.

The next day he began his search. He was lucky. He quickly found a position as a custodian for Kalkaska Public Schools. Just twenty years prior, he had left this school diploma in hand, grateful that he would never have to go back. Now he was the janitor. He didn't care. At this point he would do whatever he could to keep his family together.

Ed made two dollars an hour to sweep and mop floors, scour bathrooms, and clean classrooms. It wasn't the most glamorous position, but it was the most important. This job could give Ed his life back. After urgings from the church and counselor, Jean decided to reconcile. She saw and acknowledged Ed's attempt to do what he could to make the marriage work, so just a month after Jean filed for divorce, Ed moved back home.

Unfortunately, after just six months the fighting resumed. The anger between the two was overwhelming. They both struggled to forget the past. Sometimes when people hold anger in for so long, it is hard to let it go. They felt it was impossible to start over when there was so much hurt in the way. As a result, life in the home became heated once again. Jean knew this was not going to work. She held on for another few months, hoping that she was wrong, but she wasn't. By May, ten months after first filing, Jean made up her mind: she was going to reopen the divorce case. Ed heard rumors that she was going to refile in the next few days, and his heart sank. He knew it was the end. There was no changing the past and no further chance to reconcile.

A temporary custody and child support hearing was held on July 19, 1971, in Cadillac. At thirty-nine years old, Ed sat in the courtroom as if he were a criminal, with Jean and Ed's ex-lawyer on one side and Ed on the other. *Not only does she have my lawyer, the court wants me to pay for his fees too. What absurdity!* Ed thought as he shifted in his seat. He felt so alone and empty. The energy coming his way was negative, and he was a spectacle once again. It didn't matter that he'd made a success of himself in real estate. It didn't matter that he'd completed his psychotherapy. He was back where he started. Worse, actually.

He examined the room and felt every eye piercing through his body in judgment. Ed knew in his heart that he was not the terrible person they were making him out to be, but he chose to just listen as he was being crucified. *I quit! I won't say a word,* Ed decided. Without his lawyer, he believed he was helpless. He had no family and no support in the room. So he did just that. He listened and refused to defend himself. *It seems like just yesterday that Jean and I were getting married, and now it's over*, he thought. He drifted in and out as Jean's lawyer continued to bury him. He thought about the pain of losing their first-born child, and then the turnaround when they filled the house with laughter and the pitter-patter of feet. Now, it was all a distant memory. The family that Ed was so proud of was slipping away, and he was being made out to be a villain.

Finally, Jean's testimony was over and the decision was pending. Ed sat zombie-like while movement and whispers fluttered all around him. The longer he waited for the judge's decision, the more distraught he became. *What if I lose them? What will I do? This can't be happening!* Then Ed heard the bailiff announce that the judge had come to a decision. He froze as he watched the black-robed man sitting behind his throne. No breath escaped Ed's clenched lips because the anticipation was too great. Then, the words he feared thundered throughout the room, bouncing off each wall.

"I hereby award temporary custody and support to Jean Lantzer pending the final divorce hearing."

Ed didn't move and was still holding his breath, and then "BAM!" The judge's gavel made contact with his desk. Before Ed knew what he was doing, he had bolted towards the sound. He leaped over the wooden fence separating the judge from the gallery and grabbed the judge's neck with both hands. The courtroom erupted. People were screaming and yelling and a group of men came running. Ed was peeled off the judge and immediately put in shackles. As they hustled him towards the exit, Ed made eye contact with Jean one last time. Her look of sheer terror told Ed everything he needed to know. He was a villain, and his actions had just proved that to everyone watching.

Ed knew it was all over now. There would be no turning back. His life would never be the same. He had lost his children and was now a criminal. His eyes filled with sadness, and he concentrated on the floor so he would not see another person's glare as they yanked him out of the courtroom. He looked up to his Heavenly Father. "I'm sorry," was all he could say, and then he turned his eyes to the floor again in shame.

Two days later, Ed was shackled in the back of a five-foot cruiser heading south to Jackson Prison. The thought of spending the next six years of his life locked away was nothing compared to the thought of living without his children forever. He mourned silently so the two police officers in the front seat would not hear him. He would try to be as strong as he could. Showing weakness was not an option. He fought back the tears because he couldn't wipe them in his restraints, but the lump in his throat and the tightness in his chest were visible only to him.

Less than a minute or two into the almost four-hour trip, the cruiser pulled into a parking lot. Ed looked up in surprise as he noticed the sign that said "Cadillac State Police" above the door. *What are we doing here?* Ed wondered.

One of the police officers said, "We need to go in here for a minute."

"What?" Ed said.

"Someone wants to talk to you."

The officer opened Ed's car door and escorted him to the front of the building. *Why am I not heading to prison?* Ed wondered as he shuffled his feet back and forth. When they entered the building, the captain of the state police post met the three with a stern expression. They walked into his office and the captain said, "Sit down, I want to talk to you." He directed Ed towards a vacant chair in front of his desk, sat down, and looked Ed straight in the face. "Ed, if you had your choice, where would you be?" he said.

Ed looked at him, puzzled. "I don't have a hell of a lot of choices, do I?" He laughed sarcastically. "I'm on my way to Jackson."

"Well, Ed, we changed our minds." There was silence for a moment.

"What do you mean you changed your mind?" Ed said. He could barely breathe as he waited for a response.

"We've already got it set up. We're going to put you on a bus here in Cadillac and send you to Detroit." Ed's eyes widened. "There are people waiting there to take you to the airport."

Oh Lord, what is he talking about? Is this a dream? And if it is, please don't wake me up!

"Ed, we are not sending you to prison. We are sending you to Orlando—a place where you can get a fresh start, away from all the turmoil here."

"But I don't have clothes, food, nothing." Ed looked at his jail outfit. "Only this orange and green jumpsuit."

The captain pulled out an old shirt, slacks, and a pair of worn shoes. "These will help until you can get yourself established."

"Thank you, sir." What else could he say?

"There is one more thing. We don't want you to come back to Michigan. Is that understood?"

Okay, I get it. This is their way of getting rid of me, Ed thought. "Yes sir, I get it."

At this point, Ed would gladly take "getting rid of" over prison. He had nothing and didn't know a soul in Orlando, but things could be much worse. So for that, he was grateful. The officers knew that Ed was harmless. He was no criminal. Ed was a father in deep distress and mourning. The legal system realized that prison was not the place for him. During these years, it wasn't uncommon for the police to ship a person off to somewhere like the military instead of prison. In this case, it wasn't the military, but according to them, getting him out of Michigan would probably be the best for everyone.

16

*"You may forget that you are at every
moment totally dependent on God."*

C.S. Lewis, Mere Christianity

After arriving in Detroit, Ed was escorted to the plane. Once he was inside, his shackles were removed. He took his seat towards the back and prepared himself for the ride. Ed had never flown before. He was scared, but did his best to ignore the fear. *I wish everyone would stop staring!* he thought. Some of his fellow passengers watched him enter the plane in restraints and stared nervously. *I just have to ignore them.* Ed put a pillow behind his head and covered his lap with a blanket as he thought about ways to confiscate both. *I have nowhere to stay when I get off this plane. It could get cold tonight.*

Coming from Northern Michigan, he had no idea what to expect. He realized that he probably couldn't get away with both the blanket and pillow, so he decided the blanket would be the more useful. It was thin enough to stuff under his shirt.

With his plan in place, he tried to rest. He closed his eyes, but each time he did, his children's faces flashed before him. Emotion began to well up. *No, no, no! I can't do this right now.* He inhaled and then exhaled to release the emotion.

A stewardess stopped by Ed's seat. "Would you like to order dinner?"

Ed was surprised by the request. *Dinner?* He didn't realize this was an option. He was hungry. His stomach had been rumbling for a while now. But he knew he couldn't pay for the meal. He leaned over and whispered, "Uh, I don't have any money, ma'am."

"It's already paid for, sir. It comes with your plane ticket." She smiled.

"Oh yes, please. That would be nice."

Ed returned the smile. He pointed to the option of his choice and then eased back into his seat while he waited. When the meal arrived, Ed's stomach leaped with relief. Dinner was some type of poultry and mashed potatoes covered with a mystery sauce. Ed didn't care; he gobbled every bite. He stashed a packet of peanuts in his pocket for later. He now felt that he could get a little rest before they landed in Florida.

Shortly before the descent, Ed woke to a voice saying, "Do you want to hear a secret? I know one." Ed followed a little girl's giggle in the seat in front of him. She then pulled the string on the back of her doll again. "Gracious me, you're getting to be such a big girl!"

She giggled again and ran her tiny fingers along the black square-rimmed glasses on the doll's face. She propped the doll up on her lap as she straightened out the bright blue and white polka dot dress and yellow rickrack trim.

Ed watched her play with the doll. He choked up again as he thought about home. *I wonder what they are doing now.* He watched the girl's every move, subconsciously hoping that if he stared long enough, she would transform into one of his own children.

The girl pulled the string again. "If you had three wishes, what would you wish for?" the doll asked.

Ed thought, *That's easy: my family, my family, and my family!*

"Speak a little louder, dear, so Mrs. Beasley can hear you."

The girl hugged her doll tight as the wheels of the plane made contact in Orlando. Ed held onto the arms of his seat until they came to a stop in front of the terminal. He stuffed the blanket in his shirt while he attempted to fight back waves of fear. Not fear of the landing, but what was next. *What's in store for me? How do I survive? Where do I go?* Ed stood up and followed the pack into the airport. He knew there was only one way to survive and that was with the help of God. *Faith. I have to have faith,* Ed reminded himself as he took a first glimpse of his new home.

Since Ed had no bags to retrieve, he stood in the middle of the Orlando McCoy Jetport trying to decide on his next move. *What now? How do I find Orlando from here?* Ed was unsure what direction to take, so he stopped someone who appeared to work at the airport.

"Excuse me, sir. How do I get to Orlando from here?"

"It's ten miles north."

"Ten miles?" Ed said in dismay. "Okay, thank you."

The gentleman continued on his way as Ed tried to compose himself. *Not good. Ten miles! I have no transportation, and I have no money to hire transportation.* The fear that Ed had been pushing back was now growing. He was officially homeless. He had no home, no money, and no family. The things that meant the most to him were gone. He was at the lowest point in his life, and the only way to pull back up was one step at a time.

Ed looked at his feet. *Okay. I guess you are my transportation. Don't fail me now.* And with that, Ed put one foot in front of the other and began the long journey to Orlando.

After a long day of walking and resting here and there in the swamp, Ed finally arrived tired and hungry. He was not used to the summer heat in Florida, and quickly realized that the blanket might be of little use after all. The city of Orlando was large and overwhelming. A small-town guy, he wasn't used to huge urban environments. *I wonder if this is how an ant feels,* Ed thought as he looked up at the large buildings.

His main goal at this point was to find food and shelter. *I don't know anyone here. Maybe I should start looking for a restaurant.* He hoped that at the end of the night they would throw away the leftover food. Ed walked down alley after alley and looked in every dumpster. *I cannot believe my life has come to this!* He thought about all of his hopes and dreams. This was not one of them. He shook his head and continued his search.

Several Dumpsters contained something of use: bread, crackers, and cardboard. Ed was able to gather enough to sustain himself for the night. After downing a half-eaten cheeseburger he found behind a diner, he put the rest of his finds in his pockets for later. Night was fast approaching, and finding a place to sleep was becoming urgent.

He wandered down a narrow alley, dragging the cardboard behind him. He spotted a nook behind a crumbling brick building. Ed used the pieces of cardboard to barricade himself from the world. He then pulled out his airplane blanket to use as a pillow and nestled in for his first night in Orlando. Before fading into unconsciousness, he looked at the stars. "Dear Father, thank you for keeping me safe. I am so grateful!" And with that, he slipped into his world of dreams.

Ed lived on the streets of Orlando for four months. The alleys became his home and Dumpsters furnished his nutrition. One Dumpster in particular was well-stocked. It was behind a place called Dana's Restaurant, and it kept him alive, so he tried to sleep close by. He figured that he had had success there so why venture too far away. The little bit of change in his pocket came from bumming on the streets. *You kind of lose your dignity when you get hungry,* Ed thought. But it was the only way to survive.

Throughout the four months, Ed looked for work. He scoured the town hoping that someone would give him a chance in carpentry. He had no luck. Without an address, it was difficult to get hired. One night as Ed found his spot in the alley, he fell into hopelessness. "No one will give me a chance!" he yelled. "I can't live like this much longer! I need a miracle!" Depression was taking over, but Ed could not let it win. He was not ready to give up. Not yet.

The next morning Ed walked into the office of a sawmill. He was surprised and pleased to find one in Florida. He knew he had experience working in a mill back home and his expertise with wood could be invaluable. "Please, Father, don't let them turn me away. Open up their eyes and let them see what I have to offer," he pleaded. He opened the office door and walked in. His nerves were tense, but he had to keep it together. This opportunity was too important.

Two men standing by a desk looked up as Ed entered. "Excuse me, but are you hiring?" Ed barely got out the last word when he froze. So did one of the men.

"Ed? Is that you?"

"Yes," Ed said with excitement. At that moment, a wave of relief washed over him after he recognized that the man was a classmate from years ago—one of the classmates Ed respected.

"What are you doing this far away from home?" the classmate asked.

"It's a very long story. I'm desperately looking for work. Do you have anything?"

"Have a seat. Let's talk about what's going on."

Ed sat across from his classmate and the mill manager at a table and began to tell his long tale. When he was finished, all three men had tears in their eyes. The classmate looked at Ed with compassion and said, "Ed, I bought this mill with a group out of Detroit. I usually consult with them, but in this case I think they will understand. I would be happy to have you work for me."

The men smiled. Ed put his head down on the desk and began to cry. He had so many emotions flowing through him. After four months of living on the streets, eating out of Dumpsters and begging for pocket change, Ed finally had a job. He couldn't believe it. Both men moved away to give him space. After the story he had just shared, they knew he needed to let it out.

Ed continued to sob. As happy as he was to have the job, he was also sad. At this moment he knew he could never return home. *I lost my family. I can't go back. I can't leave. The only thing I can do is move forward.*

Ed gathered his emotions so that he could thank his classmate one last time before leaving. "I will never forget what you have done for me! Thank you."

"You're welcome, Ed."

They shook hands, and Ed walked outside and headed in the direction of his temporary shelter. He visualized himself kneeling down in praise. *It's time to start pulling myself back up.* After spending months as low as a man can go, Ed had put his foot on the first rung of his new ladder of life. With this miracle in hand, he could see one rung after another appear above him. Hopelessness turned into hope, and he knew who was responsible. A smile spread across his face. "Thank you, Lord. Thank you!"

17

"To love at all is to be vulnerable."

C.S. Lewis, The Four Loves

After a short time working at the mill, Ed rented a little apartment. He was officially off the streets. He now had the comfort of knowing that he had a warm place to go to at the end of the day. He was making barely enough money to squeak by, but he took a few dollars to buy two pairs of work pants and two shirts. The outfit he had worn every day since leaving the Cadillac State Police post was now retired. Ed threw the shirt and slacks away with pleasure, but he held on to the shoes. He had no intention of wearing the clothing again. In fact, even looking at it was difficult. It was a reminder of his pain. Discarding it was an attempt to release this pain.

His days were no longer filled with turmoil. Instead, Ed worked long hours. He figured that if he stayed busy, the memories couldn't invade his thoughts any longer.

Ed started at the bottom of the company, and before long he was given the position of outside installer. He installed everything the company built, and he was good at it. He also started to work on his parquetry again. Since he had little furniture in his apartment, the majority of the space became his workshop. During the day he worked at the mill, and in the evening he created more tabletops, hope chests, and jewelry boxes. By the time he closed his eyes, he knew he would get just enough sleep to start all over again the next day.

Ed became close with the mill manager, Bob, who, according to Ed, was a brilliant man. He could tell you how much a desk was going to cost just by looking at the blueprints. Ed respected that and respected him. They had many long talks. They often went out for coffee and a sandwich during their lunch break. It was so nice to finally have a friend again, someone to confide in and who could confide in him. No topic was off limits.

One day, Bob sat down at a table in their favorite diner with a grim look on his face. "You okay?" Ed asked.

"Well, Ed, I could be better."

"What's going on?"

"I had an affair with my secretary. A one-night stand." Ed kept his look of surprise under wraps. "The crazy thing is that I love my wife. She's everything to me. When we married, we promised that it would be forever. I knew what a mistake I had made as soon as it was over. I was weak! I had a weak moment that I can't take back."

"What are you going to do?"

"When I got home that night, my wife met me at the door. I thought, 'Oh boy, she knows.'" Bob shifted in his seat. "She had a stunned look on her face. As I traipsed towards her, I tried to figure out what to say. I walked up the steps and her look became more solemn. Then she just blurted it out. 'I just came home from my doctor's office and I have incurable cancer. I'm dying.' I just stood there, speechless, as she wrapped her arms around me."

"Oh no! Bob, I am so sorry!"

"Me too." Bob sniffled. "Ed, God is punishing me. He is taking my wife away to teach me a lesson."

"God doesn't work like that. This is purely coincidence."

"How can I be sure? How can I know that God isn't taking my beautiful wife to get back at me for what I have done?"

"Bob, the one thing I know is that God is a loving God. He loves every one of us, no matter what we do. With repentance we are all forgiven. No questions asked."

"Are you sure?"

"Yes. I have made so many mistakes, Bob. The one I am most ashamed of is that I was abusive to my family." Bob looked alarmed. "I know. I'm not proud of this. But Bob, God has forgiven me."

"Really?"

"Yes. I learned a long time ago that God doesn't guarantee that life will be easy. We will make mistakes, and our loved ones might become sick or even die. But he does promise that He will be by our side." Ed grinned. "Faith. That is all you need. God will be with you through this. Just trust in Him."

"Okay, Ed. I'll give it a try."

Bob and Ed finished their coffee and headed back to the mill.

Ed stayed by his friend's side as he watched his wife wither away. After her death, Ed watched over him closely to make sure he was going to be okay. It wasn't easy. Bob had to go through all the stages of grief, just like everyone else. But in the end, he knew he had God's love. Because of that, he knew he would see his wife again, and when he did, it would be flawless and forever.

Bob's faith continued to grow. Sadly, it sometimes takes a tragedy to wake us up, to break us open. Ed and Bob continued to have their coffee breaks and their long talks about God. As a result, their friendship grew as well.

One morning Ed walked into the office and saw Bob sitting at his desk mulling over a blueprint. "Morning, Bob," he said.

"Morning, Ed." Bob rose from his seat and faced Ed. "Hey, I want you to go out back and cure this atheist I got out there."

"What?"

"One of my guys says he doesn't believe. He doesn't think there is a god. Isn't that sad?"

"It sure is. Where is he?" Bob pointed out the window. "There. The older man in the denim shirt."

"Okay, Bob. Let me see what I can do."

Ed entered the mill yard and headed towards the man. He had no intention of giving him a sermon. He decided the best approach was to befriend him.

As Ed approached, the man was moving some lumber. "Hey, let me help you with that," Ed said. He grabbed one end and helped him stack the wood.

"Thanks. I appreciate that," the man said.

"You're welcome."

They made their introductions to each other and then the man went on his way.

Ed decided to make some kind of contact with this man at least once a day. It started off with a hello here or a wave there. Then Ed broke through. The man found out that Ed used to be a builder. He was rebuilding his home and was struggling because of his lack of knowledge about home construction. Ed received an invitation to come over to look at the project, and he accepted with delight.

Ed arrived just as the man's wife was walking out the door with a bowling ball bag in one hand and a cigarette in the other. "He's inside, just go on in," she said in her raspy voice as she headed towards her car.

She was gone before Ed could respond. He entered the half-completed house. "Hello?" Ed said as he walked into the entrance.

"Hey, Ed. Come on in."

"Okay," Ed replied as he took note of the chaos in every direction.

"Yeah, it's a mess isn't it? This is why I need your help." Ed nodded. "Let me show you around."

Ed followed and made mental notes of things that needed to be changed. It was evident that the man had no idea how to build. Ed knew he could help transform this home, and he also knew that this was his opportunity to transform the man's soul.

"So, what do you think, Ed? Can you help me?"

"Absolutely," Ed replied.

They spent the next few months, after work and on weekends, creating a beautiful home for the man's family. While they worked side by side, they talked about many subjects such as family, work, and God. At first, the man wasn't receptive to a religious discussion, but over time he opened up and started to listen. Ed used his knowledge of the Bible, which he'd read over and over. He also used his life experiences, good and bad, to explain how God works in our lives. By the end of the building project, Ed felt that he had made a difference. He had not only transformed a soul, but he had also made a friend. This new friend reminded Ed of his father. He even talked like Ervin. He missed his dad so much and was grateful to have developed a relationship with someone so similar.

The older man was not the only one to gain something out of this new friendship. Ed did too. Shortly after beginning the remodeling project, the man's daughter, Linda, stopped by to say hello to her father. When Ed first saw her, he was mesmerized. She must have been mesmerized too because her visits became more frequent. Soon they were dating. Ed was not looking for a relationship. It was actually the last thing on his mind after such a volatile ending to his marriage. But for whatever reason, Linda stepped into Ed's life and he was excited.

They dated for a short time and then Ed paid her father a visit. "Come on in, Ed," the old man said as he opened the door.

"Thank you." Ed walked inside as he tried to calm his nerves. He knew that the man was okay with the courtship, but he wasn't sure if he was ready to accept Ed's next request. "Uh, sir? Linda and I have been dating for a while now. I want you to know how much I love her."

"I know you do, Ed."

"I am ready to take the next step. I want to marry her. That is, if it's okay with you."

Ed rubbed his hands together as he waited for a response. They both had their feet planted as if preparing for a standoff. Ed could feel a bead of sweat travel down the side of his face. The man analyzed Ed's eyes, the windows to the soul. Finally he said, "Ed, you have my permission."

Relief spread throughout Ed's body. "Oh, thank you, sir. Thank you!"

Linda's dad patted Ed on the shoulder and said, "You just treat her right. Do you hear me?"

"I will. I promise."

Ed and Linda were married on November 7, 1975. They moved into a small house and began their new life together. Linda worked at an office supply store and went to college while Ed continued to work at the mill. Ed was pleased to be married again. He felt that he had been given a second chance to do things right. He hoped that this new start would bring a happy marriage and a new family. Ed would take being a part of a family again in any way he could. He made a promise that this time he would do things differently.

18

*"No good work is done anywhere without
aid from the Father of Lights."*

C.S. Lewis, Reflections on the Psalms

Ed's job at the mill was instrumental in expanding his career. It gave him the chance to make new contacts and work in facilities many carpenters could only dream of. One of those facilities was Walt Disney World.

During the mid-1960s, Walt Disney spent a great deal of time investigating the land surrounding Orlando. He was looking for his next big project. Martin Anderson, the owner of *The Orlando Sentinel*, was one of the most influential people who made the development possible by demanding that a new network of roads be installed in the area and that an airport be built for Central Florida. He won this battle and as a result gained the interest of Disney.

Word quickly spread around Orlando that someone was buying up over 30,000 acres, a chunk here and a chunk there. The buyer was a mystery and people speculated about who it might be. Disney officials contacted Anderson about their plans and asked him to keep them under wraps. The secret was kept until a reporter leaked the story in October of 1965. Walt Disney World officially opened in 1971, and by 1975 Ed was sent to build and install cabinetry in several of the added exhibits and golf shops.

His work was exquisite, and it gained the interest of Barnett Bank. This was one of the bank chains that dominated Florida at the time. Mr. Barnett was rebuilding his office. It was originally one story. They decided to add two more stories on top of it. He had designated the third floor as his office. He put in mast oak starting from the elevator, going all the way around the building, through his office and into the reception area, then all the way back to the elevator. He had hidden hinges from floor to ceiling. Ed was sent there to help with building and installation.

Shortly after Ed arrived, one of the electricians got ahead of himself and cut a couple of holes in the plywood that he couldn't cover up. Mr. Barnett came down to the bottom floor to find Ed. He had heard about Ed's building abilities and knew he was the man to fix the problem. When he saw Ed, he said, "Ed, we have a mess upstairs to straighten out. Can you help?"

"Sure. What happened?" Ed said.

"Follow me and I will show you." Ed and Mr. Barnett entered the elevator and made their way to the top floor. "There," Mr. Barnett pointed.

Ed analyzed the situation. "No problem. I will have this fixed in no time," he said.

He looked through bundles of one-inch oak plywood. He took the two pieces containing the holes out and replaced them. By the time Mr. Barnett appeared again, the job was completed.

"That was quick! I am very grateful for your help" said Mr. Barnett. Ed accepted the kind words with a nod. "You know, my receptionists are in need of new desks. Would you be willing to build them?"

"I would be happy to, sir."

Ed made a mental note of what Mr. Barnett wanted the desks to look like and went to work. He was excited about taking on the challenge. While Ed was building the desks, Mr. Barnett found out about his parquetry and inlay work. Since he was transforming the third floor of his building into his private office, he decided that he didn't want a traditional office. Instead he wanted it to look more like a living room with couches, chairs, and lamps.

"Ed, I have one more request for you. I would like two coffee tables with your inlay work on the top of each. But I don't want traditional tables. I want them large and dramatic. Is this something you could do?"

Ed felt excitement build up. The thought of incorporating his parquetry work into this job was perfect. "I would be honored, sir."

Ed spent the next few weeks creating two masterpieces. He carefully laid each diamond wood piece with Elmer's wood glue on the tables forming stars, cubes, and diamonds into tessellations. He used different types of oak to create variation in the design. Once the glue was dry, he filled the cracks with a lacquer and sawdust mixture. The final steps were to sand the tables and apply low-sheen polyurethane.

The tables were oversized with exquisite turned legs. When they were complete, Ed proudly delivered them to Barnett Bank. He brought one in at a time and placed them near the entrance to the elevator. A helper held the elevator doors open as Ed picked up one coffee table to set it inside. Ed's face turned pale as he realized he had a problem. He couldn't get the tables through the opening! They were too big.

"Oh no! I measured every door in this place, but I forgot about the elevator." There was no way to get them to Mr. Barnett's third floor suite, and the elevator was the only way up. Ed called Mr. Barnett from the lobby phone. "Uh, sir, we have a problem," he said.

"What is it?"

"The tables won't fit in the elevator. I can't get them up to you." There was silence for a brief moment.

"Don't worry about it, Ed, I will take care of it," Mr. Barnett said.

The following Sunday, Mr. Barnett hired a crane operator. When Ed arrived, there were state police officers barricading the front of the building. Ed watched as a large window on the third floor was removed, and the two tables were hoisted up by the crane and put in through it. Once the tables were safe and sound in their new home, the window was put back in place.

Ed was in awe. He couldn't believe this was what Mr. Barnett meant when he said, "I will take care of it." Ed's job at Barnett Bank was now complete and he was ready to move on to the next one. Before he left, Mr. Barnett said, "Ed, I can't thank you enough for your beautiful work. I will treasure these tables forever. They will never leave my office."

"I don't think you have a choice. It looks like they are stuck there permanently," Ed said.

Both men laughed as they said their final goodbyes.

Ed was then sent to the local hospital to install cabinets. When the hospital project was coming to an end, a visitor arrived who would change the course of his life.

As he was pounding one of the final nails into the oak, he heard a voice behind him. "Are you Ed Lantzer?"

Ed looked around in surprise. "Yes, I am. Who are you?"

"I'm Frank W. Murphy." The man held out his hand. "Nice to finally meet you." Ed accepted his gesture. The man's handshake was firm. "I heard about the work you did for Mr. Barnett. I was hoping you could come and look at a project that I have going."

"What is it?"

"I am remodeling my office building. I want to move out of my old office and into a new one. I'm having a little trouble. Mr. Barnett said that you are the man to call to come in and clean up the mess."

"Yeah, that would be me." Ed grinned.

"I want you to come over and fix things for me. Whatever the contractor can't do, I want you to do. Are you interested?"

"Yes, I'm interested. When can I look at it?"

"Tomorrow?"

"I'll be there."

The next morning, Ed walked into the partially completed new office. He didn't know it at the time, but this job would last for seven years. By the time Ed finished the office, Frank was more than impressed with his work and problem-solving abilities.

On the last day of the job, Frank approached him and held out his hand. "Ed, I want you to meet me at my home tomorrow morning. I want you to come and work for me."

Ed eagerly agreed. The mill had just sold, and there was a great deal of confusion there, so Ed decided to take Frank up on his offer. He worked for Frank for a short period of time, and before long he became Frank W. Murphy's right-hand man.

Frank was a prominent man in Orlando. He was an investor and owned several successful companies. He had started his career as a writer for *The Orlando Sentinel*. His father-in-law, the aforementioned Martin Anderson, owned the newspaper and was one of the six most powerful men in the state.

Anderson's rags-to-riches story added to his notoriety. During the depression, he quit school at fifteen to start his career in the newspaper business. He met Texas newspaper tycoon Charles E. Marsh, who sent him on a train with only fifteen dollars in his pocket to run the *Orlando Sentinel*. Within a few years, Anderson owned the paper. Not only did he become responsible for the new road network and airport, which brought Disney World to Orlando, but he also became good friends with President Lyndon B. Johnson. This friendship facilitated many of these transformations, including bringing a naval recruit training station to Orlando, and using his newspaper to help elect many political officials such as congressmen, senators, and governors. As a result, he became a very powerful man.

Since Anderson owned the paper and Frank had a love for fishing and boating, it made sense for Frank to write a column for boaters. Frank also managed the first computer system at the *Sentinel*. He held that role until a year after Martin sold the newspaper to the Tribune Company. It was now time for Frank to make his own way. After the paper sold, Frank decided to earn his living as an investor. He had earned the nickname "Speedy" as a child. The name stuck and he wore it well as he consistently moved towards success.

One of the companies that Frank started was called Checkmate Enterprises. This was the company that Ed worked for. As Frank's trusted aide, Ed had many responsibilities. He was Frank's personal carpenter, gofer, and on occasion, babysitter for Frank and his wife Marcia's three children. After a while, Ed had the power to hire and fire employees. Anything that Frank needed, Ed was there. Because of this, they developed a strong bond. Frank knew he could count on Ed and Ed on Frank.

Ed was now in the thick of this new world. He had gone from homelessness to building mansions. He spent time in a world of the elite: people with class, money, and power. It was an education that no college could instill. Ed observed human behavior in this new crowd. *How do these people act differently than the people in my world?* He realized that in some ways, they were very different, but in the most important ways, they were the same. They sought after the same thing that Ed was searching for: a sense of belonging and love.

Frank had a love for island hopping. One of his favorite groups of islands was the Bahamas. It was a 225-mile trip from Orlando, and since Frank had a pilot's license, he could be there in under an hour.

Frank pulled Ed aside one day and said, "Ed, are you interested in taking a ride with me on my plane? I want you to look at something."

"What?"

"The Bahamas."

"The Bahamas? Are you serious?"

"Very serious."

They left just before lunch. As they flew over the Atlantic Ocean, Ed was in awe. *Such beauty! Lord, your creations are marvelous!* Ed thought watching the sparkles bounce in every direction as the sun hit the water. *Diamonds as far as the eye can see.* They finally reached their destination and Frank escorted Ed to his property in Green Turtle Cay. Frank and Marcia were building a new vacation home there. In Ed's eyes, it was a mansion. He had never seen such beautiful land, and the home was spectacular.

"This is what I wanted to show you, Ed," said Frank.

"This is amazing. Thank you for sharing this with me."

"Ed, this is the next job I have for you."

Ed was puzzled and thrilled at the same time. With a half-laugh and half-cry, he said, "Please explain what you mean."

"I would like you to build all of the cabinetry inside." Frank crossed his arms in amusement as he waited for Ed's response.

"Frank, I don't know what to say. Thank you for trusting in me. Thank you for this opportunity. You have no idea what this means to me."

"I know, Ed. You adding your craftsmanship to our home means a lot to me too."

Ed spent the next few months flying back and forth from Orlando to Green Turtle Cay on Frank's plane to complete his work. They also went by boat on occasion. For the first time in a very long time, Ed really felt worthy. He finally understood that he had a place in this world. Even with his flaws and mistakes, he was reminded that he and wood were a magical combination. *This is my gift. This is my purpose*, he thought. *This is why I am here on this earth. Through wood, I can touch others. I can give them joy.*

When the cabinetry was finished on the inside, Ed built a doghouse outside for the Murphys' beloved pet. He built an exact replica of their new home. The craftsmanship was impeccable.

Finally the house was ready to be unveiled to many of the Murphys' friends, family, and colleagues. The rooms were buzzing with laughter and excitement. Life on an island does something to the human soul. It's as if Heaven is only a step away. Ed could feel the energy coming from each spirit that walked the hallways as they toured the masterwork. Near the end of the gathering, Frank said, "I have one more thing to show you."

He escorted the clan outside to the backyard. One by one, they gathered around the miniature mansion that Ed had created. "Look at the gift my man has given to my family." Oohs and aahs emanated from the crowd as they inspected the doghouse. "How about a round of applause!" Frank vigorously clapped. "What magnificent work, Ed!" He continued to clap as the others joined in. A single tear journeyed down Ed's cheek as he shyly accepted the applause. *Wood is my destiny. I know it. Lord, just show me how you want me to use it now. I have been waiting since I was a child for you to reveal your plan for me.* Ed smiled brilliantly as he received congratulations from the guests. *I am ready, Father! So ready! Show me the way.*

19

*"We may ignore, but we can nowhere
evade, the presence of God."*

C.S. Lewis, Letters to Malcolm

Ed may have been ready for his purpose to be revealed, but he was not prepared for what came next. Ed and Linda had been married for seven years, slightly longer than the amount of time he had worked for Frank W. Murphy. The last few years had been rough. They had had very little communication. Linda continued to work at the office supply store, and this job seemed to be taking up more and more of her time. As a result, she and Ed had drifted apart. As much as they initially wanted to make the marriage work, they now had very little in common.

Ed was also focused on his job with Frank and his woodwork. By this time, Ed had added a garage onto their small home. He worked during every free moment creating more wood pieces. He was gathering quite a collection. It felt as if Ed and Linda were no longer husband and wife, but roommates. As distant as they had become, they still loved each other. At least Ed thought so.

One day, Ed heard whispers that Linda was having an affair. He was filled with disbelief and anger. He decided to confront her.

"Is it true?" he said.

"What are you talking about?" Linda asked, confused.

"Are you really cheating on me?"

Linda fixed her feet into the ground so that she would not lose her balance. It took her a moment to speak. "Ed, I am in love with someone else," she said, and looked away in disgrace.

Ed was silent as he tried to take in what she had just revealed. Then he blurted out, "Who is it?"

"It doesn't matter, does it?"

"Of course it matters! I need to know who stole your heart. Please tell me."

"It's the son of my boss."

"The politician?"

"Yes, and I want to be with him."

"Are you kidding me?"

Ed's head flopped down in dejection. He knew there was no competing with someone like that. This man was on the rise in the Florida political scene. Ed was just a lowly carpenter. He knew that he couldn't convince Linda to change her mind. It was obvious from her face and body language that she was done with him. It was over. The best thing he could do was just let her go.

He reminded himself that he might not be an up and coming political figure, but he was preparing to work for someone much more powerful: his Heavenly Father. He considered the possibility that this door was closing for a reason. Even so, Ed was sad. Actually, devastated was more like it. He had hoped that he could use this marriage to redeem himself as a husband, but that was not meant to be. It wasn't God's plan for him.

Linda picked up her purse and clenched the strap with her right hand. I'm leaving now," she said. She scanned the room. "You can have all of this. I don't want a thing." Ed's heart skipped a beat as he watched her head towards the door. He wanted to say something to stop her, but there were no words. She glanced back one more time. "Ed, you can stay in the house for now. We'll have to sell it. When it's sold, you can pay me my share." Ed's slow nod showed how depleted he was. Within minutes, Linda was gone, and their seven years together was over.

Now Ed was alone again. He paced the floors trying to make sense of it all, trying to make sense of this new loss. The house seemed so empty. The floorboards creaked as he plodded back and forth. *Will I ever find someone to share my life with completely? Will I ever find my soul mate?* Ed had his woodworking to keep him busy, but it didn't stop the secret longing for that special person. You know, the one person tailor made from God for each one of us. *Maybe it just isn't meant to be for me. Maybe God has a reason,* Ed considered. But he knew he wasn't ready to give up on that dream. Not yet.

Ed walked over to a bookshelf he had put together out of leftover lumber. He wanted to relax, and reading had always helped. He scanned the books and picked one at random. He made his way to his bed and slid under the covers, clothes and all. He opened up to the first page and read the title aloud, "Mere Christianity by C. S. Lewis." Ed made it halfway through the second page and then drifted away as the book rested on his chest, keeping him company through the night.

"Ed? Ed? Are you listening?"

"Yes, Father. I'm listening," Ed responded in his unconscious state. As Ed continued to sleep, he felt the Lord softly take his hand.

"Come with me."

Ed placed his worn fingers against the warmth and strength of his creator's. They walked hand in hand into a dark room.

"Where are we?" Ed asked apprehensively.

"We are in your future, son."

Just then, a light purer than Ed had ever witnessed before appeared. It danced around the room and rested on seven wooden panels. Each panel connected to the other, creating a whole. Ed gasped and his eyes brightened. "Beautiful!" was the only word he could mutter.

"Look closer, son." Their hands disconnected, and Ed moved nearer to the panels.

"My diamond pieces?" He ran his fingers over each shape.

"Yes."

Ed continued to analyze what the Lord was revealing.

"Is this Da Vinci?"

"No. This is Lantzer," said the Lord.

Ed was confused. "Lantzer? I don't get it."

"Ed, this is your first job. This is what I want you to build."

"But Father, this is humanly impossible. No man can create this." Ed stood back to scan the whole composition. "How do I make the curves with diamonds? Father, this can't be done."

"Look closer. It can be done."

Ed rubbed his chin as he analyzed the configurations and then rejoined his master.

"This just seems so overwhelming. Father, you know my struggles. I can't even draw."

"Ed, I will give you the tools that you need. Your hands will be my hands. Let me work through you. Trust me. That is all I ask. Just trust me."

"Of course I trust you."

"Another thing. I want you to tell my story from the female perspective."

Ed was now completely confused. "Female?"

"Son, I have created each one of you with both male and female qualities. Your creativity comes from your female side. This is where I want you to be when building. Do you understand?"

"Yes, Father," Ed replied without questioning.

"This work is only the beginning, son. There will be more to come. We will talk more about that later."

"Okay."

"One more thing, my child. I want you to know that you are loved."

Ed's eyes stung as they filled with emotion. He flashed back to the four-year-old boy standing before his mother, wide-eyed, as he looked up at her in shame while she announced, "You don't know how to love!"

"My love for you is beyond what you can see or feel. Remember how you felt when you held your beloved daughter in your arms? Remember the love you felt for her as you bundled her up tight and escorted her down the dark corridor to me?"

"Yes," Ed said as his voice cracked.

"That is just a glimpse of my love for you. I want you to show my love through these panels. I want you to show every one of my children who have felt unloved that there is no such thing. My love is unchanging. It is eternal. Most important, it is never too late to accept it."

Ed fell to his knees before His majesty and bawled from his head to his toes. For the first time in his life, he felt enveloped in a feeling of absolute tenderness. The love from his biological father was the only thing that had ever come close. God's bright light wrapped around Ed and gently lifted him back up.

"Ed, I sent my son to die for you. It is time for you to unveil your purpose to the world. Every one of my children has a purpose. Yours is to use your gifts to reach the unloved child. Do you understand?"

"I understand."

"I will provide for you. Even when things become difficult, and they will, just remember that I will take care of you."

"Okay, Father. I know what to do. I am ready."

"I also want you to recognize that there are no coincidences. I will send you the things and people that you will need, when you need them."

"Okay, Father."

"Just so you know, your daughter is with me. She is filled with such light and beauty. She will be waiting for you."

Ed glowed as he took in this information. He tried to picture what his dead daughter might look like, and then suddenly, without warning, he bolted upright in his bed as C. S Lewis fell to the floor. He rubbed his eyes trying to focus on his surroundings. "What was that?" Ed nearly wailed as he replayed the dream over and over in his mind. He memorized each detail, not wanting to forget a thing. He then rose from the bed and made his way to the garage.

First, Ed had to figure out how to build the frame for the panels. He knew each panel measured four by eight feet, the standard size of a piece of plywood. He selected pine. He then built a frame out of ash and attached it to the back. Since ash is a very hard wood, it would give the panel the strength it needed to hold up to the weight of the pieces Ed planned to apply to the front. Ed also decided to double-frame each panel for added security.

The first of the seven frames was now constructed. He knew the next job was to begin cutting diamond-shaped pieces. *It will take thousands. This could take weeks,* Ed thought as he shaped one after the other.

Ed spent night after night cutting each diamond to perfection, and at every bedtime, he read C. S. Lewis. He felt an instant connection with Lewis and somehow knew his words would be vital to him. He remembered what God had said: "There are no coincidences."

Ed began his exploration of Lewis's work with *Mere Christianity*. He couldn't put it down. As he read, his connection to what Lewis was saying grew stronger. He felt that Lewis was speaking right to him. Ed finished the book after a few evenings and decided to make a trip to the library to find more of Lewis's work. The next volume he selected was *Surprised by Joy*, Lewis's autobiography. He was surprised to learn that his life and Lewis's had many similarities, such as the loss of a mother at a young age, one physically and one emotionally; the use of art to escape from a painful life; a hatred of school; bullying; having been born with a sense of purpose; homelessness; a physical defect; trouble showing love to others, and as a result, having embarked on a journey to find it. Ed also noticed something else. The two women who had abandoned them as children had taught them about numbers and symbolism. This similarity stood out for Ed. He was aware that what his mother had taught him about symbolism and numbers played a role while searching for his new angle. He also had a feeling it would play another part soon, although he was unsure how.

Ed had not yet glued one piece of wood onto the plywood backing. He was still trying to map out his plan in his mind. So, he continued to cut diamonds and read Lewis. After conquering all of Lewis's nonfiction works, Ed turned to his fiction. This was the moment that God's plan for Ed and Lewis's work merged into one.

After Lewis had spent years as an atheist, he went out to prove that Christianity was false, but instead found the truth: that Christianity was real. He came to the realization that Christ was Lord. Lewis believed that Jesus could be one of three things: crazy, a deceiver, or the Lord. After extensive research, he ruled out that Jesus was crazy or a deceiver. That meant there was only one answer: he must be Lord.

Lewis felt compelled to tell the world about his findings, to share what he had learned. After writing his nonfiction works, he realized that he was unable to reach the people who really needed to hear his message, the people who didn't know the truth. Like Ed and every one of God's children, Lewis had a purpose that was given to him by God, and he decided that he would devote his life to fulfilling his destiny. So, he began his great work of fiction, *The Chronicles of Narnia*.

The day Ed finished reading the series, he realized that his plan was clearer. *Like Lewis, I will use symbolism within each panel to tell this story.* "That is it!" he cried. The vision from God was now spread out before him, and he could see each detail of each panel with perfect clarity. "Father, it is time to begin!" Ed was so excited. He swayed back and forth as he began to sing, "Oh Lord, my God, when I in awesome wonder consider all the worlds thy hands have made." Ed's world had now cracked wide open. He picked up each volume of his first "coincidence" and neatly stacked it on his bedside table as he continued to sing. "Then sings my soul, my Saviour God, to Thee. How great Thou art, how great Thou art."

There was one more thing that Ed had to take care of before he could totally plunge himself into his new work: he had to talk to Frank. He tapped on the outside of Frank's office door.

"Come in," Frank said. He looked up from his stack of paperwork. "Hi, Ed. What can I do for you?"

"I have a couple of things to talk about. Do you have a minute?"

"Sure. What is it?"

"Linda's gone."

"What do you mean she's gone?"

"She left me, Frank. She says she's in love with someone else."

"Oh, Ed, I am so sorry. What are you going to do about the house?"

"I'm not sure yet. I guess I'm going to try to sell it. She wants her share, that I know. I'm not sure where to start though."

"Hmm. I see."

"Frank, that's not the only thing I want to talk to you about. It's time for me to leave this company."

A look of surprise came over Frank's face.

"Why?"

"I have a new project that I am preparing to start. It doesn't pay much." *Actually nothing,* Ed thought as he tried to remind himself that the Lord had said He would provide. "But it's something I have to do."

"I understand that, Ed. I know that feeling all too well. Sometimes we have to take risks to achieve our goals."

"Even though I am not sure how I will keep a roof over my head and food in my belly, I am assured that this is not a risk."

"Well, that is good then. You need to follow your instincts. They rarely steer you wrong."

"Frank, I want to tell you how grateful I am for everything you have done for me."

"You're welcome, Ed," Frank said with a grin. "I am happy for you. You will be missed around here, though."

"I know. I will miss you too," Ed said. "Before I leave, I have something for you." Frank waited as Ed stepped out into the hall, then reappeared with a hope chest covered with Ed's handiwork. "I want you to have this, Frank."

Frank looked at the chest and grinned from ear to ear. "I don't know what to say. Thank you, Ed. This is beautiful!"

"It's the least I can do for all that you have done for me."

"You have done a lot for me too, Ed. You have been a good friend."

"You too."

Frank pulled his wallet out of his back pocket. "I still owe you a paycheck too, don't I?" Frank counted out a thousand dollars and handed it to Ed. "This should do."

"Frank, this is too much."

"Ed, take this and start your new life. It is the least I can do."

"Thanks, Frank. I will never forget you."

"Nor I you."

They shook hands one last time. As Ed left, he knew he would carry Frank's friendship with him and he would feel his impact as he journeyed through the next phase of his life.

20

*"Friendship is unnecessary, like philosophy,
like art . . . it has no survival value; rather it
is one of those things that give value to
survival."*

C.S. Lewis, The Four Loves

Ed walked into Dana's Restaurant and headed towards his usual seat. He placed a single rose on one of the diner's mismatched tablecloths. He had been eating Dana's food since his Dumpster days, and now he prayed that the Dumpster would not become his source of nutrition again. Since he had walked away from his job and mentor to begin his work for the Lord, this was a real possibility. He had enough money to get by for a while, but he knew it wouldn't last long.

"Morning. What will it be today?" the waitress asked with a warm smile as she poured ice water into a mason jar with one hand and black coffee into a mug with the other.

"Morning, darling. How about the usual?"

"Of course," she said as if she were silly even to ask.

"This is for you." Ed beamed as he handed the long-stemmed rose to the woman.

"Thank you," she said demurely as she accepted the flower and turned to put in his order.

The deep lines and pockets in Ed's face were becoming more pronounced, and his slicked back hair was thinner. He noticed but tried to ignore the fact that he was aging. He thought that his thin mustache helped to at least make him feel distinguished. At fifty-three years old, it was inevitable that he'd show his age. *No one is immune,* he thought.

Ed realized that the possibility of finding his soul mate at this point in his life was remote. He attempted to accept this, especially now that he had more important things to do with his time. Nevertheless, he loved to make women smile. He recognized that many of the waitresses he had met over the years seemed happy on the outside, but deep down there was sadness in them. There was worry behind their bright smiles. *I wonder what makes them so blue,* Ed often asked himself. *They deserve nothing but the best. They deserve to feel happy.* As a result of this realization, Ed decided to start bringing his waitresses flowers. Sometimes they were real and sometimes fake, depending on his financial situation. It was his way of brightening up their day. Whatever was going on in their private lives, he felt that if he could make them feel special, even for a moment, the gesture was worth it.

Ed sipped his black coffee as he overheard his waitress talking to the owner's wife, Billie.

"Look, the French toast man brought me another rose," she bragged.

"Why are you still calling him French toast man?" Billie said.

"What do you mean?"

"He has been coming to our diner for over a year and you still don't know his name?" Billie said. The waitress looked crestfallen. "I want you to stop calling him that and find out who he is. Do you understand?"

"Yes, I do. I didn't realize . . ." the waitress said as Billie handed over the plate of plump French toast topped with powdered sugar.

This simple demand from Billie was the beginning of a collaboration between Dana's Restaurant and Ed that would change the lives of both. A few weeks later, Billie found out that Ed was selling his home. Since her daughter was looking for a house, she asked if they could come over and look at it. When they arrived, Ed greeted them at the door and invited them in. The place was a mess. Since Linda had left, Ed had done very little house cleaning. He struggled to forget his second wife. He knew it was over, but that didn't stop his longing to have her back.

Billie and her daughter stepped over dirty clothing and empty soup cans as Ed took them on the tour. Ed took them in every room and then he asked, "Would you like to see the garage?"

"Yes, we would," Billie said.

Ed held the door for the two women and followed them in. His tools were scattered and sawdust blanketed the entire floor.

"Sorry about the mess," he said. "This is where I spend most of my time."

"Are you a woodworker?" Billie asked. Just then, she looked towards a wood panel that was leaning against a wall and gasped before Ed could answer. She pointed towards one of Ed's practice pieces. "What is this? What is this called?" she said breathlessly.

"This is inlay—parquetry," Ed told her.

"Well, this is just beautiful!" Billie looked closer in astonishment. She then turned to Ed in utter shock and said, "You won't believe this, but I saw this in a dream." Their eyes locked as Billie continued. "In my dream, I was down at my restaurant. There is a long wall there. I walked in and saw this wood panel on the wall with inlay work, all different shapes and sizes. It was the most beautiful stuff, and I was standing there rubbing my hands over it saying, 'This is so pretty. This is beautiful.' I had never seen anything like it before. I didn't even know what inlay was or that it even existed, yet God was showing it to me. I could feel God there, and I asked, 'Where are You?' Then I heard Him say, 'I am in all shapes and all sizes and all forms. And I was within you before you were born. And I had my arms around you.' I looked at the panel again and gazed at all of the different shapes and sizes. When I woke up I thought, *What a strange dream.* Now, I come into this garage and here is this piece placed against the wall. Just exactly like I saw in the dream. I can't believe it! This is my dream!"

Ed smiled and said, "Well, I had a dream too, and I am going to make the Lord's Supper out of this stuff."

Ed explained his vision for the panels. He also explained that he realized he couldn't work and create the mural too. When he was finished, Billie looked at Ed and said, "I want to help you. Please, let me do what I can to help support you."

Billie's daughter bought the house and they agreed that Ed could continue to work in the garage. Billie and her husband, Dana, set Ed up in a little trailer behind the diner. On October 11, 1985, he began laying the first of over a hundred thousand pieces of wood on the seven panels. Before long, the staff and patrons of the diner joined the crusade. While Ed worked day and night, they salvaged pieces of wood from local Dumpsters. They also used their own money to buy wood and supplies to keep the project moving forward. Most important, they made sure Ed had a roof over his head and food in his belly.

Ed remembered the words, "Don't worry about it; I will take care of you." He beamed as he glued one piece down after another. *Thank you, Father, for bringing these people into my life right when I needed them. You always keep your promise, don't you?* he thought. Ed felt the answer to that question in his heart as his diamonds spread out from the middle of each design, covering more and more of the plywood backing.

Ed knew he didn't have much to offer these people who had become his earthly angels. *How can I ever show my gratitude to them?* he thought. The answer came like a flash of light. *I will use some of them as models. Perfect!* And that is just what Ed did. He first asked Dana, the diner owner.

"Of course, Ed. I would be honored," Dana said.

He then enlisted four of the patrons: a Denny's cook, a local building supply man, a water salesman, and a man who was also a carpenter. Their faces, bodies, and Dana's pointed finger were incorporated into Ed's work. They would be forever a part of the mural. This was a gift that Ed felt proud to give.

One evening as Ed was working, Billie entered the garage. "How is it coming along, Ed?" she asked as she looked at his progress in awe. There was no answer. "Ed?" she said again. Ed snapped back to consciousness and then flashed a smile. Billie repeated her question. "How is it coming along, Ed?"

"Very well," Ed answered.

"Ed, I just want you to know what you have done for all of us. People around here are just buzzing about you. You have moved so many of us. You have given us something to believe in. A glimpse of our Lord."

"Billie, I couldn't do this without all of you. You are God-sent. You know that, right?"

"Yes," she said with pride. "Ed, I want to start a nonprofit corporation to help the hungry of our community. This is in part because of this work and your inspiration. When the panels are completed, can we use them as a fundraiser to help feed these people in need? We can set the panels up for people to view and their donations will go to buy food."

"Of course. I would be happy to do that for you," Ed said quickly without really thinking about what he was committing to.

"Okay then, I will get the process going," Billie said. They both smiled. "Do you have any idea when it will be done?"

"Soon," Ed announced confidently.

"Wonderful! I look forward to the unveiling."

"So do I, so do I." Ed's eyes sparkled as he went back to work.

Ed returned to the panel that was lying horizontally on two sawhorses. He took in a deep breath and began chanting, "Chu, chu, chu, chu," over and over again. Within minutes, he had drifted back into his unconscious mind or "the zone," as Ed liked to call it. This was the special place where he went to create. It was a place where nothing else existed except for God and his work. Ed found several ways to enter that place: chanting, humming, or singing. On this day, he chose to chant.

Ed shifted on his stool as he leaned in to grab a bottle of Elmer's wood glue. He squeezed a portion onto the plywood backing and spread it out into a plate-sized area with a small piece of cardboard. He clutched a recycled cottage cheese container and tilted it downwards as diamond wood pieces trickled out, forming a pile next to the glue. Then he placed one piece at a time in position as he continued the tessellation he had started earlier. One wood diamond butted up to another, and then another.

This continued for hours. Ed had no sense of time in his unconscious state. There were no distractions and no thoughts, just movement and momentum. Ed spread more glue, grabbed another container, and made a pile of diamonds next to the previous one. This pile was a lighter wood grain in contrast to the other, darker wood. He stopped for a moment to stare at the first panel he had completed. It was leaning against the studs of the garage wall next to several of the other panels. Ed's eyes traveled around the majestic face, beard, and hair. A sphere of light framed the face in a way that made it glow. He stared at the inverted eyes. He remembered the day he had told Billie that he just couldn't get the eyes right. A day later she had come to him and said, "I had a dream last night, I heard the words, 'Tell Ed to invert the eyes.' When I woke up, I remembered the dream. I didn't know what that meant, so I looked it up in the dictionary and it said to reverse position."

Ed continued to gaze at the inverted eyes. Like the Mona Lisa, no matter where he was working in the room, it seemed like the expression from the panel followed. Somehow this gave him a sense of peace and protection. He then returned his focus to the panel in progress.

Before Ed began the first panel, his biggest problem was figuring out how to make a curve with the diamond shape. His solution was to cut the diamond in half. He had already been cutting it in half vertically to make a straight line, but if he cut the diamond in half horizontally, he ended up with a smaller line. This revelation allowed him to turn a corner, which moved him from parquetry—creating geometric shapes—to marquetry, creating pictures out of the wood.

Ed was now on the last figure out of a total of thirteen that he had lovingly placed in his mural. This historic figure was sitting at the end of a table. Ed's emotions welled up as he realized that he was nearing the end of his first God-given task. He laid one half piece after another as he curved around the dark hair. The gentleman's head tilted down with an intent look on his face as Ed gave him hands. His right hand was holding a pencil and the left hand rested on a book. Ed created three moneybags that dangled from the figure's left hip. He attached the moneybags to a sash around the waist, where he alternated a lighter wood with a darker wood in a decorative pattern to create depth and the illusion of drapery. The man was seated on two large books standing vertically as if he were placed on a bookshelf. Ed titled one *I Love* and the other *Agape. This says it all,* Ed thought as he placed the final pieces around the edge of the panel.

After he had completely covered each panel with diamonds, he stood them up around the garage, adding more eyes to watch him as he continued to work. Once he had securely glued thousands of diamonds onto the seven panels, he began sanding. First he used a belt sander to level out each piece so that they would all blend harmoniously. He also sanded the edges to make them flush with the plywood backing. Ed then gathered the sawdust and put it in a metal can. He added lacquer and mixed the two together. Then he spread the mixture over each panel, filling in every crack between each piece of wood. After hours of drying, Ed started up the belt sander again to take off the excess mixture. Last, he sanded each panel with a palm sander and fine grit sandpaper to create a smooth surface. He glided his bare hand over each panel to make sure it was smooth enough. *Oh yes. Perfect!* he thought as he prepared the final step of sealing the artwork with a coat of polyurethane for protection.

Fourteen months and twelve days after the first diamond piece had found its permanent home in the center of the middle panel, the mural was complete: seven glorious panels that when put together revealed true love. Ed stood back and analyzed each one. Together they measured eight feet tall and twenty-eight feet long.

"Here it is, Father," he said. Here is your masterpiece."

Emotion welled up as he looked at each work. Images of Ed's children came to him as he stood there. *Oh, how I miss them*, he thought. He moved from one panel to the next, taking in each of the symbols he had embedded into the work. He then stood in front of one of the panels and ran his hand over a single word. He began to cry.

"My beloved, you are now with me every day." He stared at his daughter's name, which he'd hidden in the wood. He actually hid all of his children's names in the panels in a way that only he could recognize. "These panels are now my children," he said. "Through them, you live. Just like I told you when we first met, I will live through you. That will always be so."

Ed knelt down in the middle of the room and began giving thanks.

21

"*Reality is not neat, not obvious, not what
you expect.*"

C.S. Lewis, Mere Christianity

The last fourteen months had not always been easy. Ed had so many wonderful supporters around him, especially Billie and Dana. He couldn't have fulfilled God's request without them. But while he worked day and night, he also had to battle his inner demons. He carried so many things from his past with him. They were embedded deep down. He masked them and hid them as much as he could, but he was not always successful. When his supporters looked at Ed, they saw a man full of faith and devotion. They saw a genius. But, they also saw glimpses of a man who was human and imperfect.

Things happened during Ed's time at the diner that showed how human he really was. Once, he tried to commit suicide. He disappeared one day and he left a note addressed to Linda. He knew she was gone, but he had a moment when he felt that he couldn't go on without her. The note said that he was going to drown himself in a nearby lake. When Linda was told about it, she said she wanted nothing to do with him. Billie was so distraught that she cried, thinking her dear friend was dead. Police officers and divers searched the lake for days and they found no sign of Ed. Everyone was sure that his body was rooted somewhere at the bottom. Two weeks after his disappearance, Ed walked back into the diner. Billie cried, "Where have you been?" Ed just smiled and said, "I'm back." And that was it. No explanation. Ed never revealed what happened or where he had been.

Billie also noticed that Ed acted strangely on occasion. One minute he was happy, and the next, almost like a flick of a switch, he was snappy towards her. She really began to worry about his well-being.

One day he told Billie, "I can take a saw and saw the panels up."

"Oh, Ed, you wouldn't do that." Billie said.

"Don't you tell me what to do. I can do it if I want to!" Ed had a fear of losing his panels, his new children, and this was his response. Unfortunately, Billie and the others had no way of knowing that.

On another day, Ed didn't show up for his meal. He always ate breakfast, lunch, and dinner at the diner, but on this day there was no sign of him. Billie went to Ed's trailer behind the diner and knocked on the door.

"Ed? Can I come in?" she said.

"No, get away! Get away from that door!" Ed yelled.

"No, I want to come in and talk to you, so I am coming in." Billie said.

She turned the doorknob and it was unlocked. As she entered apprehensively, she found Ed curled up in the fetal position on his bed. It was evident that he was having some sort of a breakdown. Billie knelt by her friend.

"Ed, I think I should call your family. You are sick. Who do I call?"

Ed gave her his oldest daughter's phone number. Donna was now an adult and Ed knew that she still cared for him. "Call her. She will take care of me," he told Billie.

Billie called Donna, and she was in Orlando by the next day. When Ed saw his daughter, he just snapped out of it and was ready to go back to work. He acted like that several times, so Billie realized that she just needed to leave him alone for a while and he would be okay.

Ed knew that he had struggles. He knew he was not perfect. Sometimes he wondered how God could choose such a misfit for such an important job, but He did. Ed took that job very seriously, and he was now done with the first part of it.

Saturday night, one evening after the mural's completion, one patron after another entered Dana's Restaurant. Each person was dressed in their finest clothing. With the lights dimmed, every person was handed a neon green lightstick before making their way to their table, which was covered in white linen. The once scruffy diner had been transformed into a place of elegance. Patrons and employees faced front as they impatiently waited for the coming reveal. Excitement and eagerness filled the room.

As Ed entered, all eyes were on him. A silk handkerchief glimmered as it peeked out from his gray suit breast pocket. The only good tie that Ed owned rested perfectly on his chest with its repeating Romeo and Juliet pattern. The mural, massive and majestic, was covered in blue plastic and red ribbon to create anticipation among the crowd. Forty lightsticks were strategically placed along the top. Bread was passed from table to table as Ed draped a white cloth over his left arm. Everything was designed to replicate the scene behind the blue plastic. Ed not only felt that doing so would add drama and hint at the action in the mural, but also that it was important to give thanks for the sacrifice that had been made for each one of them. To that end, he picked up a chalice filled with grape juice and offered sips to each person. As each one partook of their communion, they grinned with the curiosity and wonder of a child.

After Ed made his rounds, he set the chalice down, sauntered towards the mural, and turned to face the crowd. He cleared his throat.

"Ladies and gentlemen, what we are going to do tonight is attempt to transport you to the original Last Supper."

Elated whispers traveled throughout the room. Ed handed a pair of scissors to a small girl standing near the front. She walked over and clipped the middle ribbon. Her bright eyes lit up as the blue plastic fell from the center panel, revealing Jesus Christ facing the crowd with his arms and hands extended out towards the audience. Ed could almost picture what it must have been like to be there as Jesus offered bread and wine to the twelve disciples, declaring, "Do this in remembrance of me."

Applause swirled around the room. A song Dana had written began playing in the background, heightening the ambience. Dana had never written anything before, but Ed's work inspired him so much that the words just poured out of him. The group sang along with their sheet music in front of them. The harmony was warm and loving. When the song came to an end, the final ribbons were severed and the rest of the mural was exposed. The people rose to their feet as Jesus and the twelve disciples greeted them, each surrounding the table at the Last Supper. Cries, laughter, joy, and flashes from Instamatic cameras bounced around the diner.

"This is a true masterpiece!" yelled a voice from the crowd.

Another said, "It's spectacular!"

Ed stood back with tears of joy in his eyes as he watched the crowd gather around the panels to analyze each symbol he had strategically incorporated into the story. He felt like a proud father, with each one of the panels his child. He had created each disciple in the mural with symbols that related to the way he was martyred for his continued preaching of Christ, except for John, who was the only one who lived to old age. In John's case, his garment displayed an alpha letter and fish symbol.

Jesus' inverted eyes had no detail and neither did John's. Ed had left them out to signify that Jesus was without sin. John was the disciple Jesus loved, and because of that, when Jesus looked at John, He saw him without sin. Ed used this symbolism to show the unloved children of the world the story of redemption. Through Jesus they are sinless. Ed also added words in various languages, such as Greek and Hebrew, which represented God's love for us all.

After hours of evaluation, the onlookers found even more symbols.

"We could be here for days and continue to find more," one person announced with glee, and Ed nodded in agreement as he thought about the hidden personal symbols that only he would understand.

Finally, the clan began to exit the diner one by one, each stopping by Ed to praise his work. Ed was looking forward to spending some time alone with his mural before he called it a night. As the last guest was leaving the diner, he felt a warm hand on his shoulder. Ed turned and there was Billie with a brilliant smile on her face. They made eye contact, and Ed said, "Billie, these panels cannot be used for your corporation. I need to go home. You can keep the panels up for one week, but after that I need to take my children home to Michigan."

"What? But Ed, without the panels, there is no corporation," Billie said.

"You don't need the panels. You can do it without them, Billie. I know you can."

"But they belong in the corporation."

"I am sorry, but I just can't hand them over. It is time to go home."

Ed was now alone. He walked to the center panel and stood in front of God's sacrifice, the sacrifice he had made for each one of us. Ed looked right into his sinless face.

"Am I doing the right thing, Father? They want to take my panels, my children. I understand that I owe them more than I can ever repay, but it doesn't feel right. I don't feel like this is the time or the place to hand them over."

Sadness permeated his whole being as he put his right finger on the only square piece in the mural. This piece was Ervin's. Ed reminisced about the day Ervin had cut, polished, and handed it over to him. "This is for you, son," he'd said. "Keep it with you so that you will always be reminded of our time together." Ervin had passed away a few years before, and after Ed heard the news, he pulled the cube out of his wallet. He knew he would have a place for it someday, a very special place. Ed polished his tribute to his dad with the corner of his suit coat.

"This is the perfect place, Dad," he said. He moved back to observe the cube on the right ring finger of Jesus' hand. "Dad, this represents a wedding ring and our marriage to our savior. It also represents my love for you. I wish you could have been here tonight. I wish you could have seen my work. I think you would have been proud. Thank you for all of your gifts in my life. I will never forget you."

Ed had not really let himself grieve for his father. Now, the grief was flowing out of him like a tidal wave and he didn't know if he could ever stop. Then, a calm came over him, warmth and peace. The tenderness he had felt in his dream was all around him.

"I know this is what I have to do, Lord," he said. "My work is not done. It is not time for my children to be released to the world, not yet."

Ed kissed each panel and made his way back to the garage.

One week later, by the time the sun had risen over the Orlando palm trees, Ed was in his dilapidated truck with an old gypsy wagon following behind. Inside the weathered wagon were Ed's seven panels, and he was steering towards Michigan. As he passed each mile marker, he thought about his friends in Orlando and all they had sacrificed for him.

"I am so sorry. I hope you will someday forgive me," he said.

Ed imagined the astonished faces of Dana and Billie when they realized that he and the panels were gone. They knew he was leaving, but Ed didn't say goodbye. Dana asked Ed to have a cup of coffee with him before he left. But, as Dana made biscuits for the next day while he waited for their last visit over a cup of the strong brew, Ed slipped away without a word.

Ed wept. The picture continued to flash before him as the distance between them grew farther and farther. *I know I am doing the right thing, but why is my heart breaking for them?* he thought. *I know I couldn't tell them I was leaving in person. It would be too difficult. I don't think I could take their disappointment. I have always disappointed the people I care about. I guess that will never change.*

His wheels continued to roll down I-75. *Am I doing the right thing, Father? Yes, I know I am*, he thought. As he neared the Michigan border, he felt a surge of nervousness. He had been gone over a decade. A lot had happened during those years. He didn't feel like the same broken man who had once been escorted out of the state in shackles. He now had a reason to get up each day, a reason for being alive and breathing in air. He hoped that was enough to gain the acceptance from the people back home. *Once they see what I have created, they will surely see that I am not a bad person, just misunderstood*, he thought. He remembered the words he'd heard before he was escorted out of his home state: "Don't ever come back." Ed knew that was so long ago. He hoped they would leave him alone. He longed to be home again. He longed to be near the lost family that he loved. *I love them so much, even if they don't know it.* Now that his purpose had been revealed, he needed to complete it in the only place that was truly home: Kalkaska.

22

*"The Past is frozen and no longer flows, and
the Present is all lit up with eternal rays."*

C.S. Lewis, The Screwtape Letters

The gypsy wagon carrying Ed's prized possessions swayed
back and forth as he pulled into Kalkaska. He thought
about a few of the stops he'd made on his way home. One
was Great Lakes Bible College and the other was a church.
Ed was so excited about his panels that he wanted to share
them along the way. As he pulled into his hometown, a
feeling of nostalgia overwhelmed him. He looked right and
then left, taking in all of the familiar places: the gas station
on the corner and the longstanding Sieting Hotel across the
street. A few things had changed, but for the most part it
still looked like home. The large trout fountain was still
sitting in the center of the town square. Ed nodded as he
drove by and felt as if the trout were welcoming him back. *I
hope he is not the only one happy to see me.*

All of Ed's children were now adults. *How time has
flown by*, he thought as he counted off their ages. He had
had short visits from a few of his kids over the fifteen years
in Florida after they'd turned eighteen. Ed and the children
had hopes of rekindling their relationships, but each time
he disappointed them with his inability to communicate,
and each time they returned to Michigan. He prayed that
they might be able to start over, now that they were all
grown up and some had families of their own.

Ed had alerted Donna, his oldest, that he was coming
back to town, and she helped him find a temporary place to

live until he got back on his feet. Without an income, it wouldn't be easy, but a local real estate broker loaned him a small trailer located near the south end of town. Ed was so grateful and relieved that he would not have to sleep in his truck.

The trailer had a small detached garage, but had neither heat nor electricity. It was getting cold again in Kalkaska, and Ed knew he had to figure out a way to stay warm. After he'd settled in, he waited until it was dark. He trudged through the snow with a flashlight towards the electricity pole closest to the trailer. How do I put this? Basically, Ed stole electricity from the pole. He actually said that he "borrowed it." I smiled as he shared the details with me. It was as if he were a small child in deep mischief putting his hand into the cookie jar. Was it wrong? Yes. Was it necessary? Yes. At the time, it was his only way to survive, his only way to keep from freezing to death.

Ed found an electric heater. He now had what he needed to function—at least for a while. After he'd "borrowed" electricity for a short time, it was shut back off, but Ed did his best to stay warm. He bundled up in a ragged snowmobile suit and went to the garage to work. Working was the only way to keep his mind off the cold. There was not enough room in the garage to set up the mural, so, in a herculean way, he neatly stacked the four-hundred-pound panels against the wall, one in front of the other. He caressed each one with love, and, as if he were tucking them in for the night, carefully draped a worn blanket over the stack to keep them warm and protected. There was little room to continue his work, but he carved out a spot and went back to cutting diamond pieces, each one by hand.

The rundown blue truck he'd purchased in Florida had barely got Ed home, and before long it gave out. Now his only transportation was his own two feet. He knew that he had to find work so he could buy food, but with his past following him like a dark shadow, he was fearful that it would be difficult.

Conveniently, there was a Big Boy restaurant next door to the trailer. Ed began spending his free time there drinking coffee and nibbling on whatever he could scrounge up. This was the beginning of a long-lasting relationship between Ed and the Big Boy employees and patrons. He would sit for hours as he people-watched. It became his favorite pastime. He explained to me on numerous occasions that he'd had an interest in human behavior since he was a small child. Now as he perched day after day on his regular stool at the counter near the waitress station, he observed everyone.

He recognized some of the faces from his past, but he was looking at them with new interest. Most had changed. Ed noticed that many had aged. *Have I aged that much?* he wondered. During one of my chats with Ed he said, "You know kid, I just wanted to know what made a person an individual and what made them similar to the crowd. So I decided to find out." This helped him make sense of his purpose, his reason for creating his work for the Lord. Now that the first seven panels were complete, he patiently waited for the next vision or dream. *God said there would be more to come. When will that be?* Ed knew he couldn't begin the next phase without instruction from the Father, so as he waited, he continued his journey of human observation.

One afternoon as Ed took a break from cutting diamond pieces, he heard a "tap, tap, tap," on the trailer door. He glanced out the window and saw a police car sitting in the driveway. A surge of panic gripped him. *What do they want?* Ed knew that it was rarely good news when an officer was standing on your doorstep. He unlatched the front door hesitantly and pulled it open.

"Can I help you?" he said with trepidation.

"Are you Edgar Frederick Lantzer?"

"Yes."

"Mr. Lantzer, can you step outside please?" Ed did as he was instructed and winced as he made eye contact with the man in uniform. "Mr. Lantzer, you are under arrest for failure to pay child support."

Ed's eyes widened and he held his breath. He was unaware that there was an arrest warrant out for him. As a matter of fact, many arrest warrants had been issued over the years, but since he was miles away, he didn't know about them.

He flashed back to the court hearing as he was put in shackles, to the ride in the cruiser, and then to the plane ride to Orlando as he was conveniently shipped out of Michigan like cargo in a crate. *Now they want to arrest me? Haven't I already paid my dues? I lost everything!*

Ed seethed as the officer cleared his throat and said, "Mr. Lantzer, you have the right to remain silent. Anything you say or do may be held against you in a court of law." The officer continued as Ed peered at the ground. The realization of what was happening was overwhelming. He began to tremble. "Do you understand each of these rights I have explained to you?"

"Yes, sir," Ed answered like a small child with wide eyes. The light bounced off the handcuffs as the officer brought them into view.

"Turn around and put your hands behind your back," he said.

Ed followed orders and waited as the officer tightened one around each wrist. He was then escorted into the back of a police cruiser once again. On the short ride to the Kalkaska Governmental Center, Ed scolded himself. *Why did I come back here? I should have stayed in Florida. What was I thinking?* They pulled in front of the Kalkaska County Jail and the officer ushered him into the building.

Ed sat in the cold jail cell. He glared at the stark white block walls that appeared to be closing in on him. He scanned the room, analyzing his roommates. One man was sleeping on the cement floor, covered with a thin blanket, while two others were playing a hand of poker. Ed shook his head in disbelief. *What do I do? I have work waiting. How can this be happening?* The thought of being confined like a caged animal was more than he could bear. The final instructions from the officer played through his mind like rolling credits from a movie, the last line being, "You will go in front of the judge tomorrow morning."

Ed had no idea how long the cell would be his home. *One day? One week? One year?* He shuddered at the thought. He also fretted over the fact that he had no money, no job, and no prospects. *How am I supposed to pay?* Ed's youngest child had been five years old when he was shipped off to Florida. She was now an adult. *I must owe a fortune by now.* He was right. Ed owed $11,944.80, to be exact. When I asked him why he didn't pay child support while he was in Florida, his answer was, "Honestly, I don't know. When I first arrived in Florida, I felt that I was being shipped away from my family. I tried to move on with my life as best I could. I made many mistakes along the way. This was one of them."

The next day, Ed was released. The judge made a decision to send him to Antrim/Kalkaska Community Mental Health Services on an outpatient basis. He considered the possibility that Ed was suffering from a mental illness. He was also concerned that Ed wasn't taking care of himself. He took into account Ed's history of losing control. In the end, he decided that Ed needed help, and being thrown in jail was not the answer. So he ordered him to start counseling.

A call was placed to the mental health program, and Ed was referred to a nun named Sister Augusta. The nun had recently come to the area to develop a new outreach program for elderly people in the community—people who were suffering from mental illness and/or depression. When Ed walked into her office for the first time, he was obviously depressed. He was somber and quiet. After years of preparing his work for the Lord and completing the first seven panels, he felt hopeless. *Is it all over? I know I have more to do, but how do I move forward?* he was thinking. He had lost control of his life. Everything was now in the hands of Sister Augusta, and he was resentful. He was grateful to be out of jail, but angry that he had to report to anyone except the Lord.

When Ed appeared at Sister Augusta's door, she waved him in. "Morning, Ed. Have a seat."

She pointed to a chair positioned in front of her desk. Ed sat down and just rested there for a moment. He stared at her as he waited for her to finish scribbling something down on a legal pad. He attempted to improve his disheveled appearance by wiping his hand across his wrinkled slacks and shirt and then through his very thin gray hair. Ed really felt his age. He was nearing sixty. He thought about that for a moment. *Where has the time gone? It was just yesterday that I was young and strong. Now I am weakening. I can't give in to age just yet. I have so much to do!* These thoughts swirled around in Ed's head as he waited for the first question.

"Well, Ed, I am Sister Augusta. It is very nice to meet you."

"You too," Ed replied in a weedy voice.

"So why do you think you are here today?"

Ed went on to explain about being arrested and the back child support.

"Okay, can you tell me about yourself?"

He answered as best he could, hoping to make a good impression. He talked mostly about his artwork. When Sister Augusta tried to ask him about his family, he ignored her and continued telling her about the panels. Sister Augusta told me that as Ed explained about the mural, his purpose, she saw something in his eyes. He had a depth and wisdom beyond the normal, maybe even beyond this Earth. When describing his work for the Lord, Ed transformed right in front of the nun. He went from being blue to exuding a warm glow around him, like a street lamp shining amidst the dark.

Ed explained the vision and the months of work, almost day and night, he had spent to complete *The Last Supper*. Sister Augusta looked up and stared at him for a moment, not saying anything as she evaluated his words and his body language. Her goal during the first assessment was to get to know Ed. She wanted a picture of who this man was and what made him tick. Was he mentally ill? Depressed? And if he was, how could she help him?

She smiled and said, "Ed, I would love to see your work sometime. Would that be possible?"

"Sure. That would be wonderful!" Ed answered quickly, beaming.

The first session was nearing an end, and the only thing Sister Augusta knew for sure was that Ed was no ordinary man. There was something different about him, maybe even special. She was intrigued and wanted to know more. A connection had been made. Ed was initially angry about having to go to counseling, but after he recognized Sister Augusta's interest in his work, he wondered if this meeting had taken place for a reason. *Ed, I will bring people to you, as you need them.* The Lord's words replayed through his head. Ed sent a message above, *Is this one of those people, Father? I think it is.* Ed smiled and agreed to see the nun again, but the next time it would be in front of the panels.

Ed and Sister Augusta spent the next court-sanctioned five years meeting on a weekly basis, with each session creating a rapport stronger than the last. Some meetings took place at her office, some over coffee at Big Boy Restaurant, and some in the presence of the mural. Sister Augusta became Ed's confidant and friend. One of the most important jobs she'd been given was to help Ed take care of the court case regarding the back child support, and by the end of their working relationship, she had. After much assessment, the charges were dropped and the back child support conviction expunged due to Michigan's statute of limitations law. The law states that after a specific time frame has passed, a person can use the statute of limitations law as a defense. Since Ed had been gone for fifteen years, he was able to use this defense successfully.

Now that the charges were dropped, Ed felt a surge of adrenaline and began spending his evening hours alone with the Lord. He was ready to start another panel, and it was time for instructions. Each evening Ed knelt in his workshop and prayed. *Father, I am ready. It is time to get back to work. Show me what is next.* He sang ancient hymns until the wee hours of the morning and read as many books on religion as he could find. He checked out a variety of ancient religious writings from the local library. He felt that this would give him the clearest view of what God wanted him to create.

After spending many hours in the subconscious part of his brain, Ed finally had the details of his next two panels. They appeared before him like flashes of light. He could see them so clearly, every detail. He was now ready to start work again, and the new additions to his children would be called "The Quest" and "Moses and the Ten Commandments."

When Ed began working on the new panels, Sister Augusta was so intrigued by how he created them that she started coming over with donuts and coffee every Saturday to watch him. She was mesmerized. She sat and observed how he put a panel together. Ed showed her the process, how he cut each piece and how he started in the middle of a panel and worked his way out to the edges, without a drawing as a guide. He showed her how the wood had a different appearance depending on the angle at which he made the cut. Ed never drew a line. It was all in his head. He sat in silence until the vision was in front of him. He built the panel in his head before he glued down one piece of wood. Each picture was stored in a mental photo album, and as he moved from the center of the panel, the picture was released from his head and onto the plywood backing.

Up to this point, the majority of the wood had come either from a Dumpster or a donation, but that all changed when Ed found out about a store located near Traverse City called Rare Earth Hardwoods. The store stocked exotic woods from all over the world. Ed was thrilled that he now had access to wood from other countries. The only problem was that he had no money. He also did not want anyone else to spend their money on wood for him. If someone gave Ed a piece of wood, he considered it a gift. But if he saw a money exchange, he wouldn't accept it.

The day Sister Augusta decided to drive Ed to Rare Earth so he could look around, she called ahead and said, "Whatever wood Ed wants, put it on my bill." He walked into the building like a child entering a candy store and lit up like the star of Bethlehem.

"Oh, Sister, this is just beautiful, isn't it?" he said.

"Yes it is, Ed." She smiled and nodded.

Ed ran his stubby fingers over a piece of purpleheart. "Look at this, what I can do with this purple wood."

Then his attention moved towards two other woods of Central American and South American origin: zebrawood and blood wood.

"Gorgeous!"

Two more pieces spoke to him: the orange hue from a piece of African padauk and the dark chocolate wenge, originating from Africa. Ed began putting together a wish list in his mind. *Someday, when I have enough money, I will be back.*

As he continued his tour, Sister Augusta picked out a piece of wood that she noticed Ed ogling. When they were ready to leave, she held out the board and said, "Here, Ed, this is for you."

With a look of disbelief and elation, Ed accepted. "Sister! Thank you so very much!" He positively beamed. "I will put this gift in a panel. It will be in a special place. Thank you, my friend."

"You're welcome, Ed. I am honored to do this for you. Now let's get you back home. You have work to do."

They both grinned as they walked out the door. Ed cradled his new piece of wood like an infant and headed to the car.

After five years of working together, Ed and Sister Augusta's therapy sessions ended. Sister Augusta started a new program assessing patients in local nursing homes. As a result, her working relationship with Ed had to end, but their friendship would continue. She explained to Ed that he would be referred to a new therapist and that he should go to the agency to have one assigned. Ed actually enjoyed their sessions, and Sister Augusta felt it was important for him to continue, even though the courts were out of the picture by now.

23

"Forgiveness does not mean excusing."

C.S. Lewis, Fern Seed and Elephants

Ed walked into the Antrim/Kalkaska Community Mental Health office without an appointment and sauntered over towards the receptionist.

"I would like to speak with the new therapist," he said.

"Okay, have a seat and he will be right with you," she said.

Ed moved towards the nearest seat in the waiting area and sat down. After a few minutes, he noticed a man walking towards him. "Hello. What's your name?" he said.

"Ed."

Ed inspected the man and tried to decide whether he wanted to talk to him. He had this way of instantly reading people. He could tell if they had a light spirit or a dark spirit. If it was dark, he refused to engage with the person. Ed could tell that this man was full of light. He was less than happy to start over with a new therapist, but he was here and decided to give it a shot.

"My name is Ken Homa," the man said. He extended his hand towards Ed and Ed accepted. "Follow me, Ed," he said as he waved his hand in the direction of his office.

Ed reluctantly stood and did as he was told. *Okay Father, is this the next person that you think I need?* He raised his eyebrow in a quizzical fashion as he considered the idea.

"Please, take a seat."

"Thank you," Ed said, and sat down.

"My receptionist said that you wanted to speak to someone?"

Ed looked at Mr. Homa in confusion. *He should know why I am here. Sister Augusta sent me to him. Hmm.* He shrugged and started talking about his artwork.

Mr. Homa listened for a while and then said, "So Ed, what is going on that brings you here today?"

Ed looked at Mr. Homa with a sideways glance and continued talking about his work. Mr. Homa patiently listened again. After a few more minutes, he interrupted.

"Ed, are you married? Do you have children?"

Ed shot him another look. *What is wrong with you, man? I have already answered all of these questions with Sister Augusta. Why am I starting over? Shouldn't this information be in my file?*

He continued describing the last two panels that he'd recently completed. Ken Homa told me later that it quickly became clear to him that he was not going to get any personal information from Ed. Now they had a dilemma on their hands. Ed couldn't understand why this therapist was asking redundant questions, and Mr. Homa couldn't understand why a person who'd walked in off the street for help wouldn't answer them. Come to find out later, Ken had had no idea that Ed had been a patient there for five years. He hadn't received Ed's file yet, so he believed this was his first visit. Now he realized he was going to have to make a shift in order to help his new client. His plan was to keep Ed engaged in a conversation. If he could do that, maybe Ed would come back for another session and then they could move forward, so that was what he did.

The conversation continued and Ed did come back, many times. Mr. Homa quickly realized, like Sister Augusta, that Ed was special. He spent many hours talking to Ed about life and religion. He also spent time observing Ed at work. Mr. Homa knew that this was the most unique person he had ever met. Many people were throwing around a diagnosis of mental illness, but he did not see that at all. Instead, he saw a man who lived in a different realm from that of ordinary human beings. It was like Ed could see the whole picture of life. His view of the world came through different lenses. It was as if he had been granted a gift from God to see the world as He sees it.

Unfortunately, this made Ed appear odd. He would say things to people that just didn't make sense to us "normal" humans. Through many deep conversations, Mr. Homa could see that this was the only explanation. He also realized that Ed's brain was wired differently and he struggled with a learning disability. The long-past scarlet fever episode had taken a toll on Ed's brain and he was not able to overcome his struggles with writing. As a result, Mr. Homa felt sure that he could get Ed help.

They met every week, and as with his sessions with Sister Augusta, it was either at Mr. Homa's office, Big Boy, or Ed's workshop. Ken (by now he was Ken rather than Mr. Homa), like so many other people in Ed's past, played an important role in Ed's life. Ken's role was to help Ed attain financial assistance so he could continue his work for the Lord. This was crucial because after building the last two panels, Ed hit another lull. He had no idea what the next panel would be, and he felt depression creeping in again.

"I just feel stagnant," he said during one of his sessions with Ken.

"What do you mean 'stagnant'?"

"Well, I know I have more panels to do, but I feel like I have lost my drive. I am running out of room in the garage, and I just can't seem to get myself moving again."

"Ed, this is normal. Many artists go through periods where they feel they can't move forward. Just give it time. It will pass, and before long you will be working again."

"Are you sure?"

"Yes, I'm sure."

"Okay," Ed said cautiously.

Ed's living situation was definitely not helping matters. He needed a home that would allow his work to continue without the added worry of how to stay warm, not to mention his many requirements for electricity. When Ken realized that Ed had no money and no utilities in the trailer or workshop, he decided to do whatever he could to change that. Ken put his plan in motion and started the process to have Ed put on Social Security Disability.

While Ed waited for the disability to be approved, he continued making daily appearances at Big Boy. When he first started going to Big Boy, it didn't take long for word to spread that he was back in town. Some townspeople were happy and some were not. Those who feared Ed prior to his exit from Michigan still felt the same way. The rumors of him going mad were still fresh, even all these years later.

Now that Ed's transportation was his two feet again, he walked everywhere. If he wasn't at the restaurant sipping coffee or working, he was spotted walking around the village of Kalkaska. Ed shuddered when he saw the familiar looks from some people as they passed him on the street, often an expression of disappointment or fear. One day as he was on his way to visit Ruby in the nursing home where she now lived, a carload of teenagers drove past him. Ed observed the car as it took the first right and then disappeared. He breathed a sigh of relief as it drove out of sight. The tiny hairs stood up on the back of his neck when the kids were gone. He didn't know why, but something about them unnerved him.

Ed continued to walk towards the senior housing center, Level Acres. He shrugged off the eerie feeling he had and began to whistle a tune as he put one foot in front of the other. Suddenly, he heard a screeching noise and turned. The teenagers' car was barreling towards him again. Ed noticed that the driver's side window was down. *What are they doing?* he wondered. He stopped and planted his feet as he prepared for whatever was to come. Just as the car was parallel to Ed he heard, "Stay off the road, you crackpot!! Ed gasped as he saw what appeared to be snowballs barreling in his direction like missiles. He moved right and left to avoid as many as he could, but several struck him. The boys' laughter pierced Ed's ears as they zipped away.

Ed stood on the side of the road in disbelief. He flashed back to the times throughout his life when people had spit on him, pushed him off his bicycle, or thrown rocks at him. He had a lump in his throat as he wiped away the remaining snowflakes on his jacket. He pulled the flaps of his furry aviator hat back down to cover his ears and gazed above.

"Father, don't they know who I am? Don't they know I am your son?"

He wondered if coming back to Kalkaska had been the right choice, but he knew it was. It was his home after all, even if no one really knew who he was. *Misunderstood, that is what I am. Someday they will see.* Ed shook his head and continued on his way.

Visiting Ruby was not easy, especially after what had just happened. Ed began to feel pangs of depression, but he tried to push them away as he walked into the office. An older gentleman was standing behind a counter as Ed entered.

"Hi, Ed. You back to see your mother?" he said.

"Hi, Burr. Yes I am."

"Well, it's good to see you again, and don't be a stranger, okay?"

"I won't. Thanks," Ed said as he felt a droplet in his eye. He quickly forced it away and held onto his composure. *What a nice man,* Ed thought. *I felt like an outcast just a moment before, and now I find kindness.* Ed smiled above and then walked out of the office and towards Ruby's apartment.

Since Ervin was gone and Ruby was becoming quite frail, Ed felt a duty to check on her. All of the years away in Florida had softened Ed's memories of her. Not all of the memories, though; it was difficult thinking about their strained relationship. But she was still his mother, the woman who had given birth to him, and she was in the final phase of her life. Ed realized that he had to let the past go and forgive her as best he could.

"Afternoon, Mother," he said as he walked into the tiny apartment.

Ruby was sitting at the kitchen table. She looked up and simply said, "Edgar."

After taking just a few steps from the door, Ed found himself in the kitchen. He pulled out a chair and joined her at the table. "How are you doing today?" he asked.

"Just fine," Ruby grumbled.

"Can I get you anything?"

She shook her head. He observed how she had aged. Her hair was completely white, and her pronounced nose appeared to be larger than he remembered, now that the rest of her had diminished with time. The once robust woman was now withering away. *I spent my life in fear of this woman and now look at her*, he thought. Her sagging

160

eyelids appeared too heavy to hold up as she glanced at Ed and then looked away. *I wonder if she thinks about how she treated me. I wonder if she is sorry.* Ed could only hope that this was the case because he understood that he was unlikely to hear any words of regret from her.

Ruby looked at Ed again. Ed asked, "So, do you like it here?" His eyes traveled around the living room and kitchen combo and then to the small bedroom and bathroom. The whole apartment was barley bigger than a hotel room, yet he was sure it was all she needed.

"Yes. I do. I have my own space, but I can go into the community center to visit friends when I want to. It works out pretty well."

"Good, good." Ed nodded in understanding. "Mother?" he said nervously. Ruby looked at Ed again as she waited for him to continue. "I never meant to be a disappointment to you." Ruby's hard stare penetrated through Ed as he watched her replay the past. "Do you know that?"

"Yes," she replied.

Her eyes relaxed and that was the end of the conversation. That was the closest thing Ed would get to an apology from his mother, and he accepted that. It was enough. It was time to let it go and forgive her once and for all.

The hours slipped away and Ed realized it was getting dark. It was November, and wintertime in Kalkaska County could be brutal. Ed needed to get himself back to the trailer before darkness completely covered the village. He zipped up his donated coat and placed the furry hat back on his head. He walked over to Ruby and gave her a slight kiss on the cheek. She winced and said, "Be careful, Edgar."

"I will, Mother. I will be back soon. Okay?"

"Okay."

And with that, Ed disappeared into the cold evening.

He retraced the route he had taken earlier. His cheeks burned as the gusts of snow blew into his face. He kept his bare hands in his pockets and walked faster and faster. *I hope I don't run into those teenagers again*, he thought as he neared South Cedar Street, Kalkaska's main thoroughfare. He was relieved to see the familiar walking bridge near McDonalds that was positioned over the

Boardman River. *McDonalds, Big Boy, and then the trailer. I am almost there.* Before Ed could reach the bridge, however, another gust of snow blew his way. He tried to cover his face to protect himself when he heard a screeching sound, again. He turned and the only thing he saw was metal and rubber and then blackness.

The car quickly sped away as Ed lay face down in the snow, unconscious. Was it the teenagers? Had they come back? No. It was a young man traveling through Kalkaska. He was driving his mother's car too fast for the wintery conditions. As his speed exceeded the posted limits, he lost control, just as Ed entered Cedar Street. Unfortunately, there was not a car or person in sight when the accident occurred. No one saw it, and no one knew that Ed was injured and unconscious in the snow. The car had thrown Ed far enough that he wasn't visible unless someone was looking for him. Seconds, minutes, and then hours ticked away as the end of Ed's life on Earth was closing in on him.

Two hours later, a village police officer was patrolling the streets. As he neared the south end of Kalkaska, he spotted a mound in the snow. At first glance, he didn't think much of it, but then he looked again. He pulled the cruiser over to the side of the road and walked towards the mound. Ed was covered in snow by now, but parts of his coat poked through here and there. When the officer saw him, he began to run. He knelt down and wiped the snow off and felt for a pulse. It was very faint. Ed was barely alive. The officer ran back to his patrol car to call for help and grabbed two heat packs. He squeezed and shook them vigorously as he ran back to Ed. He placed the warming packs on each of Ed's sides and took off his coat to place over him while he waited for help to arrive. "Hang on, buddy, hang on!" the officer pleaded as he listened for the distant siren. Finally the ambulance arrived, and they carefully put Ed on a stretcher and whisked him off to Kalkaska Memorial Hospital.

Ed was in the hospital for what seemed like eternity. His fractured leg was in a cast, and his bruised and battered body was healing. After being discharged, he spent time in an assisted living home. His new transportation was a wheelchair—for a while, anyway. Ed was happy to be alive.

"Father, thank you for sparing me. Is this your sign that it is time to get back to work? I got it! I got it! The message is loud and clear!"

Once Ed had healed, he spent more time in his subconscious mind, waiting for the next vision. He spent days praying, singing hymns, and waiting. Finally he saw it. Every detail of every panel was clear. He knew where every piece of wood would go and what kind of wood he would use. "Ah, beautiful, Lord! Beautiful!" He went back to work and began cutting diamonds.

When Ed was strong enough, he decided to walk to the library and then visit Ken Homa for one of their talks. He entered Ken's office carrying a stack of books in one hand and a cane in the other. He leaned the cane against his chair and made himself at home. Ken chuckled as he watched Ed reach over and carefully place the books in the seat next to him.

"Ed, you look so much better. I am glad you are healing so well."

"Me too," Ed replied. "I haven't felt better in a very long time."

"What do you mean?"

"You know when I was hit by that car? I thought my life was over, but God spared me. He spared me because I have work to do." Ken nodded. "You know, I haven't done that much work since Florida. It is time, Ken. God is telling me that I have work to do, and I better get down to it." Ed laughed. "So, I have made a decision to completely hand my life over to my work—I mean God's work. There is absolutely no turning back now."

A bright smile spread across Ed's face. From this point on, he would let no obstacle get in his way. The remainder of his life would be dedicated to the mural and to the Lord.

Ken Homa's contribution to Ed's work finally came through. Six months after filing the paperwork, Ed now had an income and Medicaid to help pay for his medical bills. It was a small income, but it was all that he needed to continue his work.

After one year of many talks, Ken and Ed parted ways. Ken's role had been fulfilled, at least for now, and Ed began the next phase of his job.

24

*"There are far, far better things ahead than
any we leave behind."*

C.S. Lewis, *Collected Letters of C.S. Lewis*

After Ed had healed and left the assisted living facility, he spent time living in a senior apartment complex until he finally found his new home. It was in an old abandoned schoolhouse. The schoolhouse, which was south of Kalkaska, had been sitting vacant for years. The owners of the assisted living home introduced Ed to the family who owned the schoolhouse property, and they gave Ed a very good deal. He could lease to own the building at an affordable price. He had just enough money to afford the monthly payment and a little left over to buy wood on occasion. The rest of the wood continued to come from Dumpsters or donations. The family also had a large garage on the property where they allowed Ed to build his new panels. They put up a wall to divide the large garage to create a workshop for him in the back. Ed also built a 12' x 12' shed onto the schoolhouse to use as sleeping quarters and installed a wood stove for heat.

Ed couldn't have been happier. He spent the next several years completing one panel after another. In his spare time, he fixed up the schoolhouse to create a showcase for his work, and he constructed a little garden outside. He renovated the interior and covered the exterior with red brick siding. As far as he was concerned, this was the closest thing to Heaven on Earth that he could find, his own little "white picket fence" dream. *A home. I finally have a home. My home!* Ed felt blessed beyond measure. Now he went back to work, day and night. As he completed a section of panels, he placed them in the schoolhouse among the others, adding more and more children to the growing family.

Ed's Big Boy family also began to grow. Since the schoolhouse was five miles south of the restaurant, walking there was difficult. Ed's response to this problem was to ride a bike. He had acquired an old one while he was at the assisted living home and began riding it into town when it was time for his coffee break. Ed always looked forward to spending time with the waitresses. As he'd done years before at Dana's Restaurant, he would bring them a flower or candy. He often selected a waitress he felt needed to be uplifted. He would talk with her and find out what her interests and problems were, and then he would do what he could to help.

On the other hand, Ed also began revealing another side of himself. As much as he loved women and wanted to help them, he also battled his feelings of mistrust. He had been hurt throughout his life by the women he thought had loved him. When he started to feel a pang of doubt towards a woman, he would lash out by saying something like, "Women are good for nothing!" or worse. It was his way of protecting his heart, and he realized that through his counseling sessions. He created an invisible shield around himself that would go up when he needed protection and go down when he felt safe. Like the windows in a car, with one push of a button in his mind, the shield would be raised or lowered. It was the only way to move forward, the only way to turn off his emotional distrust, but there were times when the shield would get stuck, and before he could get his heart to safety, he'd be hurt.

There was one woman Ed trusted like a daughter: the manager of Big Boy. From the moment Donna Fredell took over the restaurant, they developed a friendship. As with Sister Augusta and Ken Homa, he knew that Donna had a role to play in his life. She began to look after him like a father. Ed dreamed of having a close relationship with his biological children, but it never quite worked out.

Donna saw how hard Ed worked and that he barely ate enough to keep a person alive, and this worried her. She knew a person couldn't live on black coffee alone. Now that

Ed was so deep into his work, he would literally forget to eat or sleep. "All right, you old fart," she would say. "You need to take better care of yourself! Do you hear me?" Ed would grin and agree, just to appease her, and then move on his merry way. Joking with each other was their way of communication.

One day, Donna turned the corner in the restaurant kitchen and there was Ed trying to sneak a hash brown. "Uh oh, we're in trouble," Ed laughed as she shooed him away like a child. She smiled and was thrilled that he was eating something. Ed thought about how much he trusted Donna and how grateful he was to the Big Boy staff for watching out for him. A few years before, the previous manager had started giving Ed access to the soup and salad bar for free after he'd gotten sick from not eating. Ed would get into "the zone" and work for hours without eating or sleeping, so they devised a plan to make sure he would stay healthy. The only problem with the plan was that Ed was so prideful that they knew he wouldn't accept the food.

The solution was to create a job for him around the restaurant so he wouldn't think he was getting a handout. He became the general maintenance man. When a light bulb needed to be changed or a piece of machinery needed to be cleaned or repaired, Ed was the guy. Unfortunately, the plan didn't always work because Ed often chose just to drink his coffee.

When Donna took over as manager, she made a change. She forced Ed to eat three meals a day. If he didn't come to Big Boy for breakfast, lunch, and dinner, one of the staff members would call him or send someone to look for him. From that day forward, Ed would be seen at Big Boy Restaurant morning, noon, and night for his meals, and Donna and her staff could rest easy because their role in his life was being fulfilled.

When Ed was not at Big Boy, he worked on more panels. Before long, the schoolhouse interior was full, twenty-eight panels in all. The panels were sectioned off into different scenes, each telling a story in the life of Christ, and each telling Ed's hidden story through symbols. On one particular day, Ed stared at them as he thought about how he had made the panels from his feminine side, his creative side, just as God had asked him to do. He noted how interesting this request was; he had a love/hate relationship with women, yet God had asked him to create from that place. *Interesting!* Ed thought. *Was this for a reason, Father? Is this your way of helping me reconcile that conflict?*

He scanned from one grouping to the next. There was *My Father's Love*, which depicted the Last Supper, Moses and the Ten Commandments, The Quest, a manger scene called *My Mother's Love*, and a trilogy showing three stages of Jesus' last day on Earth. In the trilogy, Ed used the wood given to him by Sister Augusta to create an angel as a tribute to her. After he had placed the last panel into the room, he stood in the middle and wept uncontrollably while his children surrounded him, as if they were hugging him. "Father, I am in awe of you! Thank you for this gift," he said. "I understand it isn't complete yet, but the Holy Spirit is so present in this room. I just pray that others will feel it someday, all of the unloved children in the world. I am so grateful, Father!"

As Ed created more of his panels, he realized that he needed more workspace. The property owner decided to take down the wall in the garage and transformed the entire 24' x 30' garage into a workshop. This allowed Ed the space he needed, and it gave him room to work with the property owner and his son. Ed taught them his craft. They spent hours with him in the workshop creating their own tabletops and boxes.

The property owner's son spent most of his childhood sitting in the workshop talking with Ed as he learned the trade of woodworking. The two became very close, and the boy looked up to Ed as a teacher and mentor. Ed also developed a friendship with the boy's dog, a large German Shepherd named Dog. When the boy was at school, Dog followed Ed around everywhere he went. He would lie in the workshop as Ed worked, and Ed kept cookies on hand just for him.

The schoolhouse was transforming more and more. Ed had now lived there for a number of years, and during that time he continued working on the exterior. Before long, the old schoolhouse that had once housed local school children now looked like a chapel, and this chapel housed his precious children inside. On the outside, he found angel statues and placed them around the building, each angel representing one of his biological daughters. It was Ed's only way to keep them close to him and his heart.

After years of living in the schoolhouse, Ed decided that he wanted to put his name on the deed. By now he had paid $5000 towards the property, and he wanted the security for him and his panels. The owners agreed, but when they went to switch the deed, they found out that they couldn't. The problem was that the way the property was zoned, the schoolhouse land had to have at least one acre split off from the owner's land. Unfortunately, there was only a half an acre. They tried to solve the problem by buying up the other half from the neighbor, but he wanted $10,000, and that was too much for them. So Ed was not able to get his name on the deed to the property that he had been purchasing for years. As you can imagine, this made him very upset, and even though the property owners did all they could, this development caused conflict between them.

As time went on the conflict worsened. One day, Ed was out in his garden pulling weeds. This was one of the places he felt closest to God. Each day, he broke away to pull the pesky invaders. Ed knelt in between the cucumber plants and tomatoes as he pulled a fistful of weeds at a time. The summer sun beat down on his face and penetrated his body. It had been a while since he had felt the sun's warmth. He breathed in the fresh air and then released. "Ah!"

Ed had always felt a connection with nature and the trees and all of God's beautiful creations that adorned the landscape. He began whistling as he worked his way down each row. When he reached the end of the last row, he carefully pulled himself up, and his now-seventy-year-old bones creaked. He dusted off his slacks, walked around the schoolhouse, and headed for the front when he heard movement. He stopped in his tracks and turned back. He retraced his steps from a moment earlier just in time to spot a dog tiptoeing towards the garden. This was not his buddy Dog, but a new dog that the boy had brought home.

Actually, the boy was no longer a boy. He had just turned twenty years old and had recently married his girlfriend. He decided to build a home for himself and his new wife on his parents' property. After his home was complete, he added a red heeler puppy to their family. This pup was not calm like Dog. Instead, since his breed was used for cattle herding, he liked to bark and pull on people's pant legs. The red heeler would see Ed and Dog and run up to join them, but Ed couldn't handle his hyper demeanor. Ed was aging and no longer had that kind of tolerance.

When Ed saw the red heeler in his garden, he tensed up and ran towards him. "Get, get!!" he screamed. The dog took one look at Ed and took off. "Stay away! I mean it!" Ed yelled. His heart was racing with rage. He tried to slow it down, but the idea of someone or something destroying his hard work was more than he could take. His heartbeat finally slowed as he watched the dog move out of view.

That was not the dog's first visit to the garden, and it wouldn't be the last. This behavior caused the conflict between the property owners and Ed to increase. The owners were also becoming upset with Ed because he had a habit of filling up every space he lived in with "junk." To Ed, it wasn't junk. He would pick up any piece of furniture or object he found along the side of the road, or he would take things that someone was going to throw away. His reason was that he knew there were people who had nothing. He felt that if he filled his world with this stuff, he could help people when they needed it. It was also plan B for Ed. He was filling his world with things so that if he had to move again, he would have what he needed.

By now, the yard was full. It even got to a point where Ed pulled in a flatbed semi-trailer that was given to him so he could store his finds in there. Needless to say, the property owners were not happy. Ed was oblivious to their feelings. In his mind, he was being a good citizen.

Now that Ed was buying a home he couldn't legally own and the red heeler was becoming an issue, tempers became heated between him and the family. As a result, both sides said and did things to each other that they wouldn't normally say or do. Ed decided to start marking his own property lines by putting up posts. It was a message, loud and clear, that their onetime friendship was over. Ed no longer talked to them or waved. Instead, they lived side by side as if they were strangers. This was the beginning of the end for Ed's little "white picket fence dream," and he knew it.

As the autumn of 2003 arrived and day turned to night, the boy was in his yard when he noticed smoke starting to emerge from Ed's living quarters. He watched the smoke for a moment thinking that maybe Ed had left the wood stove door open or forgotten to open the damper on the flue. He waited for Ed to exit the shed, but he didn't. After a few minutes, the boy panicked and screamed to his wife, "Call Dad and tell him to meet me at the schoolhouse." He grabbed a couple of fire extinguishers out of his company truck and started running.

The boy and his dad were running from different directions when they arrived at the shed simultaneously. They yanked open the door and there was Ed sleeping. He woke just as they blew through the door. The curtains behind the woodstove were completely engulfed in flames, and the fire was spreading fast. Ed was coughing as they picked him up and carried him outside and placed him on the lawn. The boy and his father then gripped the fire extinguishers and a garden hose and attempted to put the flames out as they waited for help. The bright blaze grew and grew as sirens from the north closed in. Finally, the firemen pulled their hoses and started to bombard the flames until they slowly faded. Ed was spread out on the grass as paramedics tended to him. He had inhaled a lot of smoke and he wasn't doing well, so they transported him to the hospital. Thankfully he was okay, and even though Ed and his neighbors were feuding, he was grateful that they had been there to save him. He was also grateful that the flames had been dowsed before they reached Ed's beloved children.

After the fire, the shed was condemned by the fire department. There was extensive damage, and the powder left from the fire extinguishers was considered hazardous material. A hazmat team was required to clean up the chemicals before Ed could inhabit the building again. Since he could not afford the reconstruction or cleanup, he had to move.

Ed (center) as a young man.

Ed in 1966.

Ed in middle age.

The National Trout Memorial.

25

"It is not our business to succeed, but to do right. When you have done so the rest lies with God."

C.S. Lewis, Yours, Jack: Spiritual Direction from C.S. Lewis

Ed moved back to the senior apartment complex, but his children stayed in the schoolhouse, so he rode his bike as often as he could to be with them. He also gave an occasional tour of the panels.

While he tried to figure out his next move, he began feeling that God was ready to send another person to help him on his mission. He knew the person would be instantly recognizable, and he knew it would be soon. Just days later, he heard a knock on the schoolhouse door. He shuffled to the entrance, and with confidence, drew the door open. Directly in front of him stood Sister Augusta, and next to her was a woman with bright blue eyes and a brighter spirit. Ed took one look at her and said, "Oh, it's you. The Father said you were coming." Deb Swanson smiled at Ed, not knowing what to say to that. "Please, come in." Ed waved them in. "Would you like a tour?"

Sister Augusta and Deb entered the low-lit room. Deb looked around and almost felt the room spin as she looked at the panels for the first time. "I feel His presence," she said to Ed. The feeling was so strong that she had the urge to bolt from the schoolhouse. It was as if she weren't worthy of standing in front of the Lord. Not yet anyway.

Ed escorted Deb around the room explaining each panel in detail. The more she learned about the symbols and hidden meanings in each panel, the more her amazement grew. She was most amazed by the realization that this little man had cut and glued each piece of wood onto the panels—thousands and thousands of tiny little pieces.

When the tour was complete, they made their way back to the middle of the room. Deb was overwhelmed, and she had so many questions. She couldn't believe what she had just seen. She had no idea that something like this existed, but it did and she was in its presence.

"Ed, I am overcome with emotion," she said. "What you have created here is beyond explanation!" Ed grinned with pleasure. "Ed, I was sent here," she continued. "It was the most bizarre experience of my life. Can I share my story with you?" Ed nodded even though he already knew that she was God-sent.

"I have been a court reporter for twenty-five years in Grand Rapids, Michigan," she began. "I loved my job, but after visiting a dear friend of mine in the hospital before he died of a brain tumor, I felt the calling to get involved with hospice. I walked to my friend's room and stood in the doorway and watched him lying in his bed. For the first time in a very long time, there was peace radiating from his face. No pain, just serenity. And then, a gentle smile graced his face. He was asleep, but a beautiful ray emanated from his face, a glow. At the other end of his bed stood a hospice nurse. She was looking at him with the most loving eyes, as if she was giving him comfort and relieving his pain just with the penetrating love from her eyes. It was at that moment that I knew I wanted to be a part of that. Shortly after, I started volunteering with Hospice of Michigan."

Ed's heart warmed as he continued to listen. "One day, while having lunch with a co-worker in our jury room at the courthouse, I stood up and blankly stared out the window over the downtown skyline and said, much to my surprise, 'I have to go north. I don't know why, but I have to go north.'" Ed smiled. "I typed up my retirement papers that night and handed them in the next morning. Everyone thought I had lost my mind: my co-workers, my elderly father, my siblings, and my grown children. I have never lived anywhere else, but I was now on autopilot. No emotion, no worries, just directed like a hand on my back guiding me where I was supposed to go."

Deb took a breath and continued. "Then I had to ask myself, 'Where is north?' I got on the Internet and found a beautiful Victorian home for rent in Elk Rapids. Somehow, I knew this was it. After the owner, Paul Hresko, showed me around, I signed on the dotted line and moved up here a few weeks later.

"After I had been up north for a while, I started to get anxious. I knew I needed to volunteer or something, so I asked Paul where the local hospice was located, and he referred me to Sister Augusta. I met her this afternoon for the first time, and she told me that there was something that I had to see. And here I am. When you said that the Father said I would be coming, I knew this was why I was sent up north. I still don't know the reason, but I know this is the place."

"Deb, I am getting tired. I need to find a home for my children, a permanent home," Ed said. He reached into his pocket and pulled out his keys to the schoolhouse. "Here." He placed the keys in Deb's hand. "My job is nearly done. Before I go home to my Father, I need to find a home for my Pinocchios."

Deb held onto the keys for a moment trying to understand what Ed was asking of her. He was getting older, and he had just lost his home again. He could feel it was time to start thinking about what would happen when he left the earth. It was time to start planning for their future.

Within weeks it was apparent why Deb was brought into Ed's life. The first reason was that she was to help take care of Ed emotionally. They spent hours in deep conversations about life, death, and dying. Since she had an interest in helping the dying pass to the other side, she found that Ed had so much wisdom on the subject that he helped her immensely. As a result, he decided to start taping his thoughts and ideas regarding life and death on his old battered cassette recorder during his evening hours. These hours of recording were special to him, and so was his friendship with Deb. They both gave him a sense of peace and warmth that he hadn't felt for a long time. After a year, he had recorded fifty-four tapes for Deb. She tucked them away for safekeeping and for future use.

The second reason Deb met Ed was to introduce him to a person who would become one of the most essential people in his life: Paul Hresko. When Deb returned to her new rental after meeting Ed, she told Paul's wife, Patti, about the panels. Deb was so blown away by what she had seen that she insisted her new landlords go see the work for themselves.

As soon as Paul walked into the schoolhouse, he knew his life would never be the same. The interesting thing was that it wasn't about how magnificent the work was or how intriguing Ed was. Instead, an instantaneous feeling came over Paul that revealed to him that Ed would become his purpose. There was a sense that God had been leading him towards something very important, and until now, he had had no idea what it was. As soon as he walked into the sacred space, he knew. This was it. Paul was to help Ed take care of the needs of the panels and the needs of Ed, and he realized at that moment that he would do whatever he had to do to make both of those things happen. He would help find a home for both. He strongly felt that he had no choice.

The first mission was to help Ed with the schoolhouse deed issue. Since he had paid $5000 for a home that he could not legally own, there needed to be some resolution. Deb and Paul helped Ed find a lawyer. This lawyer talked to the property owners, and they agreed to pay Ed back his $5000. The family essentially bought the property back from Ed.

After Ed moved back to the senior apartments, he worried because there was no room for the panels there. For the time being, the panels were left in the schoolhouse. This caused Ed so much anxiety that he entered a deep depression. It was a struggle to eat and sleep knowing that he was separated from his beloved children.

Ed, Deb, and Paul worked together to set up the first foundation for the panels, a foundation to protect them now and in the future. Deb used her connections in the legal system in Grand Rapids to contact a lawyer, and the foundation was quickly established and proudly named My

Father's Love in honor of Ed's Orlando angels, Dana and Billie.

26

"Only a real risk tests the reality of a belief."

C.S. Lewis, A Grief Observed

Ed knew there was one person with a lot of connections in the community to help rescue the panels from the schoolhouse and find them a home: Sister Augusta. The nun immediately got to work and found a vacant pole barn south of the schoolhouse. The family that owned the pole barn worked hard to fix up the space so they could give Ed's work a proper welcome. Finally, the panels were safe. Sister Augusta and the owners of the pole barn agreed to create a place where many people could experience Ed's vision. They invested a great deal of time and money to make that happen. During the day, the barn would be open by appointment, and at night the panels were securely locked up with chains and paddle locks. Ed was initially grateful, but soon this feeling turned to fear.

Since the fire at the schoolhouse, people around the community worried about whether Ed was stable enough to take care of himself and his mural. There were rumors that Ed had started the fire on purpose. This was not the case, but people often heard Ed say that he would burn the panels before he'd let anyone get their hands on them.

So when word of the fire spread, so did the rumors. The mural was now becoming a life force of its own, and people were concerned about the panels' safety with Ed. According to them, he had just tried to set them on fire. Ed heard whispers around town that a group of people had put together a petition to take over guardianship of him and his panels. The worst part was that Ed believed that Sister Augusta was part of the group. It is unclear whether this was true; Sister Augusta always did what was best for her friend, but the only thing that mattered was that Ed believed it to be true.

Ed was now living thirty miles away from the panels and was told that he had to call in advance to visit them. Between whispers of the petition and now this, he felt that his children were being taken away from him. *They are my children. How can they take them away from me?* he thought. He had created and nurtured each panel so lovingly, and now his ability to parent them was in question. *I am not crazy! Can't they see that? I just want to protect my children from the evils of the world. That's all. I want to keep them safe! Father, I miss them so much. How am I supposed to live like this? How am I supposed to live so far away from my children? How am I supposed to protect them?*

Ed struggled with these questions day and night. Fear was overtaking him, and he knew that he needed to build up a defense. He needed to plan his next move. Losing his panels was not an option. Since he no longer had the ability to stay with the mural whenever he wanted to and now felt like a visitor instead of the creator, Ed refused to go see them at all. It was just too painful. It was like visiting a child behind bars. There was nothing he could do to free them. There was nothing he could do to get them back. *I will get them back. I just don't know how yet*, he thought. Depression dug a groove deeper and deeper into his soul. The darker Ed's thoughts became, the more intense his fear grew.

When the panels had first gone to the barn, Sister Augusta had started paperwork to create a corporation for them and Ed. She filed for a DBA (a DBA is a fictitious business name) and started paperwork to have the panels gifted over to the new corporation. After Ed heard the rumors of her involvement in taking over his guardianship, he felt that the purpose of the paperwork was to steal the panels from him, and he no longer trusted her. I know that Sister Augusta's intentions were good. She just wanted to help Ed, but he felt like a mother bear who needed to protect her cubs.

Prior to this, Ed and Sister Augusta had had many long talks about the future of the work and the best place for the panels to live permanently. The My Father's Love Foundation met at Big Boy to discuss all of the options. They had several ideas, and one involved land owned by local Native Americans along the banks of the Manistee River. The Native Americans saw the panels and were so moved that they wanted to incorporate Ed's work into a recreation center on their land.

Ed crossed off idea after idea in his mind. He then remembered God's words: "I will provide for you. Even when things become difficult, and they will, just remember that I will take care of you." *I have to have faith! I trust you, Father. I know you will take care of this.* Ed knew he was losing the only family he had left, again. But he also knew that with God's help, he would never let go.

One afternoon, Ed made an urgent call to Paul Hresko. "We've got to get them out of there! We've got to get them out of there!" Ed announced. With this, Paul understood it was time for him to step into his God-given role. It was time to help a man whom, for whatever reason, he was supposed to help. They both knew there was only one way to get the panels out of the pole barn, and that was to steal them back. Paul understood that both Sister Augusta and the owners of the pole barn had their hearts in the right place. He struggled with this. Paul hoped to handle the situation in a way that would honor everyone involved, but he also knew that these panels were Ed's. It didn't matter if the whole world questioned whether Ed could take care of them. Paul prayed for an answer, and it was crystal clear: if Ed wanted to hang each panel from a tree, he could do that. They belonged to him, and he could choose how to care for them. Paul felt called to help Ed physically and help him with the panels, and if that meant stealing them back, he was going to support him.

One day Paul asked Ed, "How are we going to do this? I have never moved anything like this before."

"We are going to need a truck," Ed said. He then went on to describe it.

"You mean like a big box truck?"

"Yeah. Do you know anyone that has one?"

"No."

"Okay. We'll just pray about it. Don't worry, the Father will take care of it," Ed said with confidence.

This was Wednesday, and Ed selected Saturday to implement their plan. They had three days. Besides finding a truck, they both knew that another obstacle was Sister Augusta. Every time Paul brought people out to view the panels at the pole barn, she would show up within minutes. Her role was to protect the panels, and she took that role very seriously. Both Ed and Paul wondered how they would pull this off without a confrontation with her.

On a Friday night, Paul called Ed. "You are not going to believe this. I found a truck!"

"Wonderful," Ed said with joy.

"I was so worried that we didn't have a truck yet and we were planning on moving the panels tomorrow, so I remembered what you said about praying about it and the Father would take care of it," Paul said. Ed smiled. "So after work, I prayed all the way from Kalkaska to Elk Rapids. I pulled into Elk Rapids, and this cube truck pulled up on Bridge Street right in front of me, and I literally almost t-boned it." Ed's smile was now spread across his entire face. "The truck pulled right in front of the office building where I was going, so I pulled in right behind him. By now my heart was literally going boom, boom, boom!" Ed and Paul laughed. "Then the guy gets out of the truck, and I know this guy! I said, 'Nate, what in the world?' He said 'I'm sorry. I'm not used to driving this thing.' He was very apologetic. Once I kind of calmed down, I realized, 'Wait a minute here.' I began putting two and two together. Come to find out, the truck belonged to a mutual friend of ours. They just bought it, and he was driving it to them. They hadn't even seen the truck yet. So I called them and said, 'Hey, I almost creamed your truck, and can I borrow it?'" Laughter erupted again. "My friend asked when and I said, 'Like tomorrow.'" There was a brief pause. "Guess what."

"What?" Ed asked.

"I have the keys in my hands. We have our truck!"

"Amazing!" Ed sang.

"Here I was praying because you said to pray and poof! There it was, right in front of me. You couldn't miss it!"

"I am not the one that didn't believe. It was you that didn't believe. I told you all along that the Father would take care of it," Ed said very calmly.

And He did, just as he had so lovingly told Ed so many years ago in Florida. Ed finally believed without question. Worry would now be a thing of the past. He now knew that God would provide no matter what.

The next morning, Paul and a couple of men he had gathered to help load and unload the panels picked Ed up in the brand spanking new cube truck. Ed opened the passenger side door and carefully slid in. Paul and Ed looked at each other and then Ed's eyes filled with tears as he beamed.

"The Father did it again," Ed said.

"What do you mean?" Paul asked.

"We don't have to worry about Augusta."

"Why?"

"The Father took care of her."

"Ed, what did you do?" Paul asked in a panic.

"She was sent out of town." Ed began to half laugh and half cry. "Not only out of town, but God sent her out of the country for her job."

"Ed, I am beginning to believe anything is possible with the Lord!"

They both laughed as Paul turned the steering wheel south towards Ed's pride and joy.

Their secret mission went as planned. After explaining to the owner of the pole barn what their intentions were, Paul apologized and thanked him for all he had done for Ed and the panels. The owner's role was so important in Ed's journey. He provided a home for the panels when no one else could, but it was time for Ed to take them back. It was time for him to set up a new home for his children.

Before picking up the panels, Paul had found their next home, just as the Lord had instructed. He ran into a man he barely knew at the Traverse City Cherry Festival. He told the man about Ed and the panels. The next words out of the man's mouth were, "My family owns a warehouse in

Kalkaska and there is plenty of room in there. Let me talk to my parents and I will get back to you." After the man's parents visited Ed and the panels, they knew they had to help. They even spoke to their spiritual nun, who lived in Dublin, Ireland, and she said, "You need to help this man." So without question they did. They agreed to give Ed enough space to house all twenty-eight panels and plenty of workspace to continue his work for the Lord. The most amazing part was that they gave Ed the space for free. He didn't have to pay one penny for rent, just the utilities he used.

Ed thought about the family's unconditional kindness as they closed the back of the truck with his children securely placed in the box. *Father, I love you so much!* he thought. Paul put the truck in gear and pressed the gas pedal. Both Paul and Ed looked back as the truck moved forward. For a moment, they worried that someone might run down the driveway to try to stop them. Ed looked at Paul and said, "If we make it out of here, I think I might reach over and kiss you."

"I'd rather you didn't," Paul said.

They both roared as the wheels of the truck made contact with the road, and as he had years before as he left Orlando with his first seven children safe in a gypsy wagon, Ed knew without question that he was doing the right thing.

27

"Joy is the serious business of heaven."

C.S. Lewis, Letters to Malcolm

Twenty-five thousand square feet surrounded Ed. He slowly turned 360 degrees taking in every inch of his new warehouse space. *I can't believe this! This is more than I could ever ask for.*

Ed thought about how he had chosen to divide up the room. His workshop, which held a variety of saws, tools, and workstations, was located around the perimeter of the area. He began preparing the workstations for the people God would send next after He revealed why he had granted Ed so much space. *A teacher and her students will be coming soon. Get ready.* "Oh yes, Father! I see it! This will be marvelous! I have so much work to do," Ed said.

He divided up the space. He had no idea how many kids would be coming. He just knew that God would send enough to touch their hearts and to show that they are all worthy, beautiful human beings. That would be the message after all, whether they recognized it or not. But Ed knew that someday they would understand.

Located in the center of the warehouse was a room that Ed had built specifically to hold the panels. He used a portion of the $5000 he'd got back to buy yellow prefab log siding. He attached the logs horizontally around the exterior of the new structure. He stepped inside the room and walked by each panel, all of which were secured to the interior walls. The stories were placed in a strategic order.

As he paused in front of his children one by one, he inspected his signature, 6-22-34, which was embedded somewhere in the wood of every panel. The digits held deep meaning. They represented not only the love for numerology he got from his mother, but also God's will for him. Ed thought about the passage in the sixth book of the Holy Bible, Joshua 22:34. The King James Version says, "And the children of Reuben and the children of Gad called the alter Ed: for it shall be a witness between us that the LORD is God." *Father, I am a witness for you, and the signature that I chose to sign my work with represents that. Thank you for giving me the most beautiful gift. Thank you for selecting me for this job. I am so lucky! You have chosen me to share your love with the world through my work.*

Ed began to weep. *I know that I am a misfit. I know that people don't understand me. They try to label me. They try to tell me that I am crazy! But Father, you understand my heart. You believe in me. No matter what I have done, you still love me.* Ed pushed the tears away. *I know that I have sinned, Father, and I know that I will sin again. But you will never turn your back on me. You will never treat me like a black sheep, and most important, Lord, you know that I can love.*

Ed walked over to a vacant spot in between two panels. *I am ready to start my next panel. I know what you want. You want me to go back to the beginning. It is time to share the story of Adam and Eve.* Ed could already visualize the new panel resting in between the older siblings. It was as if they were protecting the vacant spot for the new arrival. *I have so much work to do before my students arrive. They feel like misfits too, don't they, Lord? Is that why you are sending them to me? I will do my best to help them, Father. Okay?* Ed started whistling as he strolled out of the room and towards his workstation. He stacked several pieces of wood and then began sawing as he waited.

Ed prepared for the next phase of his work and life. He completed the Adam and Eve panel; he continued collecting "junk" and filled every empty space in the warehouse with his finds; and he created a food pantry for people in need. He built the pantry in remembrance of the years at home with his wife and children, the happy years. Ed explained to me one day, "When I was building houses, I would sell them for cash. I would go to the bank and get all of the cash, and then I would go home and put the money on the table for the kids. Thirteen thousand dollars was the most. They would play with it all night." He laughed. "Then my oldest daughter would do the math, and we would put ten percent in an envelope, and the rest would go in the bank for the next project and to support the family. Then the kids would go to school, and they would find families that were struggling. They would come home and we would have a family meeting to discuss what families needed help. We would figure out how much money the mother needed, because there usually wouldn't be a husband there or he would be so drunk he couldn't find the door. So we put that much money in a plain white envelope with no address and no return address, and that night one or two of the older children and I would go out on the road and leave it in their mailbox. I miss that."

Ed decided to build the pantry in the warehouse to continue helping families. He also built another room behind the gallery space. This room was initially to be a place where he could get away from the sawdust. After years of working with wood and developing allergies to various species, Ed needed a place just to breathe. His doctor warned him about the possibility of his developing breathing problems, but Ed was too stubborn and too dedicated to his work to listen or to wear a mask. He was not willing to walk away from his purpose, so the small room was the best that he could do.

Before long, the room became Ed's home. He began living in the warehouse illegally. He knew it was against the law to live in a commercial space, but he found it difficult to leave his work at the end of the day, and the fact that he literally worked day and night made it silly to leave. So Ed put a bed and a chair in the room and secretly made it his home.

Ed also put together a second board of directors for the My Father's Love Foundation. Deb had moved back to Grand Rapids after completing her mission for him, so Paul and Ed worked together to decide what the future looked like for the panels. They decided to apply for a 501(c)(3) exemption to establish a nonprofit organization. The one thing Ed knew for sure was that he would not allow anyone to pay one penny to come and see his work. He was adamant about that, so Paul helped him apply for nonprofit status.

The second board of directors consisted of Ed, Paul, and a group of businessmen from the community. The goal of the new board was to help launch Ed's work into the world so that the panels could begin to do their job of showing love to the "unloved." The problem was that every time the board was close to setting up an exhibit, Ed would sabotage the whole thing. The biggest issue he faced with the board was that in order for them to do their job, the panels had to be legally gifted over to My Father's Love. But each time Ed attempted to put his signature on the document, he could not go through with it. He just wasn't ready. Not yet. The panels were the only home he had. They were his anchors. His fear of losing his children was still at the front of his mind, and he struggled to overcome it.

Paul continued to hold the position of president of the board, and he also continued to help Ed in any way he could. He was the plant manager of Alken-Ziegler in Kalkaska, a large automotive manufacturing plant. Ironically, the plant was literally next door to Ed's warehouse. Since Paul's job was to take care of Ed's and the panels' physical needs, he told Ed that he could walk over to his plant anytime he needed him. Paul told his receptionist to let Ed through to his office without question.

Ed did not hesitate to make his daily visits to Paul's office. It didn't matter if Paul was in a meeting or on the phone; Ed would walk through his office door with his tattered clothing, sawdust in his beard, and a dirty travel coffee mug, and just plop down in a chair.

One day, Paul was in an important meeting with a group of General Motors buyers. A meeting like this is typically very businesslike. Paul and the buyers were sitting around a conference table wearing blue suits, pressed white shirts, and striped ties when Ed entered the room. Ed walked in with his coffee mug in hand and joined the group at the table. As he sat down, the dust from his clothing floated around him as if he were Pigpen from a Charlie Brown cartoon. The buyers looked at Ed and then at Paul like, *What in the world? Who is this guy?* Ed noticed the men's glares and said, "Oh, don't mind me." Paul did his best to stifle an outburst of laughter. He had spent years working for General Motors as a buyer, and now as a plant manager, so he realized how odd this must seem to them. It could have been a "Saturday Night Live" skit. Ed picked up his mug in a "Cheers!" fashion and said with his Dana Carvey grin, "Oh, by the way, Paul is my secretary." Paul couldn't take it anymore, and he burst into laughter. Ed chuckled as he looked at his friend. He knew at that moment that Paul would take good care of him. With Ed nearing the final years of his work and life, he knew that God had sent him the right person.

28

"The task of the modern educator is not to cut down jungles but to irrigate deserts."

C.S. Lewis, The Abolition of Man

Two years after Ed had begun preparing for the arrival of the teacher and her students, it was finally time. Everything was in place and Ed was reeling in anticipation. For the next month, he rode his bicycle by her school every day. As he traveled to Big Boy for breakfast, lunch, and dinner, he patiently waited for God to reveal the teacher's next art lesson. Little did either of them know that it was about to become the biggest art lesson of her career.

I had no idea that I was to become that teacher. Let me share the moment when my life and Ed's intersected.

Ed and I officially met in April of 2005. He had turned seventy-three a few months before. Of course I had seen him around our small town over the years, but I had no idea who he was. A few months before meeting him, I had noticed an elderly man riding his weathered bicycle past the alternative high school where I was teaching the arts at the time. When I first saw him, I flashed back to times when I had seen him throughout the years: at church; riding his bicycle along a busy highway in the winter; and sitting in our local Big Boy Restaurant sipping coffee. I had paid little attention to him, until now.

As the days went by, I noticed him riding by my school every day. I started watching for him while getting in and out of my car or looking out my classroom window. I wondered who he was. What was he doing? He looked disheveled. He was a small man and always wore a dirty hunter-orange hooded zip-up sweatshirt. His gray scraggly beard seemed grungy with wood shavings embedded here and there.

One day as I was driving toward the school, I noticed him digging in a Dumpster across the street at the Wayne Wire manufacturing plant. Now I was really intrigued. Who is this man? What is his story? Is he homeless? Is he looking for food? I could not get him out of my mind.

One beautiful April afternoon as I was sitting at my desk, my principal entered my classroom. "LaShelle," he said, "I just received an email from the superintendent. Do you think you and your class would be interested in working with a local artist?"

"Who is it?"

"His name is Mr. Ed. I guess he created some kind of mural made out of wood."

"Mr. Ed? Like the horse?" I said. We laughed. "I've never heard of him."

"Apparently he wants to teach his craft to local school kids. The superintendent thinks you and your kids would be the perfect choice. I guess he looked at the mural the other day and said it's incredible."

I tried to imagine this mural in my head, but without more information, it was difficult. "Okay, set it up," I said. "I have to see this. Where is his studio?"

"I'm not sure, but I will find out."

"Sounds good," I said. "Let me know."

A few days later, my principal, the superintendent, and I drove to the warehouse to meet Mr. Ed. We pulled out of the school parking lot, drove less than a minute, and pulled into a driveway. *What?* I thought to myself. *He works kitty-corner from the school?* I could not believe it. We drove alongside an old brown warehouse and pulled into the back. As we entered the building, I walked in first. There among sawdust and tools stood the same man I had been observing every day for months. I was astounded. As I stood there speechless, Mr. Ed shuffled over to us, and slightly hunched over, held out his worn hand.

"Hello, I'm Mr. Ed," he said warmly.

I grasped his hand and said, "I'm LaShelle. Nice to meet you."

He stood barely five foot six and wore the same orange hooded sweatshirt I'd always seen him in. He seemed tired, as if he had lived a strenuous life. Beyond the thinning gray hair, beard, and wrinkled skin were tender amber eyes. I got the feeling, however, that there were demons deep within. As we made eye contact, I knew this man was very special. We instantly had a connection. It was like two old souls meeting again.

"Would you like to see the panels?" he said, smiling like a proud parent.

"Absolutely!" I said.

He escorted me deeper into the warehouse and first directed my attention to hundreds of wood mosaic tabletops, jewelry boxes, and hope chests. They were magnificent. "These are my practice pieces," he said.

"Practice pieces?" This amazed me. They were masterpieces all by themselves.

"I use these pieces to figure out a variety of configurations with the wood diamonds, and to work out color harmony, how each piece of wood species looks next to another."

This makes sense, I thought.

"Each piece of wood that I use is natural, no stain and no dye."

Mr. Ed then turned my attention to a room he'd built in the middle of the 25,000-square-foot donated warehouse space. We walked to the doorless entrance and there they were: the panels. I hesitantly stepped in and my jaw dropped. "Wow!" was all I could say at first. I just stood there in sheer amazement. I had never witnessed anything like this mural in my life. "I can't believe this!" I repeated over and over.

The first grouping that popped out at me was seven panels put together into one unit. These panels were of the Last Supper. I thought, *Da Vinci has nothing on you.* They were beautiful. As Mr. Ed provided my first tour of his life's work, I felt something happening inside me. This felt like a holy place. It seemed as if God was in the room shining his love down on us. My soul was completely awake for the first time in a very long time. I will never forget that moment.

After an hour I rejoined my principal and superintendent. We gathered near the door. Mr. Ed said,

"Thank you for coming." I scanned the room and noticed what appeared to be a small room that he'd built in the back of the area that held the mural. Inside were a chair and a bed. I realized at this moment that Ed was secretly living there. It was against code for him to do that. He had been given permission from the owner to work on his panels there at no charge, but legally that was all he could offer Ed. Yet there it was, the secret room he had built. He had no water, no bathroom, and no kitchen. It dawned on me that he was homeless.

I looked Ed in the eyes and said, "I will consider the project and let you know soon."

Ed smiled with a hopeful glance. "Okay."

I was unsure how I would pull it off, not knowing if my students would warm to something like this. These alternative education students lived volatile lives, much like Mr. Ed. Many of them spent time in and out of jail. Some were teen parents, and some were also more or less homeless. I felt that I could give them a gift by introducing them to Mr. Ed, yet I knew that it would also mean a large shift in my curriculum, not to mention figuring out how to meet my required state guidelines. I had a lot to think about, and not lightly.

As Mr. Ed escorted us the rest of the way to the door, he turned and looked at me and said, "Oh, by the way, I am looking for a nude model for the Eve panel. I am considering redoing her. Are you interested?"

My cheeks turned scarlet as my principal and superintendent laughed like schoolboys. "No, thank you, but I do appreciate the offer," I said. We then exited and headed for the car as all three of us bellowed.

After leaving the warehouse that day, I had a difficult time deciding whether I should agree to participate in the project. It would involve two hours a day learning a rare art form that the kids otherwise would not be exposed to. I went back and forth for months. The first meeting with Mr. Ed had taken place in April, near the end of the school year. The plan was to begin the project the following school year. I questioned whether my students would engage. I worried about how they would communicate with Mr. Ed.

He was different from anyone they had met before, yet he had more in common with them than they knew.

Summer came and went and I was still unsure. "Can I really pull something like this off? Do I really want to mess with my comfortable routine?" I asked myself these questions over and over. In early October, I finally made a decision. I decided against the project. It just seemed too difficult.

That afternoon, while walking down the school hallway, I ran into my superintendent. I told him my decision. I explained my concerns. He looked me straight in the eyes and said, "You know, if it doesn't work out, you can always end it then." I am sure that everyone around me noticed the light bulb beaming above my head. Of course! That was all I needed to hear. My intuition was telling me to go for it, but I needed a logical voice to tell me the same thing. That simple advice changed my mind and my life.

That same day, I contacted Mr. Ed to tell him that we had decided to do the project. I could hear the excitement in his voice as he said, "Wonderful!" We selected a day to begin: November 1, 2005. I realized that I had a tremendous amount of work and planning ahead of me and less than a month to prepare. I stood there for a moment and took in a deep breath. A smile spread across my face. I thought about the poem by Robert Frost, "The Road Not Taken." I felt myself standing at the fork in the road of my life's journey. I looked both ways. It would be much easier not to do this project, but by taking the road less traveled, I could strongly feel the difference this decision would make in other lives. I wasn't exactly sure how or why, but I somehow knew it would be important.

Before I knew it, Halloween had arrived. We were to begin the project the next day. I talked to my students about Mr. Ed and explained that he wanted to teach them his craft. That was all I really knew at that point. My students were ready. Apprehensive, but ready. Mr. Ed was anxiously waiting.

That evening, I planned to take my nine-year-old son, Ty, trick-or-treating and then call it an early night. As we were heading for the first house, something told me that I had to document the project. I knew it was crucial to begin in my classroom before I took my students over to meet Mr. Ed for the first time. I wanted to get their thoughts and feelings on tape prior to going to the warehouse. The problem was that I didn't own a camera. I was a single mother living on a teacher's salary. Basically, I was broke.

As I was driving Ty house to house while he gathered candy, I called Best Buy and applied for a credit card over the phone. I nervously waited as they processed my information, but I was approved.

I found out that they closed at nine p.m. It was already almost seven, and I knew time was slipping away. I had to have the video camera by morning, and my only chance to get it was in the next two hours.

My son had made plans for us to meet up with his friend Travis and his parents to continue trick-or-treating in a local subdivision. I didn't want to spoil his evening. We all walked around the subdivision, and Travis's mom and I chatted casually. I was feeling anxious and continued to look at my cell phone clock. She noticed my behavior. I explained my situation and she generously said, "You go. I will take Ty the rest of the way. You can pick him up at our house later."

"Are you sure?" I asked.

"Yes, go!"

I smiled, gave Ty a big kiss, and darted to my car.

Best Buy was a thirty-minute drive. It was going to be close. On a normal day, I was a cautious driver and carefully calculated how fast I should drive without risking a speeding ticket. That was not an option. I prayed that nothing and no one would get in my way so I could make it there before nine. It was too important to catch the first day of the project on tape. I could never get that moment back, and the documentation would not be the same without that footage.

Just my luck, I caught every red light. Finally, the bright yellow and blue Best Buy sign was in sight. I glanced at my clock and it was 8:40 p.m. I did not let myself relax until I had sprinted through the front door and come to the finish line in the electronics department. I quickly explained what I was looking for and how much I had to spend. By the time the clock had struck nine, I was walking to my car with a new Sony DVD digital video camera and a stack of mini DVDs.

29

"You have not chosen one another, but I have chosen you for one another."

C.S. Lewis, The Four Loves

I stood in front of my class armed with my new video camera. When you work with at-risk teenagers, you see attendance fluctuate on a daily basis. On any given day, I might have one student or twenty, depending on what was happening in their turbulent lives. On day one, I had eight students: Will R., Will B., Nicole, Jesse, Cody (Tex), Haley, Richard, and Zack.

I posed the question to each of them: "What are your expectations going into this project, and what do you hope to learn from Mr. Ed?" The answers varied. I heard responses like: "I know a little about woodworking. I want to learn to do it right;" "I want to learn to teach my dad. He is into woodworking;" "I think it will be fun to make something cool;" "To pass this class;" "Maybe I can make something, sell it, and get rich;" "I think this class will be awesome. I want to make something out of wood;" "I just hope to gain a new style of art out of this;" "I don't even know what is going on, just that it is something out of wood."

Zack, the comedian of the group, explained, "Uh, I am expecting to get out of this class in an hour and twenty-five minutes so I can get home and go to bed." You could hear laughter around the room. He then said, "Besides that, I expect to actually learn how to do something in art because I am not really the artsy type of person." When I approached Will B., he looked at me stoically and said through his earring-pierced lip, "Nothing. Graduate. That's all." I replied, "Maybe you will feel differently on the last day."

My thoughts were scattered as I turned off the camera and we packed up to head to the warehouse. Everyone left the room ahead of me. I turned around at my classroom door, took one last breath, and turned off the lights as I encouraged myself, "Let's do this!"

We walked our first of many walks to the warehouse as a class. I still couldn't believe how close Mr. Ed's workshop was to our school. We were there in less than five minutes. The project would not work any other way. Our budget was very tight, and we had no way of transporting our students to another building on a daily basis. This limitation became one of the first signs that the project was actually out of my control.

My students entered the building first, and I followed as Ed greeted us. His upper false teeth were so old that they shifted when he smiled. I could tell that my students were apprehensive. They hesitantly followed Ed into the room where the panels were located. I noticed that he had a long glass table set up in the middle of the room and a chair for each student. I followed the group with my video camera, recording every moment.

My students gaped as they stood in the presence of the mural. This was not a reaction I had witnessed from them before. It was evident that they realized they were entering a sacred space. They sat down and Ed strolled to the head of the table, but he continued to stand. All eyes were on this scruffy man. It appeared that he had not showered in weeks. The fact that he didn't have a shower meant that that was probably true. As I watched through my lens, I had no idea how my students were going to respond to him. It could go either way. They could either listen to what he had to say or mockingly walk out the door. I prayed they would give him a chance as I zoomed in on him.

I chuckled to myself as Ed stood in front of the group holding his dirty convenience store coffee mug. He wore the same outfit and the same hunter-orange sweatshirt as before. I wondered if this was his only outfit. He was dressed in layers. He started with a blue t-shirt and then added a soiled white-collared shirt. On top of that he wore a tan jacket and then the orange sweatshirt. I noted how my students were just in t-shirts, yet Ed was bundled up. It was the first day of November, but the weather was still mild.

Ed cleared his throat and began his first lesson. He opened by explaining marquetry and the uniqueness of his work, and then he said, "You are a unique individual." Then he gently pointed to the class. "There is nothing like you. There will not be anything like you again. You are very unique and your mind is the same way." Under the rough exterior of this man was a sparkle. His aged amber eyes twinkled with joy as he spoke. "We have a large concept that we would like to present to you. My words might be a little strange to you because my training is different than yours."

Ed went on to describe various ideas for a future home for the panels, and then he asked, "What would you like to see done with this?" Each student looked around the room in awe as their eyes went from one panel to the next. Will R. spoke up and said, "I would like to see it displayed to the whole world." The rest of the class remained silent. Ed smiled and said, "Don't be bashful. Let me tell you a few things about me." Ed pointed to his head. "Part of my brain is damaged. I was hurt. I can't get it to activate like I want. I've been called a half-wit most of my life. The only reason I can stand up is because I got out of that wheelchair." Ed looked at the wheelchair that became home after he was hit by the car. He had strategically placed it near the entrance of the exhibit as a reminder of God's gifts. "What you are looking at is a lifetime of studying and reading, but I can't write. So this is my book. This mural is my writing." Ed held out his right hand towards several panels. "I want you as a group to surpass this effort and build the last panel, with each one of you contributing." He took a sip of his coffee and shrugged his shoulders. He then grinned "Okay?"

I scanned the class with my camera and documented their stunned reactions. "We would like you to become responsible for this work. If your teacher and I can agree, the legal paperwork will be made out that when I die, you will be in absolute charge of this work." I turned my camera on each student again to catch their wide eyes as they squirmed in their seats. "I can tell you these panels are priceless, probably worth millions, but they cannot be sold." Ed snorted. "You're not going to sell them and spend the money." The whole room erupted in laughter.

Zack said, "Wow, I am sitting around millions of dollars right now."

"Yeah," Ed smiled. "What do you want to receive from coming over here and being involved? Because that is what is important, what you guys want, not what I want."

I asked the class, "What do you think? Any opinions?"

I aimed the camera towards Cody. "Speechless!" he said.

Zack looked at me with a serious expression. "This is a lot of pressure."

"It should be put in a museum somewhere," Nicole said.

"Why do you feel that way, Nicole?" I asked.

"Because it is awesome and nobody else does it."

"Because it is one of a kind," Jesse added.

"It should be kept in this town because of the history of it," Will R. said.

"Well, it should be kept in this town and have a place where everyone can come and see it," Richard responded.

"We should build a place for it!" Will R. said.

Cody responded, "This town isn't developed enough to have a museum where everyone around America can just come and see it. It needs to be in a bigger city, where it is protected more."

"You mean you don't have the ability to protect it?" Ed asked.

"I'm not talking about protecting it from any wrongdoing. I just mean protecting it in general," Cody said.

"Let me explain." Ed walked towards the table. "Can I join you at the table?" The group sang in unison, "Sure." Ed pulled out a chair, placed the red and white mug on the table, and removed his coffee-colored glasses, which nearly covered his face.

"Whenever you display something out of your mind, you make yourself vulnerable to the comments of other people. Man, they can just kill you," Ed chortled. "They laugh and tease, but I think we have something here that they can't laugh at for you to present. I have a lot of crazy ideas, and

200

we need a little more stabilization. That is where you guys come in." I scanned the room again. "This mural is all that I have done in my entire life that is worthwhile. I have built houses, office buildings, a house in the Bahamas, built part of Disney World, but this . . ." Ed paused. "This means something. It means something to me, and I have a feeling that the science can mean something to you also."

"It means a lot. It will mean a lot to a lot of people," Will R. said.

"I think this will be the next Passion of the Christ. When everyone finds out about it, it will blow up just like that," said Richard.

"We have stayed undercover for this moment. To me, it's very historical. I have dreamed about this for years, and you are an answer to my prayers and my dreams, and here you are today." Ed half laughed and half cried as he thought about years before when God had said a teacher and students would be coming. "I hope it will mean something to you."

"It is not about the money," said Cody. I quickly turned the camera on him and asked, "What is it about?"

"It's about the passion!"

As soon as those words passed his lips, I froze. I mentally scrolled back to the day Cody had moved to our area from Texas. That was how he had received the name "Tex." He appeared angry and scary at times. I flashed back to several weeks before, when I privately asked him about a fictional paper he had written during my creative writing class about a school shooting. I had only assigned three pages. He had written twelve. The protagonist was the shooter, and the location was our school. You can imagine my concern.

When that paper hit my desk, it started a flood of action: the principal, the superintendent, the counselor, the police, our school lawyer. But after I talked with him, I knew he meant no harm. He explained that he had watched a boy in Texas being bullied. As a result, he had taken his own life. He said that writing was a platform to be expressive and to explore the world around him. It wasn't what he said that convinced me; it was his heart and passion that I recognized deep inside.

As soon as I had sent Cody back to class, I raced to the phone to call the police officer who was on his way to Cody's house for a search to tell him to stop and turn around. He did, hesitantly. I wanted Tex to know that I trusted him, although he had no idea what was going on behind the scenes. I hoped I had made the right decision. I knew I was taking a huge risk. That simple phrase, "It's all about the passion," had given me my answer. I wanted to weep, but I told myself to knock it off and stay focused. So I turned my camera back to Ed.

"In this room," he continued, "there are twenty-plus years of nothing but inlay. There are two other portraits to finish the story, but I would like you people to put the last one together yourselves, not me. Hopefully I am around to help you understand it: the woods, the colors, and the harmony. But that's all." Ed paused again. "I can see it, but I am getting tired. I am ready to go fishing." Ed sat back in his chair. "We are going to launch this thing like a rocket. It will go just like that because it has its own inertia. It's going to fly!" My students nodded in agreement.

"When I first went to Disney World in Florida, there was nothing there but swamp. I mean there wasn't anything there. Once in a while, there was a house built on a piece of dry land. But that's it, just snakes and gators. Walt Disney said, 'This is where I want it.' And everyone else said, 'Whoa, this guy, he's really out there.' Ed laughed. "Now it's there. Disney did what he said." A look of pride came over Ed's face. "And I was one of the few independent carpenters who worked on my own building there. If you go through the castle, on the left-hand side, you will find a dollhouse. I designed that and built it: everything in there but the carving. Also out at the golf course, both the men's and women's locker room. That is my design. All of the cabinetry, everything in there I built. If you go out to the country store, I designed and built that whole building."

"What inspired you to do this work?" Cody asked.

"This is my life's work. I was given this job before I was born, actually. It was a tremendous study. I wanted to be able to share with individuals of my own plateau, background, and concept, what a lot of reading and a lot of study and a lot of fun you can get from two pieces of wood. That is all that's there. Two little pieces of wood put together and multiplied and multiplied. It is the study of societies and how they think. It is there, every society that I could study. When I was out west in Oregon, I was given the name Red Hawk by a group of Cherokee Indians that I met. This is a given name because of what they saw in me."

"What does Red Hawk mean?" I asked.

"That it does not prey on anything dead. It only eats things like field mice or small rodents, but it catches them itself. It is an endangered species. It is protected all over the world. Um, you could say that I am endangered also. Not too many like me anymore."

I then asked the class, "Any more questions?"

"How do we start out learning your technique?" Will R. asked.

Ed explained that they would start with an unfinished jewelry box. He had piles of them. They were his practice pieces, so they were left undone. He told the students to pick one that they wanted to finish. The first step was to decide what needed to be done to complete the box. Once they accomplished that, they could move on to designing their own tabletop.

As Ed exited the room to gather supplies I asked my students one more time, "What are your thoughts?"

"This is crazy. I mean this is a lot of pressure. This guy has been working on this his whole life, and he wants to leave it off with us. He wants to trust us with his whole life's work," Zack said.

"Do you feel that you have the potential to carry this out?" I asked.

"I know we can do this. I just hope it is good enough for him. I wouldn't want to disappoint him."

"I don't want to mess anything up," Nicole added.

I asked Nicole the same question. "Do you think you can carry this out?"

"Probably not. I am not good with art," she responded.

Zack then jumped in. "Nicole, it's not just you. We're a team. We have to work together."

"We are a team!" Cody said as he patted Zack on the back.

"We are a team!" Zack threw an arm in the air.

"There is no 'i' in team. There is 'we' in team," Jesse said.

"It will be a great opportunity to get our names in the books as part of the creators of this," Will R. said.

Richard responded, "This is about what he has done his whole life, not us."

"And he wants to bring us in on it. He wants to share it with us," Will R. said.

"How does that make you feel?" I asked.

"Actually, it makes me feel very welcome," Will R. answered. "That he's generous enough to have us help him finish his masterpiece and give us a shot at working with him. It also gives us a chance to be a part of history. This makes me very happy and very proud."

"It's a big responsibility," Richard said. "I feel that it's gonna be a lot of work, but it's gonna be fun along the way and to work with everyone here. I think it's gonna turn out to be a great project."

Ed shuffled back into the room with his arms full of white plastic buckets. The buckets contained hundreds of wood diamonds, each a different species. As Ed demonstrated the seven configurations that could be formed with the wood, I stood there reverently, still holding my camera.

A lump started to form in my throat, and tears welled up in both eyes. I could literally feel the great energy all around. It had been so long since I had felt Him. I tried to pinpoint the day that I had lost my faith. It could have been sitting by my daughter's bedside while a machine forced her to breathe after another suicide attempt. I had begged and pleaded with her to fight. I willed her to choose life, not death. She had been diagnosed with bipolar disorder in the eighth grade, but I could look back and see the signs from the beginning. We moved from one medication to another, trying to find the cure, but nothing worked. Instead, her mental health deteriorated and she continued to struggle.

Maybe it was watching my son wither away as doctors tried to diagnose why he was so ill. After months of testing, we finally found out that he had Crohn's disease. He was only nine. Maybe these experiences played a role, but that wasn't it. It was actually years before, five to be exact, when my husband had unexpectedly given up on our family. After twelve years of marriage, he decided he was done. Me? I was left to pick up the pieces alone. We had spent all twelve years living a Christian life, I thought the perfect life, but just like that he was gone, and so was everything that I believed in.

I fought so hard to find my way back to God, but I had lost my way. Now, for the first time in years, I could hear Him—faintly, but He was here. It felt like a whisper in my ear: "I am here. Just open your eyes and look. I have always been here." It was as though the dark shadow that covered my entire body was slowly being removed. It was the invisible shield I had created long ago to protect myself from pain.

I shook my head and gathered my composure so my students would not see my emotion. At this moment, I knew I was a part of something special, and I knew that I had just recorded the most important moment of this project: the new connection between my at-risk students and Ed.

As I continued to watch each student link diamonds together on a piece of cardboard, I thought about their lives. All had enrolled in our alternative high school for a reason, such as truancy, learning disabilities, homelessness, or because they had been ordered to by a court. I watched Nicole and Jesse as they sat side by side at the table. I thought about how they had just found out that they had a baby on the way, and I could see the worry in both of their faces. I observed Richard as I remembered his struggles with writing. After he found out that he had to keep a journal for the project, he murmured in my ear, "I can't write very well." And Cody, he was one of the most creative writers I had in my writing class, but I felt the pain in every word he wrote. I noticed that Will B. and Haley had not spoken one word since entering the warehouse, but they were engaged, silently. Will R. was just trying to graduate, finally. He only had a few weeks left. And Zack, humor was his invisible shield. For most, our school was the only place where they felt like they belonged. Many felt like misfits, just like Ed.

Ah! I get it, Lord. I see the similarities. This is why you picked them, I thought. *But why did you pick me?* I knew the answer to that. I knew my secret struggles and my years of fighting to be worthy. I was just like them in many ways. I literally saw the reel of my life and visualized how just a few years before I became a teacher, I would have fainted at the thought of talking in front of people. I remembered sitting in Mrs. Hall's kindergarten class at five years old and bawling just because she'd called my name. I was so shy and sensitive. As a result, I had become the victim of many who were stronger. But now I was finally stronger myself, and now I was here with my students and my new friend, Ed, my unlikely friend, preparing to work together. God had handpicked each and every one of us years before to be a part of something extraordinary.

Before I turned my camera off for the day, I understood that this was out of my control. It was time to strap myself in and hold on tight, because the one thing that I knew for sure was, our lives would never be the same.

When I returned home that night, I made my first journal entry. It went like this:

November 1, 2005
Today was the first day of the mosaic mural project with Mr. Lantzer. I was amazed and blown away by the day's events. I felt so much pride in my students. It was like watching children on Christmas morning walking into a room, looking at the lit up tree, and viewing all the beautiful gifts. They seemed surprised by the magnitude of the project, but they also seemed excited, hesitant, and eager all in one.

I thoroughly enjoyed standing behind my camera and capturing Mr. Lantzer's brilliance and my students' questions, thoughts, and feelings about the project. There were a couple of students who seemed unsure if they wanted to engage or not. My hope is that as time progresses, they will engage and become eagerly involved and excited about their accomplishments. My goal is to take a group of students who have been considered at risk for failing and give them this gift from Mr. Lantzer. I want them to know that they can succeed. There are possibilities, hopes, and dreams for them in this world. I want to build their self-image and to let them know that they really can accomplish anything that they set their sights on. The mission for me is to use the arts to reach this group of students.

Can the arts make a difference in at-risk kids? There is a correlation between the arts and successfully reaching at-

206

risk students. Creating art has been shown to help at-risk kids. It allows them to find hidden talents that they were unaware of, and it helps them to feel successful at something. This helps to change their self-image from one of unworthiness to worthiness. Instead of being on the streets and causing trouble, they are doing something positive and creative with their talent and their time. It is constructive, and it also teaches self-discipline, which is something that most at-risk students are lacking. I want to prove this correlation to be true, and throughout this journey, I hope to change many lives. Maybe even my own.

30

"Art can teach without at all ceasing to be art."

C.S. Lewis, A Letter to I. O. Evans

The project became the talk of our school. My class numbers grew each day, and our truancy problem had considerably abated. The other teachers and their classes from our school took field trips to see what we were doing, and most of my students brought family members and friends to see Ed's mural. They were so happy and they wanted to share their joy.

Once my students had finished their jewelry boxes and began designing their own tabletops, I realized that I needed to do more than just videotape. How much footage could I take of sanding and gluing? I felt that my documentation was becoming redundant. So, as my students worked, I took a tour around the warehouse. I gathered footage of the hundreds of tabletops and boxes that Ed had placed all the way around the outside of the makeshift gallery. I crept to the room behind the panels and filmed his illegal sleeping room. I felt like I was invading his privacy, but I found it so interesting that this man had created a million-dollar project but was homeless.

I examined Ed's garbage finds, which were clumped together along the walls of the building. There were piles of wood, mattresses, chairs, a couch, a brass coat rack, an old washing machine, and stacks of pallets that Ed had confiscated from manufacturing plant Dumpsters. Then I saw it. In the middle of all that mess was a table. It was very old and the curved legs were covered with peeling mint green paint. I set down my camera and tried to lift it. It was heavy. I knew it must be old because of the weight.

"What do you think?" I jumped at the sound of Ed's voice.

"What?" I asked.

"What do you think? Is this one yours?"

"Oh, I can't. This project is for my students, not me."

Ed's warm eyes connected with mine. "No, this project is for you too. Come closer. Let me tell you about this table." Ed and I moved to opposite sides of the table and Ed ran his right hand along the bare top.

"This table is from the 1920s," he said. "It used to sit in the kitchen. The lady of the house would stand behind it every day, lovingly kneading bread for her family."

"It's beautiful!"

I could picture it. How much love that table must have given throughout its lifetime, and now here it sat, lonely and timeworn, as if it no longer had meaning.

"Do you want it?" Ed asked.

"Really? You would give it to me?" My brain started swirling with ideas, one after another. There were too many to grab onto. The thought of bringing this table back to life was exhilarating.

"It's yours." Ed beamed. "Do you have a design plan for it?"

"I don't even know where to start," I said.

"I tell you what. Why don't you look through my tabletops and boxes and find a design that you like. Start with that and then make it your own. But it needs to have meaning."

I smiled in relief. "Okay. That could work."

Over the next couple of days I analyzed each of Ed's pieces, trying to find something that spoke to me. Finally, I found it. It was a hope chest. In the middle of the lid was a double star. The star was made of a very dark wood. From there, Ed had created a large diamond from cubes using a lighter wood. The design continued from there, but that was all I needed: the star and the diamond. I knew I could take it from there.

After preparing the table for gluing, I sat down and started laying my pieces. I started in the middle and selected a very dark brown exotic wood called wenge. I applied the first two pieces in the center, connecting them at their tips. Once the wood glue had hardened enough, I could continue. This was the beginning of a resurrection. I didn't know it, but my table would also be the beginning of something else—something much more important.

Each day as I sat down and laid my pieces of wood on my table, Ed sat with me. He began telling me stories about his life, each one more interesting than the next. I quickly realized that this man was more than special. I couldn't wait to get to the warehouse each day to hear more. The first day he sat with me, I placed my video camera on my table and recorded just his audio. Each day after that, I continued to record, and if I ran out of battery time, I took notes in my spiral notebook.

As the pieces on my table grew, so did Ed's life story. I was moved, shocked, saddened, and on occasion skeptical. I wondered how this man, homeless and considered a half-wit, could have lived a life this astonishing. But he did.

31

*"True humility is not thinking less of
yourself, it is thinking of yourself less."*

C.S. Lewis, Mere Christianity

After just a couple weeks of the project, I followed my
students into the warehouse, and Ed was waiting just
inside the door. He was grinning and rubbing his hands
together in anticipation.

"Afternoon, Mr. Ed. How are you?" I asked.

"Wonderful!" he responded. Then he blurted out, "I
know who you are!"

I stared at him in confusion. "What do you mean?"

"You're a Watson!"

"Yes," I agreed, still confused.

"Your grandfather saved my life."

My expression turned to shock. I planted my feet as my
knees attempted to collapse beneath me. "My grandfather?"
I asked hesitantly.

I thought about the fact that I had only known one
grandfather, and I barely knew *him*. We only met a few
times—that I remembered, anyway. Beyond that, our only
communication was through a yearly birthday card he sent
me with a dime taped inside. I loved getting that dime. I had
no idea what I could buy with it, usually a piece of Bazooka
gum, but it didn't matter. That dime represented my
grandfather. It represented the relationship I dreamed of
having with him, or any grandparent for that matter.

I remembered standing in front of his casket when I
was twelve years old. I stared at his pressed suit and the

few remaining white hairs on his head. I observed the wrinkles on his face and wondered how he had earned each one. I imagined what his life was like. What did his journey entail? I stared at his hands, so carefully placed together just below his chest. "These are my grandfather's hands," I thought. They were so foreign to me. I wondered what it would have been like to have those hands hug me, or pick me up when I fell, or pat me on the crown of my head when I made him proud. What I would have given to know those hands.

"Glen Watson. That is your grandfather, right?"

I snapped back. "Yes," I said.

My heart raced as Ed and I walked together to my table and he started to tell me the story. I sat in disbelief as I listened to every word.

"It happened when I was a young man working for my dad at the county road commission. I was driving one of the trucks down County Road 571. I was almost to Twin Lakes Road when my stomach blew up."

"Your stomach blew up?" I asked in shock.

"Yes, it felt like an explosion inside my body. I didn't know what to do, but there was one place I knew I could go to get help. I just prayed that someone was there. I was losing my ability to function, but I knew I had to stay alert until I could get there. I drove as fast as I could. When I pulled in, there was only one person there: your grandfather. He also worked for my dad. I yelled with what little energy I had left to get his attention and he came running. He gently pushed me over, jumped into the driver's seat, and hit the gas pedal. That is the last thing I remember."

As I listened, I felt emotional as I learned about the actions of a grandfather who was a stranger to me.

"If it wasn't for your grandfather, I wouldn't be here right now."

Wow! I thought about that for a moment. *Was this another one of God's connections that He had planned in advance?* Goosebumps traveled up my neck as I considered the possibility.

"When I woke, they had created a new stomach for me. It was a risky new procedure. They had tried it on two other patients prior to me, but it was unsuccessful. They died.

But God spared me," Ed said with a look that read, *Like He did so many times in my life.*

I smiled with pride as I pictured my grandfather's hands saving Ed's life. I finally had a memory that I could add to the empty folder in my head labeled Grandpa Watson. What a beautiful gift!

A week later was Thanksgiving, and my sister Tamera had come home for the holiday. She had been living in Los Angeles for nearly twenty years, and her visits were rare. She asked if she could spend an afternoon in my classroom to observe, so I decided to keep my class at the school that day instead of going to the warehouse. It was the day before Thanksgiving and we had a four-day weekend ahead. I alerted Ed and said that we would see him the following Monday.

We normally left for the warehouse right after lunch. That day during lunch I had a knot in my stomach. I tried to push it away, but it kept coming back, stronger and stronger. I just had this feeling that we had to go to the warehouse. I didn't know why, but I knew we had no choice. I told Tamera, and she said that she actually wanted to go. She was so excited to meet Ed and to see the project. So after lunch, my students, Tamera, and I piled into my Durango and the vehicle she'd arrived in and drove to the warehouse. Ed had no idea we were coming, but I knew he would be thrilled to see us and to meet Tamera. The weather had turned treacherous, so walking was out of the question.

When we arrived, my students piled out and darted into the warehouse. Tamera and I followed. As we entered, we heard a scream so piercing that every nerve in my body stood at attention. Then more screams followed. "Mr. Ed! Mr. Ed!" everyone shrieked. My sister and I ran around the center room, and there was Ed lying in a pool of blood. We all went into action. Ed was barely conscious as my students helped carry him to the Durango. "Thank God I drove today!" I said as I opened the passenger door.

Blood was pouring from Ed's head onto my leather seats and my son's Cub Scout manual. I knew those things could be replaced, but Ed couldn't. I helped Ed put pressure on the large wound with a rag as I pulled out of the parking lot with one hand. My sister stayed back with my students as I sped to the hospital. Thank God she was there!

For a split second, I envisioned my grandfather in the driver's seat many years before, but now *my* hands were on the wheel. I knew time was quickly ticking away. I had no idea how long Ed had been lying there. By the amount of blood, it looked like a while. I pulled up to the emergency entrance and the hospital staff came running. As they wheeled him away, I collapsed. Every one of my bones felt like marshmallows. Then I lost it. I could no longer be strong, and I could no longer keep my composure. Instead, I sat in a waiting room chair shaking and crying. I was so scared. *What if he doesn't make it? What if this is it?* Just one week before, I'd sat across from Ed at my table as he explained how my grandfather saved his life. It was surreal that now my students and I were doing the same. I couldn't believe it.

After what seemed like days, a doctor finally appeared. He said, "Mr. Lantzer is one lucky man. If it had been another twenty minutes, he would have died."

I tried to wrap my mind around this information. *What if we had stayed at the school?* I shuddered at the thought. There could only be one explanation and I knew it: the man upstairs. My faith was slowly being restored, day by day. I looked up and asked, "You are up there, aren't you?"

Ed survived, again. He was battered and bruised. His face was barely recognizable, but he was alive. We later found out that he had been trying to hang long extension cords to each of my students' workstations. He had pulled out a tall ladder and climbed to the top. While he was at the ceiling of the warehouse, the ladder slid out from under him and he fell to the floor. At seventy-three years old, he had survived the fall. It was a miracle!

My students were so distraught by the accident it actually brought them closer to Ed. After leaving the hospital, I met them back in my classroom. When I walked in they had colored construction paper and markers everywhere. They were making him cards. I was so proud of each and every one of them. Then they individually recorded video get well messages. I felt so moved by the changes I was witnessing in them. These kids felt love and compassion for Ed. This was something that many of them had not felt in a very long time.

On Thanksgiving Day, Ed was released from the hospital and went back to his warehouse. Tamera, my daughter, Kaleigh, and I brought Ed a traditional meal and all of the gifts from my students. Ed wept as he listened to each student's message. He looked at my daughter and said, "I have something for you."

Kaleigh followed the man she had just met to a pile of jewelry boxes. He pulled one out and handed it to her. I watched as he placed it in her arms. Then I listened as Kaleigh's fifteen-year-old soul communicated with Ed's. I'd always believed that she had an old soul. I cried so many nights as I thought about how she was too wise for her years and as a result, struggled to communicate with her classmates. "If she could only fit in, maybe she would be happy," I would say. I didn't know what they were saying, but I knew Ed could see her spirit and she could see his. I knew he understood her struggles and her fight for life. As we were leaving, Kaleigh hugged her gift close to her chest. The gleam in her eyes brought warmth to my heart. I stopped just before crossing the threshold outside. I turned around and looked at Ed. I didn't have to say a word. Instead, my eyes said, "Thank you" and his replied, "You're so welcome."

Soon after, my students and I found out that Ed had not celebrated Christmas in thirty years. "I had no one to share it with," he said. We decided that this would be the last one he would spend alone. We planned a surprise party and invited our entire school. Ed sat in his chair while he waited for us to arrive at our usual time. When the warehouse door opened, we all yelled, "Surprise!" as eighty students and teachers filled the building carrying a decorated tree, gifts, and food.

I will never forget the look on Ed's face. I guess the best way to describe his reaction would be a combination of laughter and joy. One of my new students, Katie, pulled over Ed's chair and said, "Come, sit. We have another surprise for you." Another student, Saphyre, escorted him to his seat, and then a group of us lined up in front of him.

Then I counted, "One, two, three," and in unison we sang, "Silent night, holy night. All is calm, all is bright." I watched Ed attempt to contain his emotion as we continued our out-of-tune version of the carol. When we hit the last note, we moved on to several others that we had prepared. Ed sobbed through the whole performance. When we finished, he brushed a Kleenex over his cheek and said, "You will never know what this means to me." He wiped away more of the flow from his eyes, and then his bottom lip quivered as he whispered, "Thank you."

My students grabbed the gifts we had wrapped for him: a new travel coffee mug, a sweater, and gift certificates, and then handed them to him one by one. For a split second, I could see the little four-year-old boy that he once was eagerly tearing off the green and red paper. It was difficult to keep my composure as I remembered him sharing the story of how his life had changed at that age. I wondered if he had ever received a Christmas present before. I hoped he had.

When the party ended and we began packing up, Ed pulled me aside and said, "Thank you, kid!"

"You're welcome, Mr. Ed," I replied as I watched our group begin their passage back to the school.

I prayed that we were making a difference in his life. I hoped that we had at least given him a special memory to hold dear. I know we left with a sense of compassion and love. My students gave and Ed received, but in the end we all received something that day.

Later my student Katie pulled me aside and said, "You know, this class has helped me so much." She lifted up her long sleeve and showed me a series of horizontal scars that made their way up her wrist. "I have spent years cutting myself. It was the only way I could feel something other than my painful life. I have been so numb for so long. I felt like cutting myself was the only control that I had. But now, this class has become a retreat from the pain. I don't need my razor anymore. Thank you!"

I gave her a hug as I thought about the impact we were having already. This was unexpected. When I made the decision to agree to this project, I had no idea how important that one word "yes" would become. It was the road less traveled, but it was the right road.

32

"There are no other days. All days are present now. This moment contains all moments."

C.S. Lewis, *The Great Divorce*

A few unexpected events occurred during our time with Ed. My sister Jeannine owned a production company. She donated time and equipment to take professional footage of Ed and my students, as well as of Ed explaining the symbolism in the mural for future use. *Traverse, Northern Michigan's Magazine* profiled Ed for a seven-page spread in their publication, and TV 9&10 selected our project for a segment they called "Making the Grade." It was the first time Ed had received recognition for his work, and it was the first time my students felt like celebrities. It was so exciting to watch them dress up in their finest clothing for their interviews. I documented both events with my video camera, and I even turned the camera on the magazine writer, television reporter, and cameraman to get their opinions of our unique project. All were blown away by what we were doing. We were taking students out of the classroom and giving them a real life experience, something we hoped would stay with them forever.

One year after Emily Betz Tyra visited the warehouse and interviewed Ed for the article in *Traverse, Northern Michigan's Magazine*, it finally hit newsstands. Ed was working when his ringtone, "I'm Too Sexy," blared. He removed his Nokia from the case hooked onto his collar.

"Ed, it's out!" Paul said on the other line.

"What's out?" Ed replied.

"The magazine, your story. It's printed and on the store shelves! I will pick you up for lunch tomorrow and we can sit down and look at it together. How does that sound?" Paul asked.

"Wonderful! I look forward to it." Ed's voice cracked with emotion.

"Okay, I will see you tomorrow."

"Okay. Oh, and Paul? Thanks."

"You're welcome, Ed."

Both men pressed the end button on their phones, and Ed went back to work as he eagerly awaited Paul's visit.

Paul bought several copies of the magazine and went to the warehouse to pick up Ed. They drove to a small restaurant in Kalkaska. After they were seated and had ordered their lunch, Paul pulled out Ed's copy. He waited as he watched Ed carefully open to the first page of the article. "Pieces of Him" was the title, and there was a picture of Ed dressed in his one suit, which had obviously been with him for many years. The sawdust and stains were noticeable here and there, but he stood proud and confident. It was possible that most people thought he looked dirty and disheveled, but I thought he was handsome and looked like a millionaire, and so did he.

Paul sat back in the booth while he observed. Ed was visibly moved by each word he read. He looked through the pages slowly, silently, and his eyes filled with water. It was apparent that he was struggling to keep his emotions under control.

He looked up at Paul and said, "Can you take me back to the warehouse?"

"Sure, Ed." Paul gathered to-go boxes and then led Ed back out to the Trailblazer.

Paul pulled up to the back door of the warehouse and Ed said, "I just need a little bit of time. Can you come back in a few hours?"

"Of course I can," Paul said.

Ed slid out of the SUV and waddled into the dark building holding his magazine tightly under his arm.

When Paul returned, Ed handed him a piece of paper and a pen. "I want you to pen a thank you for me. Can you do that?"

"Yes," Paul replied. He picked up the pen and held it in position as he waited for Ed's words.

"Okay, I want you to write, 'Dear Emily, Thank you so much for giving me the gift of the story you published. This has been so meaningful to me, in that it has legitimized my work and me personally. I am deeply grateful for your time, talent, and the gift you have given here. God Bless, Love Ed.'"

Paul took the note to his office and typed it into his computer. He then printed the final letter and took it back to Ed for approval.

"This is perfect, Paul. Thank you," Ed said. Then he grabbed the pen and signed his name at the bottom: 6-22-34.

After years of struggle, Ed had finally received his first glimpse of recognition. He didn't seek or need that, but it was a gift nonetheless. He was not only recognized as an accomplished artist, but even more, he was recognized as something much more important: a human being. Not as a half-wit, not the town idiot, not a crazy person to be feared, and not someone without the ability to love, but a person who was admired and appreciated.

My students admired this man tremendously, and Ed admired them. He told me that my students and I had changed his life.

"I have never been happier, kid!" he said as he kept me company at my table. "You know, you guys have given me a spark that I have not felt in so many years. Thank you for that!"

"Thank you, Mr. Ed." I said. "You have no idea what you have done for my students. They also have a spark that I have never seen before. That is priceless, just like your panels." We both grinned and agreed.

The most important gift that Ed gave my students and me was to let us watch him create his last panel. We had no idea at the time that it would become his last, but unfortunately, it did.

We entered the warehouse one day, and Ed eagerly rushed us towards the back of the room near our workstations. "Okay, everyone sit in front of me," he directed. I hit the record button on my video camera as I watched my students create a line in front of a large rectangle that was covered by a pink and blue flowered sheet. "I want all of your concentration here. Don't talk at all. You each have one minute to find the error in the pattern."

My students and I were puzzled as he yanked a corner of the sheet and revealed a 4' x 8' plywood backing. In the center was a large diamond shape created from his smaller diamond pieces. It was obvious that Ed had worked late the night before to prepare his new lesson for my students. He had decided that this panel would be a teaching panel. Our class would inspire it, and as he completed each section, he would explain his process to us.

"It is out of balance because I didn't quite get it finished," Ed said.

In the center of the diamond, Ed had embedded the letter T using a dark wood, which stood out next to the light grain of the diamond he had formed. I moved the lens back to my students as I captured them trying to find the mistake from afar. Ed then laid the panel down horizontally.

"Come," he waved. "One at a time."

One student after another spent their one minute analyzing the beginning of Ed's new child, and each pointed out their guesses. Then Ed walked in front of the panel and stood it straight up again.

"The error is right there." He pointed to a strip of diamond pieces. "Do you know how many people walk in that door and don't see the errors?"

"A lot?" the kids asked in unison.

"I see them because I put them there." Ed laughed. "Study, read, and think," he announced. "We are after your computers in your mind. We want to teach you to look at the details in every piece of artwork that you view. We have the greatest energy source right here." Ed pointed to each student. "I think we might even have a couple of presidents here." My students smiled with pride as Ed covered the panel back up. "Okay, now get to work."

This was the first of many lessons, and after six weeks, Ed had completed the panel and we had had the privilege to watch and learn. The panel was embedded with many symbols: a shield and the sword of truth right from King Arthur and his knights, a serpent eating his own tail, a letter T, which stood for the cross. Ed also used a variety of sacred numbers such as 10 for Heaven and 1 for the Great Energy. When you put the 10 and 1 together you get 101, which represented my class, Ed explained during one of his lessons.

"First thing when you go to school, you have to go to English 101. This is art 101." Then he said, "Heaven is the number 10 and it is provided by the 1, the Great Energy. You have the shield, and the best representation of the resurrection I can think of is the serpent eating its own tail. A continuous circle, which is zero, accepted all over the world by every group that I have ever studied." Ed looked at the group and said, "I have one more symbol to put in, but she doesn't know about it." Ed looked at me, and I glanced towards the vacant spot in the panel. "The book will be in here. Her book. Our book. The same book I have in front of Matthew in the Last Supper will be here."

He tapped on the future home of the symbol that represented our bond. I flashed to the day when Ed asked me to write his story. He didn't ask in the normal way, such as, "Hey, will you write my biography?" Instead he simply announced, "You are the writer. God said you were coming, and here you are."

I knew he was right. I had been preparing myself my entire life. I didn't know why or for what, but my mission had started when I was a child. I knew, so strongly, that God had an important job for me. I cannot explain how I knew, but it was implanted in every fiber of my being. What I did know intuitively was that it would involve the arts, and it was to make a difference in people's lives.

Throughout my life, I had a mental compass. I felt it when I was going in the right direction, and when I made a wrong turn, there was a scream in my ear instructing, "No! No! Go back!" Sometimes I listened and sometimes I rebelled. Whenever I did the latter, my life became chaotic and full of destruction. It wasn't until I was in my early thirties that I started to really pay attention.

I had always had a love for the arts, whether it was using words or my hands. When I was a young girl, I was often reprimanded for painting large murals on my bedroom walls when my mother was asleep. I had created a cartoon girl with large eyes, and she kept popping up on various walls in our house, similar to the way that Keith Haring drew on New York City subway walls during the night. When day broke, the subway authorities were angry at Haring, and my mother was angry with me.

Maybe "angry" isn't the right word. My mother didn't like it when I covered her walls with my paintings, but she still gave me the room throughout my life to be creative. I also built elaborate forts in every nook and cranny inside and outside our house. I painted rocks and carved little pianos out of charcoal. I then went house to house in our neighborhood trying to sell them. I only had one buyer, my neighbor, Mrs. Montgomery. She gave me a nickel and I was so proud.

In fifth grade, I wanted a built-in swimming pool so badly, so I spent one summer day digging in the back yard. My belief was that if you wanted something, you could learn how to make it. I remember waking up as soon as my mother left for work one morning, and digging all day. When she returned I had my swimming pool lined with plastic and filled with water. I even built a makeshift diving board. When my mother got out of her car and clomped towards my younger siblings, some neighborhood kids, and me swimming in the pool, I realized I was in trouble. It didn't even dawn on me that what I'd done was wrong. I didn't consider the damage to the backyard lawn. In my mind, I was creating. In my mother's mind, I was going to spend the entire next day filling the hole back in, and that was just what I did.

Creating, in whatever form, felt like home. When I became an adult, I started buying every book or magazine on writing that I could get my hands on. I had no idea why, but my compass was telling me it was important. I spent two decades preparing to write, but I didn't know what. I remember as a teenager standing in my bedroom with my best friend Dawn as we sang "Hot Blooded" into our hairbrushes. When the song ended I just blurted out, "I am going to write a book someday." She looked at me like, *Okay*, and we went back to singing. Again, I just knew deep down that art and writing would play a role in my job, my purpose. It wasn't until Ed said those words that it all came full circle.

Ed placed our symbol, a pen and book, in his last panel. It was the period to finish the panel, and it was also the period to mark the end of our project. After two and a half years, our work had come to an end. The last day of the school year had arrived, and my students were adding the final touches to their projects so they could take them home or give them as gifts to their loved ones.

The warehouse was filled with so much excitement. The summer breeze was filtering in through the open door, and it was followed by the energy of the sun. I was taking in this energy as I brushed a final coat of polyurethane onto my table.

"So you finally finished that thing, did ya?" Ed joked as he shuffled towards me.

"Yeah, and it only took me two years, but here it is." I laughed as I moved my right hand along the edge in a the-price-is-right style.

"You did good, kid," Ed said, smiling with pride.

I stared at the double star and diamond I'd borrowed from Ed and then the formations I'd created on my own. I couldn't believe what I had accomplished. I remembered how many times Ed had joked with me about my table. I would be gluing pieces down as he walked by me, and he'd say, "Ooh, I wouldn't do that." Or, "Uh oh, I wouldn't put that there." And then he would keep on walking. He chuckled as I yelled after him, "What? Why?" It didn't take me long to realize that he wanted me to figure it out for myself, to do my own problem solving.

Ed sat down at my table, and I sat across from him like we had done so many times before. As he scooted his chair closer, I thought about how each day I had come to the warehouse, I would find a gift waiting for me on my table. It was often a flower or little trinkets he'd found on his junk excursions. Most often, though, it was jellybeans or old-fashioned crème drops. Every time I found his gift, Ed would continue working as if he knew nothing about it.

One day as I was nibbling on a handful of jellybeans, he said, "You are getting a little chunky, don't you think?"

"Oh, sure, you buy me candy and then complain when I gain a pound. It's your fault, you know," I said. We laughed. As I snapped back to reality, I noticed that Ed was looking down. Sadness had come over his face. "Are you okay?" I asked.

"Well, I have some bad news," Ed said as his voice cracked.

"What is it?"

"I have to leave the warehouse. They informed me that they are selling the building and I have to find a new home."

"Oh no, I am so sorry. What are you going to do? Where are you going to go?"

I don't know yet. But it will be okay. Don't worry."

"How can I not worry?"

"Just remember, the Father will take care of it. Okay?"

"Okay," I said hesitantly.

After my students left that day, they each gave Ed a hug or a handshake and left the warehouse one by one to start their summer vacation. They had no idea that this would be the last time many of them would ever see him. Ed's having to leave the warehouse also meant that the last panel Ed hoped they would build as a class would not happen. They had spent the last two years building jewelry boxes and tabletops. They also watched and learned as Ed created a new panel, his last panel. But Ed had a dream that the students would create their own panel. I felt disappointed as I remembered the first day that Ed had so excitedly proposed the idea to them. I knew how much it would have meant to all of us. But unfortunately, it was not meant to be.

33

*"Isn't it funny how day by day nothing
changes, but when you look back,
everything is different . . ."*

C.S. Lewis, Prince Caspian

I stayed and continued to sit with Ed at my table. As we chatted, I replayed all of our previous talks. During that time, I had learned about Ed's turmoil and pain, his joy and passion. I realized how much he treasured the panels and how he feared losing them, just as he'd lost his own children. I now recognized the frightened look in his eyes as he tried to stay strong, when deep down he didn't know what he was going to do next or where he would find another home, a home that would fit his children.

I flashed back to the day he asked me to join his board of directors and thought about how just a few weeks later, he dismantled the board because we were getting too close to his panels. Ed saved Paul and me. He explained that we were the only two people he trusted. So Paul and I became the board. That deep-seated fear of someone stealing the panels was still too strong.

That day he said, "I have been trying so long to move away from this fear, a fear of losing the panels to some individual who doesn't know what they are working with. I would rather see them destroyed than have them get into the wrong hands."

"What do you foresee for the future of the panels?" I asked

"I am looking for someone to take over, and then I want to go fishing."

"Fishing?" I asked as I turned my attention to the two fishing poles, a pair of waders, a creel, and a tackle box that he'd placed near the exit of the warehouse. I always wondered if the word "fishing" had a deeper meaning. Ed would often say, "I am tired. I want to go fishing," and I felt intuitively that he was talking about dying.

"To go home to be with the Father," Ed said.

"But beyond that, when you have gone fishing and you are home with your Father and you look back, what do you want to see for the panels? What do you want to see them doing?"

"I want to see the Messiah Christ use them, in the same way that He taught me, and that they were beneficial to the world. I hope the panels will be here to use as a teaching tool for at least five hundred years. When a female walks into that room, I want her to see and feel love—a love that she will pass down to her children. Otherwise, it will cease to exist on this plane. How in the world do you get faith, hope, and love if there is no love here?"

"Do you think there is a correlation between the lack of love from your mother and the power your work has to show the female love?"

"Yes. I am showing love through the eyes of the female so that when she walks in the room, she recognizes it and feels it. I wanted my mother to recognize it. Near the end of my mother's life, she became the best sponsor of my work. When she saw *My Father's Love* for the first time, she got a group of women together and they came out to look at it, and she had them out there every week, every day that she could get a bus. She was so proud of her husband because she found him in there. And her son, who she had given up on, was in there too. I was the black sheep. I told you that a hundred times."

"So how did you feel when your mother came in for the first time to see the panels?"

"I cried."

"Did you feel like you could finally communicate with her the way you always wanted to?"

Ed choked up and nodded his head. "Uh, LaShelle, we are in a delicate area here. Well, let me start out by telling you a story. When I left the state hospital, I went to stay with Dad, and it was then that I realized how much she loved my dad and how much he loved her. Mother would be doing dishes in the kitchen, and he was nearly an invalid in the living room doing the knitting and crocheting. And he would make a little noise and she would smile. And she would make a little noise and he would smile. And my dad said, 'We have developed such a close communication that even this little noise will cause me to smile because I know what she is saying to me. I loved it.' At that moment I thought, 'Oh my goodness, if I can only get to that point.'

"Well, I think I am getting closer all the time. I use a different vehicle. When people see my panels, they stand in awe. They say, 'Here is a guy that can feel. And he has felt, and he does feel, and he is trying to install it in wood, and it's there.' Try installing an emotion that high in a piece of wood and have it reflect to someone. Communicate. I don't have to be there. I don't have to say a thing, and they will come back and they will come back and they will come back, because they feel for the first time, in many times for the first time in their lives, what real love is all about."

"It's amazing. And it's everlasting. Two people can show love for one another, but the panels can show love to the whole world, and that is everlasting. It will continue on," I said.

"Right, it doesn't belong to one; it belongs to everyone. And they are my children, and my children love. They were constructed in love. They radiate love, no matter what part of the panels you stand in front of. And that is the whole message.

"When I was building houses, I never finished a building in my life without someone buying it before it was finished. They would see it and they would say they have to have it. I would create my own design. I enjoyed it so much that I decided to build a five bedroom with a television room, full basement, bomb room, and everything just off of Division and Kalkaska streets. The real estate man said 'Ed, you are never going to sell that thing this far north.' I was hanging the cabinets when a lady walked in and she looked at the house and she said, 'I will be right back.' A few minutes later, she drug her husband in, and she said, 'He owns it, and you buy it or don't come home.'" Ed laughed. "I said that is unfair and she said, 'You be quiet.'"

He laughed again. "They bought the home. And it's been like that. I never finished a home in my life before someone bought it because of what they feel. All right, let's go a step farther. Frank Murphy felt the same thing, he and his wife. Disney World, same thing. Frank finally had to put rules on me because his friends would offer me any amount of money to come in and remodel their house." He laughed. "Frank would say, 'Ed if you work for them, you will never work in Florida again.'" He laughed. "He said, 'You work for my family and we will care for you,' and he did."

"So when did you realize that God was preparing you for this mission through building these homes?"

"Well, before I got here, we sat down and talked. That is what I am saying: at eight or nine years old we are here as children running around in innocence. We have a purpose or project to do. Some parents replace that project by throwing material things at their kids, saying, 'Here, have a car,' or 'Here, have some candy.' They do this instead of sitting down and loving them.' They forget that love exists. That is why I have tried to get closer and closer to my project. But it is so delicate that I have become just absolutely protective.

"When I was a little boy, my grandfather gave me a dog, and that dog and I were absolute friends. And when I started school, the dog would run circles around me and no one could get into the circle. It was considered a mutt, kind of like me. I was probably twelve years old, and Dad sent me out to get some wood out of the woodshed and I stumbled. I dropped the wood and I grabbed the red-hot stove and Dad grabbed me and the dog jumped and was after his throat. Dad hit it with a piece of wood and he said, 'Man, I forgot about the dog.'" Ed laughed. "But I slept behind the stove for three days with my dog. When he got old and died, I buried him. He is buried in the old court square by a pine tree. He was a marvelous friend. The animal taught me to love."

"There was no judgment there. Right?"

"He was there and he could feel. He was so protective of me that even my parents couldn't touch me without them putting him outside or chaining him up."

"Can you say that an animal can love unconditionally?"

"An animal can, but people cannot because of the element of time. The speed that the animal develops, he is self-sufficient much sooner than a human, and he doesn't forget his project or purpose. And he sees God, the invisible God, and he knows He's there, and he has a job, and he does his job without any complaints. He is happy with it. He is serving the purpose that he was created."

Ed stopped for a moment and looked at me square in the eyes. "My friend, that is what I want to make sure you understood. That it is not my love that you see and feel in my mural, it is my Father's love. I reflect it from him. I don't want it misunderstood. I am not the generator of that. It is from Him."

I lightly touched my table to see if the polyurethane was dry as I came back to the present. My heart was breaking for my unlikely friend while I realized how much I had learned from him over our two years of talks. I prayed that this was not our last. I hoped that our friendship would continue. I had so much more to learn about this incredible man, and now that he would be homeless yet again, I feared for his future. We both stared at the wood formations underneath the gloss, and then I looked up at Ed and he met my gaze.

"Thank you for teaching me your craft," I said. "Most importantly, thank you for teaching my students. You taught them so much more than how to place diamonds onto a piece of wood, Ed. You taught them about life and love. You showed them that they are unique and lovely individuals, each one of them. They now know that they are worthy and special."

My emotion swelled as I continued. "Ed, I know that they will carry this experience with them throughout the rest of their lives. They may shelve it from time to time as they move forward in the world, and it may get dusty on occasion, but it will always be there. They will never forget you, and they will be forever changed."

"I told you before that you and the kids were a gift from God. LaShelle, I can't tell you how blessed I feel for His gift. There are no words to explain to you how special all of you are to me. I will also carry this with me for the rest of my life."

"As for me . . ." I paused and tried to maintain my composure. "I don't know if I told you this, but you have helped restore my faith. I spent years lost and scared, but no longer. I finally know that God loves me no matter what. I now realize that I was telling myself lies for so long. Lies like I am not good enough, or I don't measure up. I felt so unlovable that I wondered how God could love me. At times I questioned whether He was even really there. Ed, I actually spent years afraid to go into a grocery store because I was afraid to run into someone I knew. I trembled at the thought. I felt so unworthy that if I did run into someone and they asked me how I was doing, my lips would quiver and I'd stumble over my words. Each time, I walked away yelling at myself for being so stupid. As a result, when I entered a store and I recognized someone, I turned the other way before they could see me. Can you believe that?" Ed nodded, obviously remembering similar struggles. "Thanks to you, I finally know that I am okay."

"The credit is not mine. I want you to see that," he said. "You have a beautiful spirit. I saw it the first day our eyes met. God chose you for a special job because of your spirit. Remember how you said you could feel it so strongly even as a child?" I nodded. "Even your name, LaShelle, was chosen for a reason. 'Elle' is sacred. It is the oldest known female characteristic of God, and that is embedded into your name and you. God treasures you, just like He treasures all of His children."

"Yes. Finally I can see that," I said and then looked at my table again. "Ed, this table has so much meaning to me. Through my hands and our talks, it again has meaning. It has been resurrected and so have I. Thank you, my friend."

34

"We're not doubting that God will do the best for us; we're wondering how painful the best will turn out to be."

C.S. Lewis, Letters of C.S. Lewis

As I took my table out of the warehouse that day, I knew this meant the end of our school project together. I found a special home for the table in my living room, and Ed began searching for his next home. The deadline to vacate the warehouse was nearing, and Ed still had no options. When his final day arrived, Paul called him.

"Where are you going to stay tonight, Ed?" Paul asked as his wife Patti waited anxiously nearby. Since Paul's calling from God was to make sure Ed was taken care of, he couldn't rest until this was accomplished.

"Don't worry about me, Paul," said Ed. "I am going to take a blanket and go sleep behind Big Boy."

Paul and Patti looked at each other in alarm, and Patti whispered, "No he isn't. Go pick him up and bring him here. We will figure out what to do after that."

Paul agreed, and by evening, Ed was safe and secure at the Hresko residence. Ed's only income was a small Social Security check, so the next morning Paul began researching housing options for the homeless and the elderly. There was very little available, and every phone call Paul made ended in, "We are not accepting new clients at this time."

After many calls, Paul found the Homeless Assistance Recovery Program through the State of Michigan. They offered housing vouchers for the homeless, but one stipulation was that Ed needed to be officially declared homeless, and he had to live in a homeless shelter for a minimum of twenty-eight days. Paul and Patti struggled with this requirement, but they knew it was the only way to help.

Paul made a quick visit to the local homeless shelter, the Goodwill Inn, to check it out and to make sure it was suitable.

"Do you have any beds available?" he asked the attendant.

"We have one left. Is this for you?"

"No, it is for a friend of mine."

"I am sorry, but your friend will have to make the arrangements. That is our rule," the attendant said.

Paul hesitated, but he knew what he had to do. Ed had been homeless so many times in his life, but now, at seventy-five, and after creating his masterpiece for the Lord, it seemed so unfair.

After Paul returned home, he stood by Ed as he watched the four-year-old boy still rooted deep within Ed pick up the receiver and dial. Paul choked up as he noticed the shakiness in Ed's voice. Ed tried to be strong. He had no doubt that God would take care of him, but the realization that he would be separated from his children again was almost too much to bear. Still, he had no other choice. Ed slowly put the phone to his ear and said, "Hi, my name is Ed Lantzer and I am homeless."

The next morning, Paul drove Ed to the Goodwill Inn. Ed had no belongings with him except for the dirty clothing he wore. As they neared the newly opened facility, Ed said nonchalantly, "I think I know the director there."

"Really? Paul said with surprise. "What's his name?"

"Oh, I just can't think of it right now. It will come to me."

Paul glanced at Ed with a look that said, *Sure you do, Ed.* Over the years, Ed had shared stories of his life with people, and they often seemed improbable. His listeners wondered how a man like Ed could have had so many unique experiences. It wasn't that Paul didn't believe him, but he was skeptical.

Paul turned into the circle drive and pulled up to the front door. Both men exited the Trailblazer, and Paul grabbed his copy of *Traverse, Northern Michigan's Magazine* before closing the door. As they walked to the entrance, Ed said, "Ken Homa. That's it."

"What's it?"

"The name of the director."

Paul and Ed stood side by side as the receptionist pulled open the glass window.

"Can I help you?" she asked.

"I am Ed Lantzer, and I am here to check in," Ed said.

They began the check-in process, and when it was almost complete, Ed took a seat in the waiting room. Paul waited for him to sit down, and then he discreetly handed the magazine to the receptionist.

"I know you have a lot of residents here and you take good care of all of them, but I just want you to know that this man is very special. Please take good care of him," he whispered.

The woman scanned Ed's article, and emotion crossed her face as she smiled warmly and said, "We will, don't worry."

"Oh, by the way, do you know a Ken Homa?" Paul decided to just throw it out there, even if the woman thought he was crazy.

"Yes, Ken Homa is the director here."

"Thanks," Paul said with a smile as he shook his head and headed towards Ed.

The same Ken Homa who had once been Ed's therapist at Community Mental Health years before was now the director of the brand new facility that Ed would call home. This alone gave Ed a sense of peace. The one thing he knew for sure was that he trusted his old therapist and friend. He also believed that it was no accident that he'd run into the man. God was at work again, laying all of the groundwork and lining up all of the right people to help Ed continue his journey.

Paul and Ed were led into Ken Homa's office. Ken stood up and extended his hand. "Ed, it is so good to see you. How have you been?"

"I'm good, thanks," Ed said as he shook Ken's hand.

All three men sat down.

"So tell me what is going on. What brings you here?" said Ken.

Ed filled Ken in on all of the details leading him to the Goodwill Inn.

"I am sorry to hear about this, Ed, but we will do whatever we can to help you find a home."

"Okay," Ed said trustingly.

"We have another concern," Paul said. Ken listened as Paul continued. "We have to empty out all of Ed's belongings in the warehouse by the end of the month. That gives us only two weeks. Ed has a lot of stuff in the warehouse, his work and tools, not to mention all of the stuff he collected while he was there. I have secured a garage in Elk Rapids to store the panels, tabletops, and boxes, but we have no idea what to do with the rest."

Ken thought for a moment and then said, "I have a new intern here. Her name is C.J. How about if I put her on this? We will figure this out, Ed. Don't worry."

"Thanks, Ken."

"You're welcome, Ed."

Once the meeting was over and a tour of the facility completed, Ed said goodbye to Paul and was escorted to his room. As he stepped in, he moved from corner to corner, analyzing every inch. He sat on his bed and bounced twice to check the firmness. "So this is home," he said to himself. It didn't take much to make Ed comfortable. Just the fact that he had a place to sleep and stay warm, even if it was temporary, was enough.

He tried to imagine where his life would go from here. He had again lost everything. Even his panels were now homeless. He pictured them stacked one on top of the other in a dark garage. Ed could handle being homeless. He was used to it, after all, but his children? That was too much.

"Father, I know there is a reason for this," he said. "I am not sure what it is yet, but I will wait for your instruction."

Ed lifted himself off the bed, straightened out the bedspread, and headed to the cafeteria for lunch.

He took his tray of food and found a table near the back of the cafeteria. He nibbled on a few morsels as he watched other people filtering into the room. *I guess I'm not very hungry*, he thought after he managed to get down two bites. He pushed his tray away, leaned back in his chair, and began one of his favorite pastimes, people watching.

He loved to watch people. He analyzed their movements, mannerisms, and facial expressions. Ed could tell a lot about a person just by observing. The faces of homelessness were so diverse. This was a surprise to Ed. This was the first time he'd been surrounded by people in the same situation. He looked towards a young family. The parents were barely twenty, and each of them had a youngster on their lap. An older man sat alone, not making eye contact with anyone while he sipped the broth from his vegetable soup. *I wonder what his story is.* Ed watched him for a few moments. There was something different about him, something almost childlike.

Another table held a woman and her children. It was obvious that she was raising her family alone. He flashed back to Jean and his children when they were that age. Ed could see the worn look on the woman's face. He felt a pang of guilt. He wondered if this was how Jean felt while raising their children alone. *Probably.* This was the one regret that Ed would always carry with him. When one of the woman's children asked her a question, she answered with a drained smile. Ed felt compassion for her. He sensed how strong she was, yet scared. *Just like Jean must have been.* The fear was evident in her eyes as Ed held her stare for a brief second and then she quickly glanced away. *I wonder if they know how much you love them, Lord. I wonder if they understand that you will take care of them.*

Ed pondered his question as he continued to watch more residents enter. Finally, he picked up his tray and headed towards the area to discard his uneaten food. He turned as he felt someone moving in behind him. It was a young man, about twenty-seven or twenty-eight years old. To Ed, he was just a kid, alone and in a homeless shelter.

Ed nodded to him and asked, "How are you?"

"Good, and you?" the kid responded in a monotone. He appeared hardened.

Ed set his tray down and looked back at him. "I am good too. Thank you for asking. Are you here alone?"

"No. Actually, my girlfriend is here too."

"How long have you been here?"

"Well, on and off for a year. We stay as long as we are allowed and then we leave for a bit. We can only stay for a certain amount of time, but as long as we leave for a while, we can return."

"I see. Where do you go when you leave?"

"Sometimes we sleep under the bridge downtown or by Boardman Lake. Other times we couch surf."

"What is couch surfing?"

The kid laughed. "It's when you sleep on friends' or family members' couches. But they only let us stay for a few days and then we have to move on. It can be really difficult at times."

"I can imagine."

Ed looked at him for a moment and saw something very familiar in his eyes. It was toughness and sadness. *What happened in his young life to bring him here?* Ed thought about his own life at that age. He so related to the boy's furrowed brow and tightened jawbone. *This was how I felt at his age. Oh, Father, how can I explain to him that he will be okay? That you shine over him?*

"Well you take care of yourself and I will see you around, okay?" he said.

"Sure, okay. See you around."

Ed turned and shuffled towards the exit as he felt the kid watching him leave. "I understand, Father. This is why I am here, isn't it? I am here to help." Ed smiled and then turned in the direction of his room.

The next morning, Paul called to check on Ed. "How was your night?" he asked.

"Actually, it was good."

"Oh good. I am so happy to hear that, Ed."

"You know, Paul, this was the first time in a very long time that I had a shower, a warm bed to sleep in, and a warm meal. I guess I can't ask for much more, can I?"

Ed quickly adjusted to his new home. He spent his days talking with his fellow residents, helping the landscaper plant flowers around the building, and taking a daily trip on a transit bus to the local library to check out books.

Ed and I decided that we would continue our talks. Since I knew how much Ed loved coffee and books, the perfect place was the Borders bookstore. The first day I picked Ed up, he was waiting near the door in a chair. I could see him light up as I walked up to the entrance.

"Hey kid!" he said as he met me at the door.

I gave him a hug and I could hear him try to sniffle away his emotion. It had only been a couple of weeks since our final talk at the warehouse, but it seemed much longer. Ed looked better than I had seen him in so long. His remaining hair was neatly slicked back, and he wore a new patterned sweater and a navy spring jacket with light blue and white stripes.

"Wow, you look nice!" I said.

"They took me to their second-hand store and let me pick out some clothes. What do you think?" Ed asked as he stood proud.

"Very dapper, I would say." We laughed as we walked to the counter to sign him out for the afternoon.

We entered Borders and selected two brown cushioned chairs near a window. Ed waited while I ordered. I sat my caramel mocha down on the small end table that separated us, and then I handed Ed his double-cupped black coffee, just the way he liked it. He took his first sip and looked at me with a glow.

"I can't tell you how good it is to see you."

"You too, Mr. Ed. Are you doing okay at the shelter?"

"Yes. I like it there. I have been working with C.J. She set up a garage sale at the warehouse for next weekend. We plan to sell everything except for my tools. What we don't sell, we will throw away in a Dumpster. We plan to rent one. We sold one of my tables to pay for it."

"I bet that will be a relief for you."

"Yes, it will. It will definitely give me some closure."

"Have you made any friends at the shelter?"

"Oh yes. I have been helping a man there. He pretty much stays to himself, but I sit with him every day in the cafeteria. He talks to me. I guess he doesn't talk to too many people around there. I help make sure that he is taking care of himself."

"That is wonderful, Ed."

"Oh, I want to show you something."

He pulled out a yellow folder he'd brought with him and handed it to me. I opened it to find a stack of poems, all hand written. I read a few and was moved by the emotion in each one. It was apparent that the author had experienced a life of struggle, and yet I could feel the urge to overcome it.

"Who wrote these?" I asked.

"A young man that I met the first day in the cafeteria. We meet every day. We talk about so many things, like life, relationships, and God. He tells me how he has been trying to find a job, but no one will hire him because he is homeless. I explained my experience with that when I was in Orlando. I hope that I can encourage him to keep his faith and to not give up."

"I am sure you will, Ed."

"The young man hesitantly shared these with me, and I asked him if I could show you. I told him that you also teach creative writing, and I knew you would want to read them."

"Thank you for sharing these. You know, I am so proud of you. You have only been there a short time, and look at what you have already done for these people."

Ed shrugged his shoulders and said, "Well, it is my job." That was all he had to say because I understood what he meant.

"What else have you done this week?"

"Ken took me to look at some apartments in Elk Rapids."

"Elk Rapids?"

"Yes, that is where the panels are, and I want to be near them. Also it would be nice to be near Paul and Patti."

"That is true. Did you see anything that you like?"

"Oh yes. Ken thinks that after my stay here, he can get me into one using a housing voucher."

"It sounds like you are doing well. I am so happy about that, Ed."

"Me too."

When I dropped Ed back off at the shelter, I walked him to the door. He turned to me with a worried look on his face, as if he was afraid he would never see me again.

"Don't be a stranger, okay?" he said.

"I won't. How about next week same time?"

"Oh, that would be wonderful."

Our weekly visits continued for a couple of months until one day when I received a phone call from Paul.

"Ed is in the hospital," he told me.

"What? Why?"

"Ken Homa said that Ed had been experiencing stomach pain, and it became so severe that they called an ambulance."

"Are you kidding?"

"No. It gets worse. They found stomach cancer."

"Oh no!"

"They plan to operate tomorrow morning."

"Okay. Thank you, Paul. I am on my way," I said.

Ed at the warehouse.

Ed's copy of *Traverse, Northern Michigan's Magazine.*

Ed (left), LaShelle (third from left), and students.

LaShelle filming Ed and students.

LaShelle's table.

One of Ed's tabletops.

EL PASO DE LA GEOMETRÍA #'S.
RIGIDA A LAS FORMAS HUMANAS
EL VERBO SE HIZO CARNE
Y HABITÓ ENTE NOSOTROS!

An inset from Ed's first panel. (See larger images at
www.themuralwriter.com.)

The Last Supper.

My Mother's Love.

The Quest.

Moses and the Ten Commandments.

The Best Man.

Simon and the Lamb.

Rising of Christ.

Daddy.

The Veil. (See larger images at www.themuralwriter.com.)

Adam and Eve. The one on the left is the last panel.

Ed and Big Boy.

Ed at Borders.

35

"What draws people to be friends is that they see the same truth. They share it."

C.S. Lewis, *The Four Loves*

I gingerly walked into Ed's hospital room. I feared what I would find. I had no idea if he was conscious, and I did not want to see my friend in pain.

Ed was sitting up and managed a smile when he saw me.

"Hi, kid," he said.

"Hi, Ed. How are you feeling?" I said. I knew that was silly to ask, but it was the standard question, after all.

"I am hanging in there."

While Ed was giving me all of the details regarding his upcoming surgery, his hospital phone rang.

"Hello?" he said hesitantly, not knowing who it could be. Then a shine radiated off him as he said to me, "It is my daughter Donna." I watched Ed as he smiled so brightly. It was clear that hearing from his eldest child meant so much to him. It had been quite a while since he had had any communication with his children." When he hung up, he said, "She is going to come by."

"I am so happy for you, Ed," I said. We didn't talk for a few minutes while Ed sat in deep thought. It appeared that he was replaying memories of his daughter. Then he snapped backed and winced. "Are you in pain?" I asked him.

"You know what, kid? Pain is our teacher. I learned that a long time ago. We need pain to pay attention, and when I feel it, I know I am still alive." I pulled up a chair next to his bed as we began our next talk.

"You know, I was thinking about the panels before you walked in. I really miss them. What if I don't see them again? What if they never see the light of day? What if their purpose is never revealed?" I listened as a lump formed in my throat. "It can't be all over now, can it?"

"No. It isn't over, Mr. Ed," I reassured him. "You are the one who told me how God has a plan for all things. This is not the end."

Ed wiped away a stray tear. "You are right. You know, when I was a kid, one thing my mother taught me that stayed with me is that a man would never be forgotten if he is remembered by at least one person. Because of that, throughout my life I would say the names of my loved ones that passed over out loud so they could be remembered." Ed looked me straight in the eyes and asked, "What do you want to be remembered for?"

"I guess as a person who made a positive difference in the lives of other people," I said. "I feel that is the most important thing that we can do here."

Ed smiled. "How do you want to sign your name?"

"What do you mean?"

"Find a synonym for your name, what you want to be known as."

"You mean like 6-22-34?"

Ed nodded. "Yes. That is what every artist needs to do. If this is it for me, I want you to remember that. But it must have meaning."

"Okay." I replied as I tried to understand what he was telling me. "Well, I better let you get some rest. You have a big day in the morning."

"Let me walk you to the elevator."

"Will they let you do that?"

"Oh sure, I just have to drag my IV with me." Ed chuckled.

We continued to talk as we slowly neared the elevator. Without looking at me, he said, "You have been a stabilizing force in my life for the past few years, LaShelle. A good friend. Thank you so much."

Ed began to cry as he tried to say more but couldn't, and I couldn't speak as my emotion was starting to get the better of me. When we arrived at the elevator door, we stopped and I pushed the button. Ed then turned to me.

"This might have been our last chat," he said. Tears were now flowing freely for both of us. "I just want you to know how much your friendship has meant to me."

"Ed, your friendship means the world to me too," I said.

We hugged and I stepped inside the elevator. The door slowly began to close as we faced each other. I tried to etch him into my head for fear that this would be the last time I would ever see him alive. I didn't want to forget one thing about him, and I believe he was doing the same.

Right before the doors collided with each other, he said, "Don't forget the joy, kid!" And then he was gone. As I went down, I wept like a baby. I was not ready to let go of my friend. The only thing that I could do now was pray, and that was what I did.

Ed's surgery went as expected. The stomach that doctors had created for Ed years ago was again reconstructed, and they cut out as much cancer as they could find. But unfortunately, the surgery took a toll on Ed's body.

The next time I saw him, he was in intensive care. It scared me when I walked into his room because he looked so weak. He had no color in his face and his cheeks were sunken. I tiptoed to his bed and examined him. Then his eyes slowly opened. There were tubes coming out of his nose and mouth, so he couldn't speak.

"Hi, Ed. I'm here," I whispered. His familiar amber eyes looked into mine, but this time I saw fear. They were wide and panicked. I carefully rubbed his arm. "Everything is going to be fine. Okay?"

He tried to nod and then his eyes relaxed. Paul and I took turns sitting with Ed. We didn't want him to be alone.

After a week, when Ed was not recovering properly, his doctor explained the next step was to move him to a nursing home. He was too weak to undergo chemotherapy or radiation, so he was transported to Birchwood Nursing Center by ambulance and set up in a shared room.

Before my first visit to the nursing home, Paul called me and said, "I just talked to Ed's doctor. He doesn't believe Ed will ever walk out of the nursing home doors. They don't think he is going to make it."

"What? That can't be!" I said.

"I know. They say he is very weak and losing weight daily. He is really plummeting, LaShelle."

"Thanks for letting me know, Paul." I was devastated.

As I drove up the hill on La Franier Road, I thought about my friend. How could I possibly let him go? He had taught me so much, and he had shared so much of his life with me, but I had so much more to learn from him. "Please don't take my friend yet Father, please!" I prayed. I pulled left into Birchwood Nursing Center and parked. I sat in my car for a few minutes while I gathered my strength. I knew that I had to be strong for Ed, even though I felt weak. I took in a deep breath and then blew it out. Finally, I was ready, so I made my way towards the entrance.

Ed was completely wrapped up in a thin white blanket like a caterpillar in a cocoon when I entered his room. It reminded me of E.T. the way his gaunt face peeked through the covering. Ed shook as I pulled up a chair to sit near him.

"How are you?" I asked.

"You shouldn't be here," Ed murmured in his fragile voice. He glanced at me and then quickly looked away in embarrassment. "I don't want you to see me like this."

"Mr. Ed, there is nothing that would keep me away. I am here for you, no matter what. Okay?"

Ed feebly agreed. We didn't talk much that first visit. Ed was too weak and tired. I just wanted him to know that I was there. That was all.

My visits continued, and each time I saw him, I became more and more alarmed. He was losing so much weight that he resembled a skeleton. It was becoming apparent that the doctors could be right. I saw no improvement. It was so difficult to sit with him and watch as he withered away. I wondered how this could be the end for Ed. His work had not been exhibited as a whole, and he had not had the opportunity to see what a difference the panels could make in people's lives. That was the purpose after all, to show the world love. This man had lived a life without love. But God gave him this gift, this purpose. His job was to show God's love to the world. I just prayed that God would give him the opportunity to see it for himself.

"Father, just let him see what his years of seclusion and dedication to you can do for mankind," I prayed. "Please give him dignity and please let him see his children soar."

Paul sat with Ed as well. It was important to the both of us that Ed felt our presence. So we took shifts, just like we did when Ed was in the hospital. After a visit with Ed, Paul was also losing hope. And then, God sent another miracle.

36

"And so for a time it looked as if all the adventures were coming to an end; but that was not to be."

C.S. Lewis, The Lion, the Witch, and the Wardrobe

Several years before, when Ed was working in the warehouse, Paul brought the Prayer Lady to meet Ed. Jennifer received the name Prayer Lady after she submitted her life to the Lord and asked Him to take the lead. She asked for a continual infilling of the Holy Spirit to guide her life, and through those early years the Lord taught her how to listen for His voice. Jennifer wouldn't just pray, "Here is what I want, God." She would ask, "What do *you* want, God?" and then patiently wait for the answer.

Through the years, the Lord and Jennifer developed a beautiful relationship based on obedience and prayer for people in need. She didn't hear God's voice, but she knew He was there. Most of the time it was a clear impression just as real as someone's voice. It might come as a scripture or a name. God taught her to trust Him through little acts of obedience. She learned over time that the more obedient to the Lord she was, the more He communicated with her. She heard things like "Call this person." She obediently did and found out that they were having a heart episode at that moment. Then God would instruct her, "Call that person." When the person in question answered her call, Jennifer realized they were going through a breakdown. The people she called would ask in confusion, "How did you know?"

Jennifer knew because God had told her. This was the continual conversation she had with the Lord, and it started with little acts of obedience. One of those acts of obedience was for Ed.

When Jennifer and Paul walked into the warehouse, Ed instantly saw the Prayer Lady's spirit. Her brilliant long red hair and crystal blue eyes glowed as Ed shook her hand for the first time. Her beauty, inside and out, mesmerized him.

"Would you like a tour?" Ed asked her.

"Yes, thank you," she answered with a glistening smile.

Ed showed her his practice pieces and then led her into the sanctuary holding the panels. He observed her standing in front of God's Love as her light beamed brighter. Ed knew she could feel the Father all around. He also sensed that she had a close relationship to God, just like he did.

"Let me show you where the kids are working." Ed escorted her to see my students' workstations.

Jennifer then reached her hands towards Ed's. "Can I pray with you?" she said.

Ed accepted her soft hands into his. God had put the idea in her heart that Ed needed prayer for forgiveness. After all of his years of struggle and broken relationships, Ed understood that this was the prayer he needed that day. When the prayer ended, they held hands for a few more moments as they both watched their teardrops trickling down onto them.

Two years later, when the Prayer Lady found out that Ed was in the nursing home, God spoke to her again. "Go see him," He said. At the time, Jennifer was going through a deep valley in her own life. Her family was dealing with health issues, and she was going through a lot of changes in her business. It was a very intense time, so it wasn't easy to let someone else in at that point. Yet the Lord was calling her. She responded, "Wow, Lord, you really want me to reach into this man's life? Is this your will?"

After praying for days, she was sure that God was leading her to Ed. Conveniently, her office was right down the street from the nursing home, and with conviction, she walked into Ed's room for the first time. Ed was bundled up in a white sheet and she was alarmed by how frail he was. The room was barren and felt very institutional. It was apparent that Ed did not have many visitors. The room had no cards or flowers to speak of, and her heart broke instantly as she saw Ed diminished and depleted. It was not a rosy picture. Jennifer knew that God had sent her, but she was unsure why. The chances of Ed recovering appeared impossible. But, obediently, Jennifer did what the Lord asked, and she prayed with Ed.

Her visits continued, sometimes weekly and sometimes daily. It depended on the Lord's instruction. During some of the visits, Jennifer brought her sister Lara and they both prayed with Ed. God also told Jennifer to bring Ed the things he needed. His appetite was non-existent, so she picked up yogurt-covered pretzels and M&Ms in hopes of encouraging Ed to eat something. She brought flowers and a poinsettia plant to brighten up his room. She also brought him a soft brown blanket to keep him warm. The Prayer Lady felt the Lord explain that Ed needed things to fill his life, things like scripture, encouragement, and words from God. She brought him a portable DVD player and a variety of CDs and DVDs, including the Bible on CD and old-time scripture.

Bit by bit, Jennifer came to see Ed, prayed for him, and brought things that he needed, and bit by bit she started to notice improvement. He was gaining some strength, and every day that she entered his room, he lit up at her presence. Her visits were important to Ed. Sometimes they would sit at a little table in his room and drink green tea together, and sometimes they would sit in prayer, depending on what he needed that day. It was these simple things that brought Ed joy.

One day as Jennifer was praying for Ed, she felt that the Lord was telling her that she needed to have her husband go shopping for Ed. Her husband didn't know Ed well. They had met once or twice, but he didn't have a relationship with Ed. The Lord was specifically telling her to let her husband do this, so he went and, ironically, returned with the CD series of C.S. Lewis's nonfiction books. Neither Jennifer nor her husband knew the significance of C.S. Lewis in Ed's life, and when she brought Ed the gift, he accepted it with emotion and gratitude.

During one visit, Jennifer felt the Lord tender her heart and say, "Take his hands, put them in yours, and I want you to ask Ed what he wants to pray for." Just like she had done in the warehouse years before, the Prayer Lady reached out her hands and held Ed's in hers. Ed's hands were formidable. They had become tools themselves after years of working with wood.

"Ed, what do you want to pray for?" she asked him.

Ed responded simply, "That the Father's work will be completed."

Jennifer and Ed closed their eyes. "Father, please finish this great work that you have begun. Be faithful to completion, and Lord, help Ed finish whatever you have started. Also Father, please give Ed dignity in his life and let your will be done."

This prayer was pivotal. From that moment on, Ed's health and strength began to flip around. He grew stronger, his appetite returned, and he started to get up and walk. Paul, Jennifer, and I were amazed. So were the doctors. They simply said, "We can find no medical reason for Ed's recovery. I guess we will have to write this down as a miracle." And a miracle it was.

It didn't take long after Ed started to flip around that we realized God was at work again. In Paul's spare time, he was trying to raise enough money to open an art and cultural center in his community, but he kept hitting one wall after another. He felt so strongly about this idea that he called every contact he had for help. One contact told him that there was a man in Petoskey, Michigan who was a consultant for nonprofit organizations. She was so sure that he could help Paul that she agreed to pay the consulting fee! So a meeting was set up between Paul and the man, Dale Hull.

The day of the meeting, Paul had this burning feeling that he needed to ask Ed who the historical person was who had inspired his work. Paul had heard Ed mention this person from time to time, but it never seemed important, so he didn't pay attention. But now, for some reason, it was important, although he had no idea why. Paul tried to push the feeling away because he had so much to do to prepare for his meeting with Dale, but it kept coming back. He had a few hours before the meeting, so he decided to relent and drive in the opposite direction to find the answer to his question. When he sat down in Ed's room they chatted a little. Paul told Ed about his meeting and then he blurted it out.

"Ed, who was the historical person that inspired your work?"

"C.S. Lewis," Ed said.

"I feel silly asking this. I have heard the name, but for the life of me, I cannot remember who C.S. Lewis is."

"There is a CD right there on my floor, *Mere Christianity*. It is one of C.S. Lewis's books. Listen to it on the way to your meeting."

Paul reached down and picked up the CD. This was the same CD that the Prayer Lady had brought to Ed just weeks before. Now it was in Paul's hands. Paul said his goodbyes and headed towards Petoskey. C.S. Lewis's words kept him company as he drove an hour and a half towards a meeting that was about to change everything.

Paul shook Dale's hand as they introduced themselves to each other. Paul sat down and they chatted for a while about the cultural center project. During the conversation, Paul noticed a C.S. Lewis book on Dale's bookshelf.

"C.S. Lewis." Paul pointed at the volume. "I just listened to him on my way over here."

"Interesting. Do you know much about C.S. Lewis?" Dale asked as he pulled the book from the shelf and opened it up.

"Actually, not much."

"Well, I am one of the founding members of the C.S. Lewis Festival here in Petoskey."

Paul's mouth dropped. "You what?"

"Yes, we have a festival each year in the fall. People come from all over the country to be a part of it. This June we plan to add a new event, a C.S. Lewis Elderhostel celebration. We will collaborate with the Bay View Association's annual event, which also brings people into the area from all over the United States."

"You need to see something." Paul pulled out his copy of *Traverse, Northern Michigan's Magazine*. He carried this magazine with him everywhere, and this day he was so grateful that he did. Dale scanned the article and looked at the beautiful photos of Ed's panels. Paul grinned as he observed how moved this man was, and then he said, "The artist in this article was inspired by C.S. Lewis."

Dale looked at Paul with shock and then eagerness. "I want to meet him," he said.

Paul, Dale, and their wives sat in the waiting area of Birchwood Nursing Center as they watched Ed's faded frame move towards them. He was now strong enough to get around using a walker, but he hobbled at a slow pace. His cheeks were still hollow and there were dark circles under his eyes.

Dale rose as Ed neared and introduced himself. After Dale and Ed played a round of intellectual tag, each man trying to prove he was more sharp-witted than the other, Ed started to talk more about his life and his artwork. Dale told me later that when he realized that Ed had walked away from his life for his work, he was more than intrigued. The fact that a homeless man had created what appeared to be a masterpiece had captured Dale's attention and he needed to see more: he needed to see the panels.

The next day, Paul and Dale stood in front of the garage in Elk Rapids. Paul grabbed the handles on the garage door and lifted it open.

"Here they are," he said.

Dale stood in amazement for a moment before moving in. Most of the panels were stacked one on top of the other, but five or six of them were placed upright against a wall. "These are incredible," Dale declared.

Dale was no stranger to art. He had a lot of experience in the art world. He had been the executive director of the Crooked Tree Art Center, and had even personally transported works by Monet from one museum to another. Now he was standing in front of something so unique, so beautiful that it was impossible to walk away as if he had never viewed it. It was too late for that.

Dale rubbed his chin and turned to Paul. "If I can find the space, can we exhibit this work at the new C.S. Lewis Festival event this summer?" he said.

Paul was thrilled. "Absolutely!" he said without hesitation.

The next few months were very busy. While Dale and Paul went to work putting together Ed's first major exhibit, Ed went to work putting his health back together. He was gaining weight and strength every day, so he began doing the same thing that he did at the shelter: helping other residents. He visited with them and shared the word of God. He explained how God had worked in his life and how He could work in theirs.

Ed also helped push other patients around in their wheelchairs. The nurses often scolded him, "Patients are not allowed to push other patients. It is a liability and that is our job!" But when their backs were turned, he tiptoed behind them pushing one of the residents. I remember he told me on one visit with a mischievous snicker, "They need my help. What else am I supposed to do?"

"You are always breaking the rules, aren't you?" I laughed.

"Yep. You found me out."

Ed's bellow was weaker than normal, but still loud enough to wake his neighbor. Watching Ed bounce back from near death was something I had not expected. Yet here was my friend joking and laughing again. I couldn't have been more relieved.

"My doctor told me today that I will be leaving soon," he said.

"Ed, that is the best news ever!"

He smiled, but I sensed something. Was it worry? I wasn't sure. "Are you okay?" I said.

"I'm great, kid."

"But?"

"I think I am finally ready to let go."

"What do you mean?" I asked with alarm.

"I have spent my life protecting my panels. Whenever someone came too close, I would run. I am getting too old to run." I nodded with understanding. "I need people around me that I can trust. I have you and Paul, but I think it is time to put the board back together."

"Ed, I think you are right."

"One of my longtime friends came in to see me the other day, and he reminded me how important it is to have people that I trust to look after my children when I am gone."

"Who was that?"

"Lon Husbands."

"I've heard of him."

"I have known Lon for many years. He is a businessman in Kalkaska. I used to have coffee every morning with a group of men at Big Boy, and Lon was one of them. Those are good memories."

"Do you want Lon on the new board?"

"Yes. I trust him, just like I trust you and Paul."

"I think that is important, Ed."

"Yes." Ed glanced at the floor and then looked back up at me. "God has given me more time. I know I need to get my things in order before it is time for me to go fishing. It is time, kid, it is time."

As I left that day, I knew he was right. Ed would be leaving the nursing home soon, and he had been granted the most beautiful gift from God: the gift of time to complete his job. The day Ed walked out of the nursing home door for the final time was a miracle. If I had ever had a doubt that there was a God, at this moment I realized there would never be another one.

37

*"Nothing you have not given away will ever
really be yours."*

C.S. Lewis, *Mere Christianity*

When Ed was released, he temporarily stayed in a small trailer north of Kalkaska. He was now on oxygen and was still weak, but improving every day.

While he was settling into the trailer, Dale was securing a storefront in downtown Petoskey. He approached a friend of his who owned several buildings near the upcoming C.S. Lewis Festival. After his friend heard Ed's story, he generously donated a building that had been used as an art gallery for three months.

The most important thing for Ed was that not one person ever have to pay one penny to see his work. This was something he made each one of us promise, which had resulted in My Father's Love becoming a nonprofit organization years prior. "This work is for the unloved child. I don't want anyone turned away from viewing it, ever!" Ed insisted. And now, it was official. Ed's work would be on display as a whole for the first time during the summer of 2008.

Dale and Paul rented a U-Haul truck and carefully packed up Ed's precious work. Word spread around Petoskey that Dale was bringing million-dollar artwork to their town. When the truck pulled in and volunteers began unloading Ed's children, people began coming in off the street to see what was going on, and many volunteered to help. It didn't take long for everyone involved to realize that this was much more than they expected. This was something very special.

Before the panels were moved to the new gallery space, Dale realized that they were facing a dilemma. No one there had any experience displaying artwork of this size. Since each panel weighed at least four hundred pounds and there were thirty of them, it would take someone with knowledge in this field to figure out how to proceed.

Dale called Paul for help. "Do you know anyone with experience in displaying massively heavy pieces of artwork?"

"Is that really a job?" Paul laughed. "Let me make some phone calls and I will get back to you."

Paul called some of the engineers he had worked with years before at General Motors. The answer he received from them was, "No, we have no idea how to do that." Then, after Paul had hung up the phone, he remembered what Ed always said: "Just pray. The Father will take care of it." So, for the next few days he made it a priority to pray for God's help.

Several days later, Paul was in Elk Rapids for a meeting near a building he was looking at for the art and cultural center. He was meeting with a man who ran the local hydro dam, which was located near the building. They conversed for a while. Paul explained about the cultural center, and the man explained the dam, and then Paul asked, "So, have you always run dams? That seems like such an obscure profession."

The man laughed and answered, "Actually no. I am from Seattle, and I worked for museums and galleries installing massively heavy pieces of artwork."

I know what you are thinking. I am sure it is the exact same thing Paul thought. "Are you kidding me?" Paul asked.

"No."

"Well, I have something to show you." Paul pulled out his *Traverse, Northern Michigan's Magazine* article again and filled the man in on Ed and the C.S. Lewis Festival exhibit. "Would you be willing to look at the works? They are just around the corner in a garage."

"Sure," said the man.

After looking at Ed's work, the hydro dam man agreed to help. Once the panels had been transported to Petoskey, he not only professionally secured them to the walls, but he also configured a triangle using three of the panels, which would allow them to be freestanding in the center of the room. The beautiful part was that he did all the work for free.

Many other people stepped forward too. Moran Iron Works created and donated brackets to hang the panels, and others donated paint and supplies.

As the last of the panels were being secured, Paul noticed a woman walk in nonchalantly eating an ice cream cone. He silently watched her as she looked around trying to figure out what was going on. After about an hour, he noticed the woman near the back of the exhibit, crying. Paul moved towards her and asked, "Are you okay?"

She smiled through her tears and said, "Yes. You know, I left my church several years ago. Being in the presence of this work has completely restored my faith." She wiped away a tear. "I will be back in church this Sunday."

This was one of many stories of transformation we witnessed as the panels began to do the Lord's work for the first time. The once vacant gallery in downtown Petoskey was quickly being transformed into a holy place, and Paul, Dale, and I were absolutely blown away. It was at this moment that we realized how powerful Ed's work was and would become.

Finally, the exhibit was ready and the grand opening set. Paul and Dale made arrangements to put Ed up in one of the finest hotels in Petoskey during weekends, and they rented him a white limousine with a chauffeur. Selfishly, we wanted Ed to feel special. We knew that he had spent his entire life feeling special only to the Lord, and to Ed, that was all that mattered. But we wanted Ed to feel dignity, respect, validation, and appreciation from the people who came to view his work, even if it was only once in his life. As far as we were concerned, that was the least that he deserved.

One of the first events was a meet and greet at the exhibit. Paul picked Ed up from the little trailer in Kalkaska and drove him to Petoskey for this event and for his stay at Stafford's Perry Hotel. As they pulled up, a crowd began to gather outside the gallery. Paul exited the Trailblazer and helped Ed out. Ed heard, "There he is! There's the artist!" He shuffled towards the crowd in confusion. *What are they doing?* he thought. As he moved closer, the crowd surrounded him and started to clap. The clap crescendoed, steadily increasing as more people joined in. Ed was stunned. He choked up and did his best to fight back the tears. He looked at Paul like a small boy and said, "I don't understand. I am still the same person."

This was the first time in Ed's life that he had experienced this kind of recognition or compassion. Yet he was still the same person who was shunned and had once been able to clear a street, and now people were gathering along the street to show appreciation? *How can that be?* He thought about the times when he had been spit upon, hit by rocks, thrown off his bicycle, and pushed away by society. How does a person reconcile this incongruity? *Father, would they still love me if I were a ditch digger?* Ed scanned the crowd again and smiled. *My Lord, this is for You.* He modestly nodded to the group and then moved into the gallery.

After a long evening at the gallery, Paul drove Ed to the Perry Hotel. He helped Ed up the staircase leading into the yellow and white-trimmed historic hotel. Ed was growing stronger each day, but he was still on oxygen and used a walker for support. The hotel had stood tall on a bluff overlooking beautiful Lake Michigan since 1899, and it was the only one from that era that was still operating in Petoskey.

Ed felt self-conscious staying in this Victorian jewel. He had spent his lifetime never wanting for anything. He had very little, yet he had never felt poor because the Lord always provided exactly what he needed. As he peered inside, he realized that this was a lifestyle he was not accustomed to, but he tried to take in the experience because he recognized it was a temporary gift and he was very grateful.

When Paul and Ed entered his room, Paul watched as Ed looked around the space. Ed was mesmerized by the furniture and interior design. He walked around the room and touched each piece as he said, "I can't believe this." He made his way to the sliding glass door that led out to a private balcony overlooking Little Traverse Bay. He stood in the doorway as the cool evening breeze gently blew the curtains, and he breathed in the fresh air. He looked down towards the veranda below and listened to a woman playing a piece of classical music on her flute. Then he looked towards the horizon at the vibrant sunset.

Paul continued to watch Ed take in the beauty before him, then look towards Paul and begin to cry.

"Paul, I can't believe this! I just can't believe this!" Ed said.

"It's beautiful isn't it?"

"Yes."

"Enjoy it, Ed. You deserve this," Paul said, beaming.

Ed spent the next three months being treated like a celebrity. He gave tours of the panels and lectured about his work and his inspiration, C.S. Lewis, to the thousands of people who came to the event.

Ed's exhibit was also part of an annual gallery walk in Petoskey one evening. As I pulled up in front of the gallery, I saw Ed sitting in his tan chenille chair. It was placed in front of a large window with the words "My Father's Love, Marquetry of Ed Lantzer" strategically placed through the center.

Ed's face lit up as he saw me exiting my car. By the time I had reached the door, he had shuffled over to meet me. "I missed you, kid!" he said.

I leaned in and wrapped my arms around his frail shoulders, "I missed you too." Ed half laughed and half cried as he handed me a present. It was covered in white wrinkled paper. "What is this?" I asked. He just smiled as a tear appeared in the corner of his eye.

I carefully removed the recycled paper and revealed the back of a black picture frame. I turned it over and there was a photograph of Ed standing in front of the white limousine. The chauffer was holding his door while Ed grinned with pride. My friend and I took a few moments to absorb this. We both cried and remembered the journey that had led him to this moment, the journey I had been given the job of documenting. It was long and painful, but here he was, finally being recognized for the wood mosaic masterpiece that had taken away his life and given him life at the same time.

One afternoon while Ed was taking a rest from the gallery, two couples entered the exhibit. They were visiting from Evansville, Indiana. One of the couples had won a trip to stay in a cottage in a local Victorian community called Bay View, which overlooked Lake Michigan. The previous winter, Kay Sander had attended a multiple sclerosis fundraiser while her husband, Steve, an educator, was teaching an evening class. During the live auction, Kay bid on the Bay View package and won. The problem was that she had to go home and explain this purchase to Steve. They would normally have discussed purchasing a vacation package ahead of time, but for some reason, Kay felt inspired to bid. She was relieved when her husband agreed to go, and five months later they were in Petoskey, Michigan. While attending a church service at Bay View, they had spotted a write-up about Ed's exhibit in the bulletin, and a short time later they were standing in front of Ed's panels for the first time.

A man named John Myers was the docent that day, and since Ed was not there, he gave the couples a tour of the panels. He explained their history and how they had come to Petoskey.

"Well, this has to come to Evansville. Does it travel?" Kay asked.

"This is the first time it has been on display, but we would like for it to travel," John said.

"Who do I talk to?"

"Paul Hresko." John wrote down Paul's name and number and handed it to her and then said, "Ed will be here tomorrow if you would like to meet him."

The next day Kay and Steve returned with another couple from Evansville who happened to be at Bay View at the same time. The Haynies were staying at their family cottage in Bay View and had been coming there during the summer for many years. Kay and Steve were already working on ways they could bring the panels to Evansville. They had never done anything like this before. As a matter of fact, neither Kay nor Steve could be considered artsy.

They had no background in the arts and rarely went to a museum, but Kay felt the Holy Spirit guiding her, and she could not back away from this strong feeling.

When they entered the gallery, Kay immediately headed towards Ed as he sat in his usual spot. "My name is Kay Sander, and my husband, Steve, and I were here yesterday with some friends to see your work," she said. One corner of Ed's mouth turned upward as she continued. "We were so moved that we just had to come back today to meet you in person."

"Thank you. I am glad that you did," Ed said.

"I have to tell you that I have never in my life experienced what happened to me. Ever!" Tears began to appear in Kay's eyes just like they had done the day before "I felt the power of the Holy Spirit. It was a feeling like I was standing on holy ground, that this place is anointed." Ed fought back emotion as he listened. "Mr. Lantzer, it was such an overwhelming feeling that I was shaking and my knees buckled. I really could have fallen to the floor."

"Would you like another tour?" Ed said.

"Yes, we would."

Ed then personally escorted the couples around the room as he explained the symbolism embedded in each panel.

By the time Kay and Steve had driven back to Evansville, they had brought Terry Haynie on board with the plan. Terry was vice president of development for the Easter Seals Rehabilitation Center, and she had a strong background in fundraising. They realized that it would not be cheap to bring a masterpiece of this size to Evansville, not to mention trying to find a location to house the panels. But Terry knew a lot of people in their community, and Kay felt that she would be the perfect partner.

As Kay and Steve headed south, they made the first phone call to Paul Hresko and started the dialogue. Paul asked, "How are you going to get your funding?" and Kay responded, "We don't have a clue, but we will be in touch."

By the end of the summer, many lives had been transformed. As I sat by Ed's side during my visits to the gallery, I witnessed person after person walk in and leave changed. I knew they had been changed by seeing the expressions on their faces. Something miraculous happened between the time they walked into the gallery and walked back out.

On one day near the end of the exhibit, I turned my attention to Ed. I stared at him and studied him studying everyone else. It was at that moment that I realized why God had given him more time. After years of obedience, dedication, and seclusion from the world, Ed was finally seeing love—real love—for the first time. I could see it in his eyes. There is no other way to describe what I saw, except that it was pure. It was God's unconditional love. I felt it too. This love radiated out from the wood and wrapped around each person. I watched many tears of joy flow. Several people even fell to the floor in praise. Ed sat in his chair as each person stopped to talk to him and tell him how his work moved them. The panels were finally alive and doing the work God had intended. As a result, word quickly spread. If a person mentioned the word "panels" around Petoskey, everyone knew what they were talking about. Ed and the panels had become the buzz of the town, but to Ed, this was not his glory to take. He was just the vehicle. Every bit of it belonged to the Lord.

One of the most important things Ed accomplished that summer was to create a new board of directors for My Father's Love. Ed told me in the nursing home before he was discharged that he was finally ready to let go. He understood that it was time to trust. Ed struggled with trusting people his entire life because he'd been hurt too many times, but it was time to break down that wall. He recognized that God was surrounding him with just the right people to form the new board. For the first time in his life, he had complete trust in someone.

Dale, Paul, and I were joined by two of the docents for the gallery, John Myers and Harold "Woody" Woodruff. John was the executive director of the Great Lakes Chamber Orchestra, and Woody had retired from his job as an electrical engineer in the Detroit area. Ed's dear friends from Kalkaska, Lon Husbands and Larry LaSusa, the lawyer who had helped Ed resolve the deed issues at the old schoolhouse, also joined us. Ed felt that putting together this board was the only way to protect his panels after he was gone. He was done running, and he was done sabotaging his relationships. God had given him this precious time to get his things in order, and he was not going to waste one second.

38

*"Don't let happiness depend on something
you may lose."*

C.S. Lewis, The Four Loves

Word about the panels moved beyond Petoskey, and people
started coming from out of town just to see them. What was
meant to last only a few months would soon turn into a
year.

When the three-month gallery deal came to an end after
entertaining more than four thousand people, the board
agreed that Ed and the panels needed to stay in Petoskey.
But the owner of the building told Dale, "You know, you
need to get out of here because I have rented the building to
a new business."

"Oh, you have?" Dale asked his longtime friend.

"It's your own fault because you brought so many
people in here and you like the space," the owner teased.
"But now you have to get out."

"Fine. But now I need a place for a year."

There was a pause. "Well, the building across the street
that was used as a gym is vacant. You can have that, but
you will have to do all of the cleanup. It is now your space,
and you can do with it what you will."

Dale breathed a sigh of relief. Things could have gone a
lot worse.

By fall the exhibit had been relocated across Mitchell Street
after a total renovation. Just as before, many volunteers
stepped forward to help. An interior designer picked out

paint colors, and Birchwood Construction volunteered to repair and paint walls. They even built a half wall to segregate a small workspace from the exhibit. Carpet, light fixtures, and many other materials were donated, as well as the time of many people to do all of the installation. When the new gallery opened, everything was in order. *My Father's Love Exhibit, Marquetry of Ed Lantzer* was again displayed on the front window, Ed had a new chair sitting there, and an iron and wood sign that said *The Ed Lantzer Gallery* hung near the entrance. The moment Ed saw the sign he realized this was for real and he said, "I'm taking that sign with me to the grave."

The next step was to move Ed to Petoskey. If his children were going to be on display for a year, he needed to be close by. Dale found a subsidized housing complex for seniors at Riverview Terrace Apartments that Ed qualified for, and he and Paul quickly secured a unit for him. A few of Ed's practice pieces, including a game board and tabletops, were sold to buy supplies: a cube truck to transport the panels to future exhibits, furniture and necessities for Ed's apartment, and an electric smart car so that Ed could transport himself to the gallery each day. Things could not have been better. Ed had his own home and transportation. After years of homelessness, it was finally over. He had a home that was officially his. A home he felt no one could take away.

Ed went to the gallery every day. He gained enough strength to get rid of the oxygen tank and his walker. This was a very happy time. The people of Petoskey rallied around Ed and accepted him as one of their own. Dale took him to concerts and to have lunch with Ernest Hemingway's grandson, and picked him up every Monday morning to have breakfast with a group of local farmers. Ed looked forward to his weekly breakfast. They discussed topics like farming, the price of grain, cattle, and how they believed the government was cheating everyone. These discussions stimulated Ed, but his favorite discussions were about the good old days.

My talks with Ed also continued. One day when I entered the gallery, Ed was sitting in his chair by the window. Now that the novelty of being a gallery owner had begun to wear off and the summer rush had slowed, Ed found himself getting bored. He spent each day sitting near the large front window waving to each person who passed by, and before long the passersby looked for him each day to say hello with a wave.

As I moved closer to Ed, I realized that he was asleep. I gently tapped him on the shoulder so that I wouldn't scare him. He opened his eyes and grinned.

"Morning, sunshine," I said even though it was almost noon. "It's time to rise and shine."

"Morning, kid." Ed yawned and stretched.

"I see how this new gig works. You get to sleep all day."

Ed bellowed, "Yep. I do. Actually, I scared a few people the other day."

"What do you mean?"

"I was sleeping and they thought I was dead."

"What?"

Ed laughed. "Yes."

He went on to tell me the story. A good friend of Dale's from the art center was driving down the street, and she always waved because she knew Ed was going to be there. Well, on this day she waved but Ed didn't wave back. She noticed that he was slumped in his chair and thought, *Oh, he's asleep.* She got about two blocks down the street and said, "What if he was not asleep? What if he has died?"

She parked her car and walked back towards the gallery. She stood in front of the window looking at Ed like a mother waiting to see her child's chest heave, but nothing. She didn't know what to do, and she didn't dare go in because she was fearful of the worst. She called a couple of friends and they came down. They all stood on the other side of the window staring at Ed until finally the owner of the building arrived. Bravely, he entered the gallery and walked towards Ed.

Just as he reached his chair, Ed woke up and said, "Hello there." Everyone jumped. They also laughed with relief. This happened on more than one occasion. As people went by the gallery window they would see Ed either waving or sleeping. Each time he slept, the same fear gripped those who saw him as they wondered, *Is he okay?*

After Ed and I had chatted for a while, he said, "Can I take you to get something to eat?"

"That would be lovely. Do you want me to drive?" I asked.

"Oh no, this is my treat. We can take the electric car."

Ed and I went out the side door of the gallery to an alley where he kept his car plugged in. His new vehicle looked like a blue and white new age golf cart. He escorted me to the passenger side and unzipped the white vinyl door and pulled it back for me.

"Wow, no one has ever unzipped a door for me before," I teased.

Ed grinned and proudly walked to the driver's side and unzipped his door too.

I watched Ed as he gripped the steering wheel. It had been a while since he had had his own vehicle. The last one was a hunter-green van with bright pink and yellow flowers that had been donated to him when he was in the warehouse. The van had no insurance and the plates had expired, but he occasionally drove it to Big Boy to eat one of his meals or have coffee with Lon and the group of local men. The hippie-style van was so bright that it was easily spotted a block away.

Ed's electric car neared a traffic light. He beamed as he turned left into a parking lot and pulled in between the lines and came to a stop.

"Will this do?" he asked.

I looked at the Garfield's Restaurant sign and smiled. I knew how important this was to Ed. Here was my friend wanting to treat me to what he felt was a fancy meal. Garfield's is a very nice family restaurant, but it wouldn't be considered fancy. On this day, however, it was the most elite restaurant I had ever seen.

"This is perfect, Mr. Ed!" I said.

Ed scooted by my side and we walked in together. I thought about how long it had been since I'd seen Ed this happy. He literally glowed as he sat across from me in the booth. Ed normally ate very little due to his stomach issues. It had been like this since I had first met him. I think he struggled since his stomach had blown up years before, but on this day he ordered a large fish dinner. I always worried about how little he ate, so this gave me comfort. I felt that

Ed was finally living the life he deserved: he had a home, a car, a gallery, and validation, and his health was improving. As Ed nibbled, I sent a message upward: *Thank you, Father!*

We talked about so many things during our meal together. We talked about life and how he had given up so much for his work. Then he took me by surprise, saying, "I have been getting so bored lately. It can be a little depressing sitting in the gallery seven days a week. I feel like I should be working, but sometimes I feel so down that I don't want to work again. Am I wasting my life?"

"What do you mean?"

"I feel like time has slipped by. Have I accomplished my job? I feel like I have a couple more panels in me, but is it God's will?"

"Ed, maybe it is time for the board to set up your workshop in the back of the gallery. You could start a panel if you want, or you could just tinker around. What do you think?"

"That would be nice." Ed flashed a smile. "Do you know what is the hardest?"

"No, what?"

"Not having someone in my life to share my work with. I always hoped I would meet my soul mate someday, but for whatever reason, that hasn't happened."

"You are seventy-six years old. Are you saying that after all of these years you have never let go of that feeling?"

"That is what I am saying," Ed responded sadly.

"What about the ladies at your apartment complex? I hear you are like a celebrity around there."

Ed smiled. "No way. They flirt with me, but I am too set in my ways to let anyone in now. It's too late. But I still regret it, and I feel like I missed out."

"I am sorry, Mr. Ed."

"I know." Ed laughed and then said, "Do you know how I get away from the women at my apartment complex?"

"How?"

"I focus on something negative about them, like a pimple on their nose." Ed roared and I joined him.

"That is so funny!" I said. Ed then got a serious look on his face. "Are you okay?" I asked.

"Is there enough love in that room at the gallery to say that I have loved enough?" Ed paused for a minute and then continued. "Have I loved enough, or have I gone too far?"

"Ed, you have loved the perfect amount."

I smiled at him and he smiled back just as the waitress interrupted with the bill. "I've got that," Ed insisted. He pulled out a fifty-dollar note, as if he were Rockefeller, from his aged brown leather wallet and placed it on top of the bill.

"So, what do you think of this, kid?" He looked around the room with pride.

"Ed, this means so much to me. Thank you so much!"

"You're welcome."

When Ed and I returned to the gallery, he walked me to my car. I saw disappointment brush over his face. I knew how much he hated it when I had to leave. He feared that I wouldn't return. It must have been the small child still holding onto his memories of the past.

"Please come back soon, okay?" he said.

"I will, Ed. Don't worry."

I gave him a hug and then he stood on the sidewalk, and I noticed him from my rearview mirror watching me until I had pulled out of sight.

The following week I returned with the rest of the board to set up Ed's workshop. He met me at the door as usual. Ed had always been an emotional person, but this day he was crying when I crossed the threshold. He hugged me and then held out a white envelope.

"Another gift?" I asked.

"Oh yes." Ed beamed. I pulled out the letter inside and read every word. I looked back up at Ed in surprise, and tears were now streaming down his face. His voice trembled as he said, "The tests show no sign of cancer. It is completely gone."

"Oh, Mr. Ed, I am so happy for you!"

I put the letter from Ed's doctor back in the envelope and wrapped my arms around him again while his tears of joy trickled down and landed on my shoulder.

"Oh wait, I have something else." Ed sniffled while he shuffled to his chair and pulled a box off the nearby ledge. "Here you go, kid."

276

I smiled and accepted the box of chocolates. Ed and I sat near the window to begin our next talk while we waited for the rest of the board to observe the work of the electrician we had brought in to wire the back of the building for Ed's saws and machinery. We spent an hour talking about how much Ed missed working with my students and me in the warehouse.

"I want to feel that spark again. Those were the best days of my life," he said.

"Well, maybe when your workshop is put together, I can come and work with you again," I said.

"Oh, would you please?" he said. I nodded and smiled. "You know what, kid? Someday I want you to create your own panel. It should be a self-portrait of how you see yourself and how you want the world to see you."

"I would love to do that!"

I stood up and pulled out my camera. Ed gave me a look like, *Here we go again.* I always had my camera during each visit. I felt it was so important to take as many pictures of Ed as I could. I snapped a picture of his profile and then I spun him around to get the lighting just right.

"You always do this to me," Ed joked.

"Well, I can't resist taking pictures of that handsome mug of yours."

Ed roared as I snapped more photos. I stared at him for a moment, and a feeling came over me as I observed him: *appreciate, savor, and enjoy every moment I spend with Mr. Ed.* I knew this was important, and I even wrote it down in my journal. He had been declared cancer-free, but I felt so strongly not to take one minute I shared with Ed for granted.

Paul's voice coming from the back room brought me back to the present, and Ed and I both stood up and headed to his soon-to-be workshop to help set it up. By the end of the day, we had cleaned the space and hooked up his machinery and tools. We also decided to bring in more docents to give Ed a break from the exhibit so he could go back to work.

I could tell how happy Ed was to have a workshop again. He hadn't had one since the warehouse, and we all felt that this would give him purpose.

When it was time to leave, Ed walked me to the door. He hugged me again and said, "I love you, kid."

"I love you too, Mr. Ed."

"Please come back and see me soon."

"I will, and please call me if you need me for anything."

This was something I said every time I left, but he never called. Maybe it was because he continuously lost his phone or the numbers in it. As a result, I had to reprogram my number into his phone many times. This visit was no exception. Or maybe it was because he hated to talk on his phone. When he received a call, it was always very short and to the point. But I believe it was because he didn't want to burden me; he knew how much I already had to deal with as a single mother. Nonetheless, I hoped that if he ever really needed me, he would call.

Shortly after the workshop was up and running, Dale decided that he would attempt to make his own tabletop. He liked working with wood and was fascinated with Ed's work. This would also give him an opportunity to work with Ed. So while Ed tinkered around on small projects, Dale started his own.

As Dale laid his pieces, Ed would walk by and say things like, "That's not going to work."

"What do you mean it isn't going to work?" Dale would ask.

"You should know better, but I will tell you," Ed would laugh as he explained the problem.

One afternoon, Ed was sitting in his chair and Dale was in the back workshop, about 125 feet away, sawing a piece of wood that a friend had given him for his table. Ed listened and then yelled from the other room, "What are you doing cutting my walnut?"

Dale yelled back, "How do you know I am cutting walnut? Besides, it isn't yours to begin with."

Ed simply answered, "I know it's walnut from the sound. The sound the blade makes as it cuts the wood."

Dale was absolutely blown away. He was amazed at how Ed could literally tell what kind of wood a person was cutting just by listening.

After Dale finished his table, he decided to make one of Ed's game boards with a chessboard in the center and a diamond mosaic all around. Once he had finished the chessboard, he started placing the diamond pieces along the side. Ed walked into the workshop after about two rows. Dale looked up at Ed with pride and Ed said, "Three more rows and it is going to break down."

"It isn't going to break down. I know what I am doing," Dale insisted.

Ed shook his head and moved on. Dale proceeded to place three more rows on the table, and just as Ed had predicted, the shapes would not fit. Of course, Ed laughed again with a look that said, *I told you so!*

Dale and Ed's friendship grew, and much of it was built on humor. They loved to joke with each other. Ed cherished this new friendship and was grateful for the time Dale spent with him.

The next Monday morning, breakfast was scheduled. Dale usually picked Ed up at his apartment around 6:30 am. On this Monday, Ed called Dale and said, "You can pick me up at the gallery this morning."

"Gallery? Why are you already there?"

"I will explain when you get here."

Dale drove towards the gallery as the blustery snow blew in every direction. Ed was waiting near the window in his usual spot wearing his furry aviator hat and leather jacket. As Dale approached, Ed had a serious look on his face. When he entered the gallery, Dale noticed a gash along Ed's nose. He appeared beaten up.

"What are you doing here? And what happened to your nose?" Dale said.

"I crashed my car," Ed said.

"What? What happened?"

"When I was ready to leave the gallery last night, I went to unplug my car. I didn't realize that the key was on because it doesn't make any noise. When I stepped in the car, my foot accidentally hit the gas pedal. The next thing I knew, I was knocked to the ground and the car was dragging me across the parking lot. My foot was stuck between the gas pedal and the brake so I couldn't break free. I was pulled across the entire parking lot until I crashed into a fence. It was a long way. I could see the tire rolling near my ear, and I thought it was going to run me over. Once it stopped, it took me a while to extricate myself from the car. It was probably about seven o'clock and it was pretty dark out. I went into the building and found a shovel and tried to dig the car out. I dug for a while until I could actually see something. That is when I realized that I broke the front axle. I didn't know what to do, so I went back into the gallery and fell asleep on the floor."

"You mean you slept the whole night on the gallery floor?"

"Yes."

"Why didn't you call me, Ed?" said Dale. "I would have taken you home."

"Dale, it was late and I didn't want to bother you."

Ed was shaken and banged up, but we were grateful that he was okay. Unfortunately, the car was not. After examining it closely, a mechanic told us that it had been totaled.

On February 12, 2009, Ed turned seventy-seven. In sacred geometry, seven is considered perfection. Paul told Ed, "You have double perfection, Ed. This is going to be your year." Ed smiled and nodded. Things were indeed going his way. By now, thousands of people had had the opportunity to see the panels. One visitor was a rabbi from Jerusalem. During his visit, he was so moved that he asked to have private time with the panels so he could play his wooden flute in their presence. Before the rabbi went back to his homeland, he inquired about bringing the panels to Jerusalem for an exhibit. Ed was beyond excited. We also had inquiries about bringing the panels to Kalamazoo, Michigan; Cape Town, South Africa; and for the National Day of Prayer in Washington D.C. Since we were only months away from the end of the lease agreement for the gallery space, it was time to start deciding where the panels would go next.

39

*"Give me all of you!!! I don't want so much
of your time, so much of your talents and
money, and so much of your work. I want
YOU!!! ALL OF YOU!!"*

C.S. Lewis, *Mere Christianity*

Communication between Evansville and My Father's Love stepped up, and official plans for the panels to travel out of state for the first time were made. When Kay and Steve Sander returned to Evansville, many extraordinary things happened. They began by having brainstorming sessions between Kay Sander and Terry Haynie. "If it comes here, where can we have it?" was the main question.

They agreed that they needed a place with a lot of parking. The Washington Square Mall, which was the very first mall in Indiana, seemed to be the perfect solution. There were some empty storefronts, and Kay and Steve had been friends with a co-owner of the mall, Gene Hahn, for many years. They shared Ed's story and directed Gene to the newly implemented *My Father's Love* Web site. A short time later, Gene called and said, "You guys go over and see Stan. He's my property manager there, and he will show you around."

Kay and Terry belonged to a Thursday morning Bible study group that they later named The Sonshine Girls. The more they talked about the panels, the more members of the group wanted to get involved. One of the Sonshine Girls was Dr. Linda Ramsey. She wanted to go look at the storefront with Kay and Steve. She was prepared to help with the costs of the exhibit and the rent. After Stan gave the group a tour of the space, they agreed that it was perfect.

Dr. Ramsey asked, "How much?"

"Gene told me nothing. No charge," said Stan.

They all looked at each other in disbelief.

"What about the utilities? Do we do that?" Kay asked.

"There will be no charge at all. The only thing we ask is that you get insurance for the event."

This act of kindness from the Sanders' friend gave each of them affirmation that they were doing the right thing and that it was time to put together an official committee to launch the exhibit by October of 2009. They put together a nucleus of a committee. At first, different gifts and talents came from the small women's group. As their work progressed, they began to expand out to other organizations in the community.

Johnny Kincaid and Gary Jossa had been friends for more than twenty years when they and their wives became involved with Kay and the group that was bringing Ed's panels to Evansville. Johnny had been a disc jockey in Indiana for years, and Gary had businesses in marketing and advertising. Over time, their paths had crossed through business and promotions, and now they were about to cross again.

The Evansville group decided that it would be helpful to have more information about Ed to use in promoting the panels, as well as for the docents and visitors of the exhibit, so Johnny and Gary volunteered to travel north to Petoskey, Michigan to meet Ed in person and create a video biography. Neither had experience running video equipment. Gary had always been the guy to send his employees out on shoots, and Johnny was a well-known voice in radio. He'd often been involved in publicity stunts, like being encased in a casket of ice as he broadcast his commentary for hours. If you dared Johnny to do something, he would likely do it, and taking on this project of videotaping Ed was no exception.

Gary grabbed one of the cameras from his company, Johnny got a crash course on how it worked, and off they went. Johnny and his wife, Jill, left before Gary and his wife, Kristy. Kristy was known for her love of Diet Coke, and during their trips this often became a problem because Gary would constantly have to pull into gas stations along the way to buy some soda for her.

On this trip, Kristy had to stop shortly after they left Evansville, and Gary was less than understanding. He pulled into a convenience store with frustration. When Kristy returned to the car, she had a peace offering in her hands, a big box of fudge.

"Here, this is for you," she said, and handed it to her husband hoping to make amends.

"I like fudge, but either we are going to get diabetes, or it will take us two years to eat all of this," Gary said. Still, he accepted the peace offering and put it under the seat. The two of them then got back on the road and headed north.

Johnny and Gary were prepared to meet Ed. They were told that he could be a little temperamental. "He may cooperate with you or he may not," they were informed. So they had an idea of what to expect.

When Johnny and Gary arrived at Ed's gallery with all of their equipment, Ed was sitting in his chair, expressionless. He carefully watched these two men, analyzing their every move as they set up. Johnny and Gary talked with Ed about what they would be doing, and then they toured the panels. Both men were shocked at what was in front of them. The fact that just one man had created such a masterpiece was beyond their comprehension. Neither had seen anything like it, and knew they probably never would again.

As they began their first day of filming with Ed, it didn't take long before all three were comfortable, and Ed even cracked a joke or two for the camera. Johnny worked the camera. His main focus was what they were going to get on tape, but by the end of the first day, he knew they would be walking away with much more. He had just documented a man so unlike anyone he had met before. He not only saw Ed's talent, but more important, he was in awe of Ed's faith. Johnny knew that there were many talented people in the world, and many talented people wasted their gift. But Ed recognized the voice of God speaking to him, and he had actually listened to it and dropped everything in order to follow what God was telling him he was supposed to do.

How many of us would do that? Johnny wondered. He tried to imagine what he would do if God told him, "You are going to spend the rest of your life doing this." Would he have enough faith, like Ed, to step out and say, "Okay, no matter what happens, I am going to pursue that"? After meeting Ed, he hoped that his faith would be as strong.

After two and a half days of filming, they had hours of footage of Ed himself, and most of the board members sharing their experiences with Ed. Johnny and Gary felt that they had captured moments with Ed that were vulnerable and beautiful. They knew that this video would be special, and both were anxious to get back to Evansville to put it together. But before they left, they decided to take a quick day trip to nearby Mackinaw Island. A visit to Mackinaw Island is like taking a trip back in time. The movie "Somewhere in Time," starring Christopher Reeves and Jane Seymour, had been filmed there years before, and it attracted thousands of visitors every summer.

Before they left, Gary asked Ed if he could bring him lunch.

"No, thank you. Someone is bringing me lunch," Ed said.

"Is there anything else I can get for you?" Gary said.

"I love fudge. Bring me back some fudge from Mackinaw Island," Ed said.

"Fudge? Just a minute." Gary ran out to the car, where Kristy was waiting and said, "Where is that box of fudge?"

"It's right here." Kristy grabbed it from under the seat.

"Well, I need it. That is what Ed asked for."

Kristy handed it to Gary and said jokingly, "The next time I have to make a bathroom stop, don't be surprised. It was God's plan all along."

After returning to Evansville, Johnny compiled all of the footage to create a video on Ed's life. Plans were made to have the video playing constantly throughout the exhibit, and after Kay viewed it for the first time, she cried with gratitude for the Lord's continuous provisions. She was sure that it would help to make the exhibit even better.

While Ed and the My Father's Love board of directors spent the rest of the summer making arrangements to send Ed's children to Evansville by fall, the Sanders and many volunteers began preparing the storefront. Just as with the Petoskey exhibits, movers, carpenters, carpet cleaners, and painters volunteered their time to put the gallery in order and build a prayer room in the back. The painters came in and said, "We can give you two guys for one day."

"Okay, this will give us a good start and then we can finish the walls," Kay said.

The next day, she walked into the space and the painters were back again. They smiled and said, "We just wanted to complete the project ourselves."

These acts of kindness continued. A neighbor of Kay and Steve's, who owned a security systems company, came to look at the gallery after Kay inquired about options to protect the panels. He said, "We have a good camera system."

"How much are we talking about?" Kay asked.

"I will just give it to you, and I will send a guy out to install it at no charge," he said.

The Evansville group quickly recognized the generosity of the people of their community. Evansville was being transformed in an unexpected way, and if Kay had questioned before whether she was doing the right thing, this took away all of her fear.

40

"No one ever told me that grief felt so like fear."

C.S. Lewis, *A Grief Observed*

During my next visit to Petoskey, I sat next to Ed and we watched several groups of people view the panels. The first group was a grandmother and great-grandmother showing their grandchildren Ed's work. The children were in from out of town. Ed watched intently as the children recognized characters and scenes from familiar Bible stories.

An older couple also brought a friend to the gallery. This happened time and time again. Once a person viewed the panels, they often returned with friends and family. When the older couple was ready to leave, the gentleman walked over to Ed and shook his hand vigorously and said, "God sure has blessed you with a special gift." Ed graciously thanked him, but I could tell that he was still not used to the attention. Maybe he never would be.

After both groups left, Ed and I went out the back door to have lunch at City Park Grill, which was located behind the gallery. This was our usual lunch spot. Ed seemed to move more slowly and his balance appeared to be off on this day. He shuffled like he always did, but I noted that he reminded me of a toddler just learning to walk. His feet and body were not moving at the same pace.

"I fell the other day at my apartment," Ed said.

"Oh no. Are you okay?" I noticed another scab on his nose. This was not the same scab from the car accident months earlier. I also spotted scratches on his hands.

"This was my second fall. I'm having a difficult time accepting my failing balance."

"Did you go to the doctor?"

"Yes, Paul took me. They said there is nothing that they can do." We moved at a snail's pace as Ed continued. "I worry about traveling with the panels to Evansville now."

"Why?"

"I'm afraid I will fall. I am embarrassed. I don't want people to see me like this."

"Oh, Mr. Ed, I'm so sorry."

"I think I have to get my walker out again."

"That's probably a good idea."

"I am so frustrated that I don't even want to show people the panels at the gallery right now. So I sit in the window every day and watch people go by. I wonder where they are going and why everyone is in such a hurry. Some make no eye contact with anyone. They don't even know anyone else is there. I watch them go by and I wonder what their purpose is in life. There is so much that people don't understand that they need to know. They need to know that God loves them."

As I listened to Ed, I wondered if he would have been different if he hadn't lived a life with so many obstacles. Would he be oblivious just like these people? Had the obstacles helped him become the person he was? I pondered these questions as I continued to listen.

"Don't they know that they should appreciate every moment? I wish they would slow down and notice life all around them, like the way leaves dance and the way clouds gently pass by. I wish they would notice the delight in a passerby's face and the burden in another's. I wish they would recognize why they are here and that they each have a special purpose. I don't have much time left to complete mine."

"Mr. Ed, don't say that," I scolded as we entered the restaurant and were immediately seated at a table near the historic bar. This was the very same bar that Ernest Hemingway had made home on many occasions years before during his time in nearby Walloon Lake. I glanced at the black and white portrait of Hemingway placed above the bar in front of a barstool. I wondered if that was where he'd sat as he sipped his troubles away.

Ed looked at me and said, "I feel so empty inside. Many artists and writers of the past felt the same way. That is the reason for their high suicide rate, I think." I listened with concern as he went on. "I have considered it many times, but I am still here because God's love for me was stronger."

"I am so glad that you didn't." I placed my hand on his wrinkled fingers and patted.

"When I was in the nursing home, I would wake up with night sweats. I would wake up in the middle of the night and all of my thoughts were still there."

"What did you think about?"

"Dying."

"Did you think you were going to leave the hospital?"

"No. I thought my job was done, but I couldn't understand how it could be done when there were so many things I still needed to do."

"You thought you were going to die, but you weren't ready to."

"Right. It's that calling. Each one of us is called to encounter a particular experience on Earth. In our own way, we are faced with it. We have no choice." Ed paused and I watched him as I wondered what he was thinking about, and then he said, "I see you working so hard with your students and your own art studio. You are working every day towards your goal. That must be the answer for happiness, to be working towards a goal every day. I was happy until I stopped working."

"Maybe if you spent even thirty minutes a day in the workshop, it would help you feel better. Remember how you felt at the warehouse? You were happy and driven."

"Yes, I do." Ed's weary eyes made contact with mine again. "I have been searching for years for someone to take over my work when I am gone. I want it to be you."

"Mr. Ed, I don't think anyone should because it is *your* work, *your* job. This is your legacy, and I don't think anyone else can take your place. Your work will live on forever." I pointed at the picture of Hemingway. "Just like his."

Ed smiled and said, "Hemingway," and then he nodded.

The waitress came and I ordered decaf and a cup of soup. Ed said he wasn't hungry as usual and ordered black coffee. I hoped he would at least nibble on the complimentary biscuits he loved so much. I looked at him with concern as the waitress departed.

Just then, an elderly man came in with a walker. Ed and I watched him make his way into the dining area. I knew Ed was comparing himself to this man. Suddenly, as the gentleman tried to climb up to a second level of the restaurant, he fell to the floor and his walker followed. Ed sat stunned as we watched the man's relative help him up. Tears filled Ed's eyes and he said, "See, that could happen to me. I don't want people to see me like that. It shouldn't be that way." I grabbed Ed's hand again and squeezed, hoping to give him some of my strength.

When I left that day, I was very concerned about my friend. He was happy and feeling healthier than he had in a long time, but now the realization that he was struggling with physical problems had hit him without warning. My heart ached for him, and I knew that I needed to spend time with him as often as I could to help him through this difficult stage.

A week later, I was preparing to visit Ed with one of my art students, whose name was Asia. Each year I assigned an art history project in which students selected a famous artist to study. Asia chose Ed. Ed was so honored. Several months earlier, I had brought her to meet him for the first time and interview him for her project. They made an instant connection, and every time I ran into her during the summer, she pleaded to go with me to visit Ed.

Shortly after she and I made our arrangements to go to Petoskey the following week, my cell phone rang. I was surprised when the caller ID flashed "Mr. Ed." I quickly answered, worrying because Ed rarely called me.

"Hello?" I said hesitantly.

"Hi, kid. How are you?"

"I'm . . . good."

"I wanted to tell you that Lon took me yesterday to get my angel statues out of the garage in Elk Rapids. He is going to take them to Kalkaska so I can give them to my daughters."

"That is great, Ed. I know how important that is to you."

"What is new with you?" Ed asked.

"Well, yesterday was my birthday," I answered.

"Oh no, why didn't you tell me? I wish I could have been a part of that."

"I didn't celebrate this year because I had to teach a painting class last night at my studio, so I didn't do anything for it. How are you, Mr. Ed?"

"Okay," he answered. I could hear a trembling in his voice. I knew Ed well enough to know that something was wrong. "I visited my doctor in Traverse City and he gave me a clean bill of health." Ed continued to ramble on for a bit longer and then I stopped him.

"Are you at the gallery?"

"Yes."

"Would it be okay if I came to see you today?"

"Oh, that would be wonderful!" Ed's voice shook as if he were holding back tears.

"I will get ready and then head that way."

"Call me when you get into town."

"I will. Would you like a coffee?"

"Yes, please," Ed said gleefully.

"Okay. I will see you soon."

"Oh, this is going to be great!" Ed's voice shook again with emotion. "I can't wait to see you."

"I can't wait to see you too. I will be there soon."

I drove faster than usual that day because I understood that Ed needed me. He had always been too proud to ask for help, and that made his simple phone call very important. He didn't specifically say that he needed help, but he didn't have to. I heard it in his voice.

When I arrived, Ed was eagerly waiting. I handed him his cup of black coffee from Roast & Toast, our favorite coffee joint in Petoskey, and he put it aside without taking a sip. We began with small talk, and after a few moments, I jumped right to the point.

"Are you okay, Mr. Ed? Tell me what is going on."

Ed paused for a moment, and then with sad eyes he said, "I know the panels will be going to Evansville soon, but I'm afraid."

"Why are you afraid?"

"I am afraid that my children and I will be homeless again."

"Why would you feel like that?"

"Because Petoskey has become home to me. I feel safe here. I have an actual home here. When we leave for Evansville, we will go right back to being homeless again, and that will be the end of my life."

"Ed, just because the panels will be in Evansville for a few months doesn't mean that you will lose your home in Petoskey. You don't even have to be there all of the time. You can visit the panels when you are up to it, and the rest of the time you can be here." Ed nodded with relief. "I know you said that you are afraid for people to see you like this, but Ed, they are going to love you."

Ed smiled and then looked serious again. "You know what the hardest part is? Inside I feel like I am forty years old, but my body won't do what my mind wants it to do anymore." I listened, realizing how difficult it must be for Ed, or anyone going through the same thing, for that matter. I had never thought about that before until this moment, and it made me consider my own aging process in a different way. "Aging can be very depressing, you know," Ed said.

"It must be difficult, Ed. I am so sorry you have to go through this. But I have some good news for you."

"What?" Ed asked with interest.

"I will be driving you to Evansville for the grand opening. How about that?"

"Oh no, I am in trouble now! Do you think your driving is good enough?" Ed teased.

"Hey, mister! Don't you worry about it. I will get you there in one piece."

Towards the end of our visit, Ed stood up and made his way to the back of the gallery. When he reappeared, he had a large white box on the seat of his walker. He was grinning from ear to ear as he made his way back to me.

"Here you go, kid. Happy birthday!"

"Oh my goodness, what is this?"

As I opened the box, I wondered where it had come from. I knew he had had no time to buy a present. Was he collecting his "junk" again? But it didn't matter because to me, this was not junk. I pulled back both flaps on the top of the box and stared in awe at the most delicate white china with gold trim that I had ever seen. Emotion overcame me as I gave my friend a hug. "This means so much to me. Thank you, Mr. Ed. I will cherish this forever!"

"You're so welcome, kid. I want you to know how much I cherish our friendship."

"Me too."

"Thank you for coming today. I am usually good for a week or two after our visits, but then I start getting depressed again. I feel so much better now."

"Any time, Mr. Ed. You know that. Don't ever forget that I am only a phone call away. Got it?"

Ed smiled in agreement. "Got it."

When I brought Asia to see Mr. Ed a week later, he was so happy to see his new friend. He told me before we got there that keeping his new friendship alive was very important to him. He hoped that he could make a difference in Asia's life.

After we chatted for a while, Ed said, "I talked to my doctor and he said some really big changes are coming. He has been sending nurses to my apartment every day. You know I don't like anyone in my apartment. The nurses are going to be taking over my care. The worst part is they are going to make me take a bath, and I hate baths!"

"Why do you hate baths?" I asked.

"Because they aren't good for you."

"Yes they are," I said.

"Somebody told you that. I went long enough without one to find out." We all laughed.

"It's crucial. Water is crucial. Our bodies are made up of how much water?"

"That is where your fat comes in. You keep adding to it, and adding to it."

"So you think if you don't add any water, you won't get fat?"

"That's right," he smirked.

"Asia, don't listen to him," I said. "He knows not what he talks about."

"Sure he does," Ed replied.

"You are just trying to make an excuse so you don't have to take a bath."

"I took a bath last year."

"You did? And you didn't melt?" I teased.

"I take a bath once a year and that is enough."

"Well, it sounds like they are going to put their foot down on that."

"Yeah. I have to try some stuff that I don't like. They come in and make me take a bath, and they have to be there to make sure I do it. There will also be two nurses at night to put me to bed."

"What brought all of this on?" I asked.

"My two falls. Look at how long I have been doing what they are telling me not to do. That has to count for something. They have only been at it for a few years. I have been at it for over seventy, and I think I was doing pretty good."

"But we also want to keep you healthy."

"The nurse said, 'We have to keep you alive because of your success.'"

"That's right, and we have a lot to do yet." Ed chuckled as I continued. "You have to do what they say. It can only benefit you, right?"

"Well, you are sounding like my doctor now."

"It is out of care and concern."

"What am I supposed to do?"

"Just do what they say and then sit there and look handsome. Okay?"

"Okay," Ed reluctantly agreed.

Ed just out of the nursing home.

Ed travels to the new Petoskey gallery in style.

Ed and Dale celebrate the formation of the new board.

Ed drives his new Smart Car.

Ed takes LaShelle to Garfield's restaurant.

Paul, Ed, and Dale set up new workshop.

Ed waves to Petoskey villagers.

Ed at his first Petoskey annual Gallery Walk.

Some of Ed's unfinished boxes.

Ed's Petoskey workshop.

Ed puts LaShelle's number into his phone—again.

LaShelle picks Ed up for a visit.

Ed enjoys a Petoskey park.

Ed after his fall.

Ed at the gallery in Petoskey.

Ed with his first panel.

Ed and Dale Hull at the gallery.

Ed and Asia.

Ed at City Park Grill.

41

"Peter did not feel very brave; indeed, he felt
he was going to be sick. But that made no
difference to what he had to do."

C.S. Lewis, The Chronicles of Narnia

By the end of summer, Ed was giving his nurses the runaround, disobeying every chance he could. He was now relieved that the trip to Evansville was set so he could evade the new demands his doctor and nurses were making. He was preparing for another major change in his life. He had always dreamed of traveling. Over the years, he would often tell me that maybe he should take the panels and go to China or Africa. Each time he expressed this desire to travel, he would mention a different location. But now that he actually was going to travel, he was reluctant. Fear can be a powerful emotion to overcome. Fortunately, Ed made the decision to fight past his fear and move forward with the plan.

My life also went through a major change prior to the trip to Evansville. After my divorce years before, I had repeatedly brought the wrong people into my life. I had never really been alone since I was nineteen years old, and I realized that I was afraid of being alone. Every time I dated someone new, Ed would be very gracious to them, but I knew that he did not approve. Finally after another breakup, I decided that I would stay single for two years. I wanted to get to know myself without someone in my life.

This idea was very foreign to me, but I knew it was important. So, for two years I took myself out for dinners and movies. I even took myself out for New Year's Eve alone. I always brought my journal to write in so that no one would talk to me. It was difficult, but over time I adjusted and eventually realized that I was actually good company. I ultimately felt that I didn't need a man in my life. So when my brother, Larry, started telling me that he had just met my future husband and that I must meet him, I told him no.

I was surprised because my brother liked very few of my boyfriends. Even though Larry was younger and the only boy of seven children, he had taken on the father figure role in our family. He was very protective of all of us girls, and always had a judgmental eye when we brought a date home. But now he was insistent that I meet this person he was sure I would marry. I spent eight months telling him no, but he didn't give up, and once a week, he asked me to meet him again.

Finally, towards the end of summer, I agreed to meet this man. The reason I relented was to appease my brother. I was sure that once I met him, I could go back to my comfortable life alone. But by my third date with Ken VanHouten, we were inseparable, and by October 15, 2009, Ken and I were heading south to Evansville, Indiana to take Ed to the grand opening of his new exhibit. Ken was worried about me transporting Ed in my small economy car for twelve hours, so he generously offered to drive us in his Suburban.

As Ken was driving, I noted how kind he was to Ed and vice versa. I wondered if Ed approved, but I was certain that he did. At least I hoped that he did. I also hoped that our trip would be smoother than Paul's trip to Evansville the day before with the panels.

Right before Paul and his friend Rich, who called himself "the roadie," left for Indiana, Paul received a call from Dale, who said that the police had pulled him over in the cube truck as he was bringing the vehicle to Paul to load up the panels. Dale found out that the truck needed to have a DOT (Department of Transportation) number on the side as well as the foundation's name. The problem was that the panels needed to be in Evansville by that evening so they could be installed the next morning in time for the grand opening. Paul and Dale had never driven a cube truck before or transported a large load, so this was all foreign to them.

Paul made calls to find out what he needed to do to make the truck legal. The list was longer than his arm, and he worried whether he could get everything done before it was time to leave. Luckily, he found an awning place to put the numbers and letters on the side of the truck. On a normal day, the awning business was backed up, but today they had time, and within an hour the truck was adorned with the DOT numbers and the title "My Father's Love." The letters and numbers had to be a certain size and spaced a certain distance apart, and as Paul pulled out of the awning shop, he prayed that they were.

Paul then found out that he had to have a DOT physical, so he quickly found a doctor who could get him in right away, and after a strip search, he walked out with the signed form. Then when Paul got back into the truck, the battery was dead. He frantically called the mechanic who had looked over the truck a few days before, and *he* sent someone over to jump the battery. Once the truck was running again, Paul rushed to another company to get a log book. One of the requirements on the list was that he needed to log his mileage and stop at weigh stations along the way to Evansville, but he didn't have a log book. When he pulled in, he was told that the man who had the log books had just left for the day. "Of course he did. Why wouldn't he?" Paul said sarcastically.

Paul started to pull out, feeling that there was no way they were going to make it to Evansville in time, when he spotted someone flagging him down. "Wait, the man with the log books is in the back. I thought he had left. He can get you one," said the clerk. Finally, with the log book in hand, Paul and Rich headed south down U.S. 131. As they pulled through Kalkaska, they saw a large sign blinking at them. It read, "Road closed, detour ahead." Paul yelled, "No way!!" He looked at his watch and realized that they had just enough time to make it, but he was worried that each weigh station stop along the way would set them back. But luck was on their side. After making their way through the detour, they were finally on the expressway. Paul and Rich looked at each other and smiled with relief.

Just then, Paul spotted a police car pulling alongside the cube truck. Paul took a deep breath and prayed to himself, *Please God, please God.* He hoped that everything would meet code and they wouldn't be pulled over. As the police car stayed side by side with the truck for what seemed like eternity, Paul looked at Rich and asked, "Do you want to say the Rosary with me?"

"Sure."

Paul reached for the rosary he had placed near him, and they began to recite in unison. Finally, the police car sped away.

"Do you think someone or something is trying to stop us from getting these panels to Evansville?" Paul asked.

They were both sure this was the case, but they felt that each step of the way God had created an avenue to get around the obstacle.

Paul and Rich settled in for the long ride. The only issues left were the weigh stations ahead. They had no idea how long each stop would take or how many stations they would run into. As they neared the first one, Paul put on his blinker, preparing to turn in, when Rich announced, "It's closed! Keep going."

"You're kidding? That's great!"

They continued on, and when they reached the next weigh station, it was closed too, and the next, and the next. Paul and Rich couldn't believe it. At last they pulled into Evansville, just in time. They both knew that God was at work and now Ed's children could begin to do their work in Evansville as well.

Our trip to Evansville was smoother, but it wasn't without problems. Ken and I picked Ed up at his apartment at 7:15 A.M. We drove around the back of the building, and through the glass door I spotted Ed sitting in a chair with his walker placed next to him. He was sitting like an anxious school child waiting for the arrival of his bus. I grinned as I thought how handsome he looked in his blue and white pinstriped suit.

When he saw the lights of the Suburban, he grabbed his walker and met me at the door. "Are you ready for this?" I asked.

"Yep."

I handed Ken Ed's gray and black woven suitcase, and he loaded it into the back of the Suburban. The suitcase had wheels and two handles, which were not necessary. It was so light that I could tell Ed had not packed much. I wondered what he planned to wear for the four days we would be in Evansville. My suitcase was so full that I could barely zip it, although I have been known to overpack on occasion.

I helped Ed slowly get into the Suburban, one foot at a time. Later we would discover that he would not move from his spot for the entire eleven-hour trip. We made several stops along the way for food, bathroom breaks, and gasoline, but each time Ed refused to get out of the vehicle. Instead he said, "Nope, I'm good." He did let Ken order him a black coffee from Burger King early on in the trip, but that was the last thing he ate or drank for hours, and I believe he only took a sip or two of that. Ed stated, "People really don't need much food. I can go three days without eating. People eat out of boredom or for something to do. It is really only necessary to eat once a day."

"I heard of someone who only eats once a day, and he seems healthy," Ken added, trying to make Ed feel better.

Ed nodded, content that we understood he was not planning on eating, and Ken and I began to worry. How can a person travel for eleven hours without eating or using the restroom?

As the darkness lifted, the weather appeared cloudy and dreary. The vehicle was set at a warm temperature, but we noticed that Ed was cold, so Ken showed him how to control his own temperature in the back seat. Ed turned the heat on full blast, and it stayed at sauna temperature the entire trip. He began to share how much he enjoyed his Monday morning breakfasts with Dale and the farmers. His voice was so soft that I could barely hear him. He was seated behind me, so I twisted around to listen carefully and read his lips.

"There is one farmer that bought a separate house for his wife. The farmer said that it was cheaper than divorce,"

Ed said, and we all laughed. "And he pays her to cook his meals too."

"No kidding?" I asked.

"Yeah." Ed then got serious. "Maybe I will meet my soul mate in Evansville." Ken and I looked up in surprise wondering where that had come from.

"Do you want our help?" I asked. I knew how much Ed regretted not having someone to share his life with. It would be nice if he could find that now, I thought.

"I have a lot of requirements for a wife. It could be difficult," Ed teased.

"Really? What are they?"

"She needs to be creative. She needs to have her own life, and she needs to have her own money. I don't want her hand in my pocket," Ed laughed.

"That shouldn't be too hard. By the end of your trip we will find a wife for you. Okay?"

"Okay, deal," Ed said with a smile and a glimmer of optimism in his eyes.

After seven or eight hours, we stopped again for food and gas. "Do you need to use the restroom, Mr. Ed?" I asked hopefully.

"Nope, I'm good."

"How about a bite to eat?" I pointed to the bag of Honey Crisp apples I'd bought in Kalkaska at Cherry Street Market before our departure. They were to be a gift for the Evansville group. "How about an apple?"

"No, I don't need anything," he said.

As Ken and I walked into the Burger King/gas station combo with concern, Ken suggested that we buy Ed a small bag of French fries and a bottle of water and just give it to him. "Like a toddler, he might eat them if they are in front of him," Ken said.

"Brilliant idea!" I said.

Sure enough, when we gave Ed the French fries and water, he cautiously accepted. As we drove the last leg of the trip, Ken and I peeked at Ed through the rearview mirror to see if he was eating, and he was nibbling on a fry like a rabbit. Ken and I looked at each other and smiled at our success. After a while, I asked Ed, "Did you have enough to eat?"

"Oh yes. I ate more than half of them."

I breathed a sigh of relief.

Once we were in Indiana and about an hour away from our destination, Paul called to say that they had successfully installed all thirty panels during the day.

"LaShelle, you will not believe the reactions I witnessed as each panel was raised and attached. The room was filled with so much emotion. When they were all put together, people were speechless and just stood back and stared at them. The panels are already making an impact here."

"That is beautiful, Paul!" I said.

"Can you have Ed here by 6:30? We have dinner reservations with the Evansville group so they can meet Ed and celebrate."

"No problem. We should have Ed there in plenty of time," I said.

We were getting excited as we realized we were only thirty miles away. Ken and I smiled at each other, and Mr. Ed seemed relieved. It had been a long drive for him, and we all wondered how Ed would make the same trip home four days later. Then, our final exit came into view too quickly. We were right upon it, but I realized that our MapQuest directions said the exit would say Louisville on the sign. It did not. Since I was the navigator, I made a split-second decision to take the exit anyway.

As we drove, we realized we were in a rural area, and we were sure that the city of Evansville was not rural. We saw pond after pond. It seemed like everyone had one. We then came across a large train, just sitting in a yard. "Wow, you don't see this in Northern Michigan." I said. We then noticed a junkyard with a white picket fence in the front yard. In the yard stood a large tree with a bent rusted car installed into it. Ken and I looked at each other in concern. "Uh oh," I announced. "This doesn't look right."

Ed sat in silence as we kept driving, and I wondered what he was thinking. I turned to peek at him, and he was resting his eyes. I was relieved and hoped that he wasn't paying attention. I also hoped to see a sign, one that said Evansville, and possibly one from God. Finally, after thirty minutes of this, Ken and I decided to call Kay and Steve for help. They graciously directed us towards Evansville, and at 6:30 on the dot, we had Ed, tired and worn, at the Western Ribeye Restaurant to meet the Evansville group for the first time.

As Ken and I helped Ed out of the vehicle, we noticed the bag of French fries hidden under his seat. It was full, minus one or two fries. "That little stinker," I whispered to Ken as we directed Ed in to meet the waiting group.

42

*"My own eyes are not enough for me; I will
see through those of others."*

C.S. Lewis, Experiment in Criticism

The first day at the exhibit, Ed had interviews lined up with local newspapers and television stations. While he was being interviewed by a young trendy photographer from the newspaper, Ed started to flirt with her. Ken and I looked at each other wondering if this was his first try at finding his soul mate, and we realized that he would not need our help in this endeavor. Ed glanced at us mischievously as he asked her to take him to dinner. She laughed and said, "I don't make enough money to take you to dinner."

"I don't eat much," Ed replied with a chuckle.

She continued to take photographs and Ed continued to try to get the dinner date, but to no avail. He struck out on his first try. Later he told Ken and me, "Females don't laugh enough. I was trying to get her to laugh." And that he did accomplish.

When the photographer was done, I pulled up a chair next to Ed and sat down while one of the volunteers shook his hand and said, "If you plan to set the panels up somewhere else in the future, I want to be a part of it. They are a blessing. You did an awesome job!"

Ed thanked him, and before the man parted he said, "Well, I will see you tonight at the grand opening. If you need anything before then, you know how to get a hold of me. I am willing to help."

"Thank you very much," Ed said as Kay walked up.

"He is such a wonderful man, isn't he?" Kay said. Ed tried to conceal the bubbling emotion he was experiencing, but he was unsuccessful. She continued, "I don't know if you have read any of Dr. Henry Blackaby's studies, but during one of the first big Bible studies he did in our area, we were really experiencing God. The bottom line was, see where God is at work and join Him. And this exhibit is the biggest example of that I have ever seen."

"Well," Ed said as he repaired his composure, "you come down to one final thing, and that is, what is, is. History rewrites itself. The actual happenings are the will of God. It is the will of God. It is the will of God that we are here in Evansville."

"And at this moment in time," Kay added. "The people gathered here are very special." She glanced around the room at all of her volunteers. "My small women's group is instrumental in making so much of this happen. When I came back from meeting you in 2008, I went to my group and they saw the fire. They said, 'Okay, we are a part of it.' With blind faith they have done so much. Each of them has used her gifts to be a part of this."

Ed got emotional again, and then he said, "I am also so impressed with the man who owns this mall. I really appreciate him, and I think he appreciates this."

"I have many more stories," Kay said. "People with their souls and their hearts and their spirits, and what they have done for this exhibit. This is going to be amazing, Ed. Thank you for sharing your work with us."

After Kay departed, I asked Ed, "So what did you think, Mr. Ed, when you first came in and saw this?" We scanned the room.

"Boy, this is beautiful. It is really beautiful."

"Is it what you expected?"

"It is way more. The colors." Ed looked around the room again. "They did such a job here. You can imagine these walls being the purple color before, and see what they did to get this ready. The new buttery yellow blends so nicely with the panels. How they spent all of this time getting the room ready for us. Amazing."

"Do you remember all summer when we had our lunches, you expressed how worried you were about this?"

"Yes."

"What do you think now that you are finally here? After all of the worry and fear, what do you feel now?"

Ed rubbed his hand across his mouth in deep thought. "I feel amazed. This is greater than I thought it could be. I am very thankful." He turned to me and said, "The board is going to have to understand that the odds are that I won't be back in Petoskey. I am thinking about staying."

"You know what? I think you are probably right. I think this exhibit is going to give the panels wings, and they are going to be flying. This is just the first stop of many, Mr. Ed."

"Well, it can't get any higher than this or I'm going to have to go to the hospital."

"Why do you say that?"

"This is really hard on my heart. Yep. It is."

"Why?"

"It's so emotional for me. The anticipation. These people have volunteered and worked so hard, and they did it without knowing anything about me or seeing the panels."

"So is it hard on your heart because you are happy or because it is stressful?"

"I just feel that it can't get any higher than this. Nothing else will ever compare to this time here. I am quite sure of that."

"I keep thinking back to when we were in the warehouse. Those years, working and dreaming of something like this happening, and here you are. This is the first day of the panels finally traveling out of Michigan. Can you believe that?" I asked.

"There are so many new things that have started since I got here last night. From the time that I got here until now, individuals have come up and offered help. I will be flying from now on." Ed did his half laugh and half cry thing. "I won't be making that trip in a vehicle again. It will be in a private airplane. People involved in the Evansville group know a couple of pilots, and they will pick me up in Petoskey and bring me here to the airport. And someone will come get me."

"Good. It will be a lot easier on you."

"Now I have two homes." Ed's amber eyes glistened as water filled them.

"Petoskey and Evansville?" I asked as I thought about Ed's fear of being homeless again. I now felt reassured that he knew that would never happen again.

"Yep. I have been told that I can stay at the hotel anytime when I come into town, at no charge."

"What do you think about all of these people who have been volunteering over the last couple of days?" I asked.

"I think they have faith. They didn't know what this was all about, but they trusted God's will. I didn't know. I didn't know anything when I started the panels. I had an opportunity to do something and I did it. I don't know whether it is good or bad, but it is here. And you have to come to the conclusion that what is, is. And it is God's will, or it never could have happened, both negative and positive."

"I agree with that one hundred percent. Well you've come a long way, mister."

"Don't go getting me crying again. This is just overwhelming."

"I can't help it. I have seen you go from homeless to famous. And here you are."

"I'm just along for the ride. If there was some way that I could witness this and not be involved, I would," Ed said.

"I can understand that. You would love to be a fly on the wall, wouldn't you? To see people's reactions?"

"Yes," Ed laughed.

"Of all the people I have ever met, you deserve it, Mr. Ed."

Paul walked up with a young gentleman holding one of Ed's small boxes and gestured towards the man. "He worked all day installing your work and he wants to buy one of your pieces. Will you sign it for him?" Paul said.

The twenty-something-year-old man tugged at his baseball cap as he eagerly stood next to Paul. Ed held out his hands for the opened box, and Paul handed him a black Sharpie. Ed then very slowly signed his childlike signature inside the top lid. As Ed returned the box to the new owner, the man thanked him and held it tight to his chest. I sensed that he had been struggling in some way, and that holding that box to his heart was a way of healing his long-aching spirit. Maybe standing in the presence of Ed's children and the presence of God did the healing. I then looked at Ed and from his expression, I suspected that he felt the same way.

A few minutes later, a reporter from the local television station appeared. He introduced himself, and while Ed continued to sit in his chair, the man took off his coat and placed the television camera on a tripod directly in front of Ed. He sat down next to the camera and started asking Ed questions. Ed appeared to be nonchalant, or maybe it was his way of hiding his nervousness. This was not something that a man who had spent years in seclusion would be used to, but he did his best to answer every question.

They were the standard questions like "Tell me about this exhibit," "Tell me about your artwork," and "What or who was your inspiration?" Ed showed very little emotion as he answered each one. Finally, when the reporter asked the last question, "Is there anything else that you feel is important that you would like to add?" he leaned forward as if expecting something very profound.

Ed brightened right up. He turned his attention to me as the camera continued to roll and said playfully, "I think you should get LaShelle on here and talk about her involvement, as she is an artist too."

"Don't listen to him!" I squealed with crimson cheeks.

"And it is the only thing she knows how to do," Ed teased. "She's not a driver, that's for sure. Don't let her drive, even if she has a map." He chuckled. "She gets lost real easy."

As I was holding my breath wondering what he would say next, I now knew that he had not missed a thing while he was resting his eyes in the backseat of the Suburban.

Ed continued with his commentary. "She had us lost within five miles of this place. She made some wrong turns. We were thirty-five miles away and she still wanted to go on."

By now the entire gallery had erupted into laughter as Ed explained my poor navigating skills to the roomful of people. He then offered his final advice. "If you want to get lost, get directions from her." Laughter echoed around the room again as the reporter thanked Ed for his time and the entertainment.

That evening, October 16, 2009, was the grand opening of the exhibit. Susan McCool, one of the Sonshine girls, and her husband, Joe, had volunteered to organize the opening night and a dinner. The dinner was held just outside the gallery doors in the hallway of the mall, and all of the food was donated by Shylar's Bar-B-Q. Long tables were lined up and each was covered with white linen. They invited many people from local churches and the community, but most important to Ed was that they had invited the homeless population from Evansville.

As the meal was served, the Evansville group, the My Father's Love board members, church members, community members, and the homeless all shared their meal together. A saxophonist from Germany opened the evening with a beautiful version of "Amazing Grace" as large groups of people filled the gallery. Ed was well rested from sitting in his chair most of the day, and was dressed proudly in his same pinstriped suit, but he wore a fresh blue dress shirt.

As I walked around the gallery and observed the exhibit Evansville had put together, I was amazed. The room was beautifully painted and decorated, including a well-designed floor arrangement for the panels devised by Kathy Perdue, and a prayer room in the back designed by Jill Kincaid. Music stands that had been donated by H&H Music held information sheets written by Jana Kastle about the meaning of each panel. Benches were strategically placed throughout the room so that visitors could sit and quietly observe Ed's work. When I watched the video that Johnny Kincaid had produced, I cried.

I then noticed a framed sign thanking all of the organizations and individual people who had donated to this *My Father's Love* exhibit. There were both religious and secular partners who had helped bring the panels to Evansville. My heart swelled with appreciation as I read each name. I was blown away when I read a list of churches, all different denominations. This was a grassroots movement: Baptist, Catholic, Presbyterian, and Methodist, to name a few, all coming together to bring Ed's life's work to their community. When people asked what church was sponsoring the exhibit, the answer was, "The body of Christ all brought together by God."

Kay shared with me what she had written in her journal. *The Lord said, 'Don't draw a line in the sand. There are no boundaries.' No saying that I am from this faith and you are from that faith. It was just a coming together of God's community.*

These churches not only donated money, but also time. Since the exhibit would be open until Christmas, many of them were signed up for a week at a time as volunteer tour guides. Welborn Baptist Foundation and The Daniel Headlee Foundation had also given a significant grant. I wanted to know more about The Daniel Headlee Foundation, so I asked around and soon found myself standing in front of one of the most heartfelt women I had ever met. Her name was Barbara Headlee, and she shared her story about her son Daniel with me.

Daniel had been killed in a car accident when he was a college student at Indiana University in 1979, and Barbara explained the pain she had felt when a policeman came to her door to give her the news. She and her husband Jack had set up a foundation in honor of their son, and the grant from that foundation had helped launch the Evansville exhibit. Because of that, Ed had had the chance to witness the power of his work in a community that didn't know him. Now he would know for sure whether he had done the Lord justice and whether he had done his job well.

Ed used to say that when he left this dimension and met the Father for the first time, the words he hoped to hear were, "Well done, my good and faithful servant. Well done." Those words were the only thing that mattered to him. Witnessing his children at work in a foreign place, a place where he knew no one and no one knew him, was the only way he would know for certain whether he had succeeded. I believe that God graciously granted this gift to Ed for his years of sacrifice and obedience. God wanted Ed to know that he indeed had performed a "job well done."

After I talked to Barbara, I focused my attention on Ed. He was giving his first tour to a large group of people. There were cameras flashing as people listened to his description of the symbolism in each panel. Emotion overcame me again as I watched my dear friend share his masterpiece with the crowd.

I thought about his fears of coming to Evansville, his fear of people seeing him with limited balance and declining physical health. A lump formed in my throat as I noted the look of sheer reverence on everyone's face. Every single person in that room was in awe of him and his children. After touring for an hour, I could see that he was getting tired, but I knew that he recognized the warmth and the open arms from Evansville, Indiana.

When the tour was over, Ed steered his walker towards me with a weary smile on his face. I smiled back as he approached.

"You did it, Mr. Ed! You did a wonderful job! I am so proud of you!"

"Thank you, kid," Ed said with satisfaction. "By the way, I have made my decision. I am definitely not going home."

As we hugged, I felt that Ed was finally at peace. He knew that this was where he needed to be. Maybe it was because he was comfortable now that he felt the love around him, but I believe more than anything that it was because he couldn't leave his children. The thought of going back to Northern Michigan without them was just too much to endure.

I walked with Ed back to his chair near the front window so he could sit for a bit before we departed for the night. "Are you sure you aren't staying so you have more time to find your soul mate?" I teased.

"Kid, you found me out. I can't hide anything from you, can I?"

"Nope," I laughed. "Well I guess you will have to find her on your own now." We both squealed as we sat down side by side.

One person after another stopped by Ed's chair before they exited the gallery for the night. A homeless man in his early twenties stopped by to shake Ed's hand and thank him for their earlier conversation. Some of the homeless who attended the dinner lived on the streets, and some lived in shelters. This person was living at the United Caring Shelter. After the dinner, Ed and the young man sat together and talked for a long time. When the young man finished his conversation with Ed, he approached one of the volunteers, Linda Yunker, and said, "Thank you for inviting all of us. I really enjoyed the meal."

"You are so welcome," Linda said.

"I am one of the fortunate ones because at least I have a car. Some nights I sleep in my car. I don't have much gas, but I am going to bring my mother in here so she can see the panels."

"That is wonderful," said Linda.

Then the young man said, "You know, it is time to get my life back together."

No one knew what Ed had said to him, but whatever it was, it had had a powerful impact.

I continued to observe Ed's reaction as people said their goodbyes.

"You did a beautiful job," one man said.

"It's amazing to see what God allows to transpire if we use the talents He gives us. It has been a blessing, thank you. It is wonderful," said another.

A middle-aged woman was exiting the gallery when she stopped in the doorway and turned towards Ed. "My father, the two things he was passionate about were Jesus and woodworking, and if he was still alive, I think he would be sitting in here with you and probably would be studying from the master for the day."

Ed smiled and thanked her. The appreciation for Ed's work was overwhelming, and he sat back taking in every word. I could see his mind working, and I wondered what he was thinking. One thing I knew for certain: Ed now believed that every second he had sacrificed for his job was worth it.

Before he left for the evening, he saw an elderly woman heading towards him. She was crying. I could see that he was puzzled. The woman grabbed Ed's hand and started shaking it vigorously. "You, sir, are in favor of the Lord," she said through her tears.

"Well, thank you very much," he said.

"May I give you a hug?"

"Yes," he said.

She kissed Ed on his left shoulder and then wrapped her arms around him and squeezed. A moment later, she released him and looked directly into his eyes and said, "Well done, well done."

As the woman walked away, Ed watched her leave, and I could tell that he was feeling the presence of the Father all around him.

I noticed a little boy sprawled out on one of the benches. He was obviously tired after a long day. The boy observed as each person talked to Ed. He then sat up and scanned the panels around him. He stood up and walked over to a panel and put his tiny pointer finger on one of the diamonds. He then moved towards Ed and stood directly in front of him and asked, "How did you do this?"

"With the help of my Father," Ed smiled.

"Well, you and your father did a good job with all the little pieces," the child said as he skipped away and then sprawled back out onto the bench to wait for his family. Ed looked at the boy and then above with one tear resting in the corner of his left eye.

"Are you okay?" I asked.

"I am wonderful, kid. Just wonderful."

The next evening after the gallery closed, Ken and I escorted Ed to Kay and Steve's home for a pizza party. They put together a casual evening so that Ed and the My Father's Love board members could get to know the Evansville group better.

I noticed that Ed was very quiet throughout the evening. He sat in a chair in deep thought through most of it. There was no doubt in my mind that he was thinking about everything that had happened the last couple of days. Towards the end of the evening, I sat near him. Kay entered the room and said, "Ed and LaShelle, remember when Steve and I went to see the panels the first time and we took a couple with us, Judy and Tom Terrell?" Ed and I both nodded. "Well, Judy called to tell me the most amazing story. She and Tom have a winter home in Sarasota, Florida. While there, she went to the local Dairy Queen to pick something up, and she had Traverse City, Michigan on her license plate. When she stepped out, there was a young man sitting on the curb. He was in a Dairy Queen uniform, so he obviously was taking a break. He asked her, "Are you from Traverse City?" and she said, "No, but I have a place there."

"Well, I am from that area," he told her.

"Where?"

"Kalkaska."

She then mentioned that she had been to an art exhibit by an artist from Kalkaska named Ed Lantzer. The young man's eyes lit up and he said, "Oh, I learned how to do that from him. My art teacher used to take us there every day to work with him, and he taught us. I made a jewelry box for my mother!" Ed and I looked at each other in shock as Kay finished her story. She said, "It sure is a small world, isn't it? It is amazing how the Lord brings things full circle."

It had been several years since our school project, and I knew how much that time had meant to me. I often wondered if my students felt the same way. In that full circle moment, I no longer had to wonder.

Before Ken and I headed back to Northern Michigan, Ed received two gifts. Dr. Ramsey presented him with a gift from the Evansville group. It was an interlinear Bible with Hebrew, Greek, and English translations. In the bottom right corner, the words "My Father's Love, Evansville IN" were engraved in gold. Ed was so honored to receive the book, and he spent a great deal of time reading it as he sat in his chair at the gallery.

Ed still loved to learn everything that he could, and he told me that one of these days he needed to buy *Strong's Exhaustive Concordance of the Bible.* That comment led to the second gift. I whispered to Ken, "As soon as I get a chance, I need to get that for him." Ken whispered back, "Never put off until tomorrow what you should have done yesterday. Let's do it now."

We darted to Barnes and Noble and purchased the book. Before I gave it to Ed, I wrote a note to him on the inside cover. It said:

My Dear Friend Ed,
 10-18-09
My hope is that in this book you will find the knowledge you are looking for because I can never repay you for the

things you have given me as my teacher and mentor. Such things as: Strength, knowledge, love, compassion, but most of all friendship.

You have taught me to live a truly authentic life and also to discover the artist that lives within me.

Thank you for being my true friend and even though I will not always be with you, you will always be in a special place in my heart.

Forever my friend,
LaShelle

When Ken and I returned, I handed Ed his second gift. He carefully read each word, and then he looked at me and said, his voice shaking, "Thank you so much, kid. Thank you."

43

*"No man can be an exile if he remembers
that all the world is one city."*

C.S. Lewis, Till We Have Faces

Since Ed had decided to stay, the Evansville group had to make more arrangements so that he was taken care of. The owner of the HomeLife Studios and Suites where Ed was staying said that he could stay as long as he wanted at no charge. The Evansville group took turns transporting him to and from the gallery. They also kept his room stocked with food and took food to the gallery for him

The biggest dilemma, however, was how to get Ed to eat. He had struggled with eating for years, so the fact that he wouldn't eat came as no surprise to the board members, but it did alarm them. Ed would occasionally eat a peanut butter sandwich, bananas, and vanilla wafers, so these items were always on hand. If someone was assigned to pick him up in the morning, they often took him to breakfast. Ed always ordered the same thing, but it would vary depending on who was taking him to breakfast. For instance, when he went with Terry and Linda Yunker, he would specifically order six strips of bacon. When he went with Bob Ho, he ordered two eggs, no bacon. He never ate much, and each time he ordered the same amount. Ed's brain was always functioning in a mathematical way, even when it came to breakfast. Before they left the restaurant, Ed would also take time to flirt with the waitresses. He was taking his job of finding his soul mate very seriously.

Ed had another ritual. When he arrived at the Washington Square Mall he would do two things before he went into the gallery. First, he would stop at Hahn Realty, which was just around the corner from the gallery, to flirt with a gal named Q who worked there. Ed assured everyone that she was in love with him. He would then stop at a store called Just Cookies to order black coffee or a Coke with extra sugar packets to add to it. It normally took him thirty minutes to make it to the exhibit. When it was Michael and Kitty Williams's turn to take him to the gallery, Michael looked at his watch while Ed flirted and said, "Ed, I have to go to work."

"Can't you see I am talking to my girl here?" Ed responded with a smirk. One thing was for sure: he and Q had many laughs together.

One evening when the gallery was slow, Alan and Nancy Sanderson were volunteering as docents. Alan sat down to talk with Ed. Their conversation went on for about thirty minutes or so, and the impact of that conversation on Alan was as profound as always. Then Ed opened his hand, and lying in his palm was one of his diamond-shaped pieces of wood. Ed looked at the wood and at Alan and then placed the piece in Alan's hand. "Keep this for me, will you?" Alan put the diamond in the front pocket of his slacks, and at that moment made a decision that this would be a part of his getting dressed routine every morning. When he put his pocketbook in his pants, the diamond would go too.

Ed gave scheduled tours for the community and schools from three states: Indiana, Kentucky, and Illinois. The schools brought students on field trips to meet Ed and view the exhibit. As Ed watched the students make configurations out of his diamond pieces, his heart warmed. He had always had a soft spot for children, and seeing them reminded him that the purpose of his work was for the unloved child. Whether it be spiritually, financially, or artistically, this was important to him. He wanted to make sure that every child felt loved as he had not.

Educating these school children was very special to Ed. Many of the children returned to the exhibit with their parents. One little boy was five or six years old, and when he brought his parents to see the panels, they said, "He would not stop talking until we came to see the exhibit, so here we are." The William Henry Harrison High School Choir performed with their vocal teacher, Kristi Miller, in the gallery on several occasions. There were also two homeschooled families who asked to sing in the presence of the mural: the Hollander family and the Toon family. Their first visit to the exhibit was spontaneous, but after that they were invited back several times to sing.

Employees from other stores in the mall also came in to see what was going on. Two men from Sears walked in on their lunch hour and said, "We had to come see this because it is the talk of the town."

There was one gallery visitor who touched Ed's heart more than any other, a nine-year-old named Nathan. Nathan's grandparents, Terry and Linda Yunker, were volunteers, and during one of their shifts, they decided to bring Nathan to meet Ed. Ed and Nathan bonded immediately. After the first visit, Nathan insisted on accompanying his grandparents when they volunteered so that he could see Ed. The most amazing part of this story is that Nathan is high-functioning autistic. One of the biggest challenges that a child with high-functioning autism struggles with is interacting with others. They typically want to be involved with others, but they lack the skills. When Nathan met Ed, they made a connection that stunned his grandparents. Their grandson connecting with someone like that was not something they had experienced before. But each time Nathan entered the gallery, he pulled up a chair right beside Ed and sat with him for hours.

As Terry and Linda gave tours of the panels, Ed and Nathan talked. The Yunkers had no idea what they were talking about, but they were obviously in tune with each other. It was as if their spirits were interacting. Soon, Terry and Linda found themselves picking Nathan up from school and bringing him directly to the gallery on a daily basis. When Ed spotted Nathan coming around the corner, he would light up and say, "Here comes my buddy!" Nathan would grin from ear to ear as he ran to Ed and leapt into his arms. Then he would pull his chair as close to Ed as it would go and sit down to chat. If Ed was too tired to talk and needed to rest, Nathan would just sit with his new friend and rub his hand or his arm. When they weren't in the gallery, Terry, Linda, and Nathan would take Ed to see all of the historical sights around Evansville, like the Newburg riverfront of the Ohio River or the private gardens, which was really touching for Ed. Before leaving the mall, Nathan would take on the job of pushing Ed on the seat of his walker. Nathan loved that, and Ed enjoyed the ride too.

One evening after a long day, they took Ed back to his hotel. They escorted him in safely, as they always did, and then Nathan excitedly said to Ed, "I have a gift for you."

"You do?" Ed said in surprise. Ed took off his pinstriped suit jacket and sat on the corner of the bed. Nathan then handed Ed a small red gift bag. Ed first pulled out a photograph that Nathan and Ed had taken together. "This is wonderful! Thank you!" Ed said.

"There is something else," Nathan said eagerly. Ed then reached back into the bag and pulled out a wooden praying cross. His heart swelled with joy.

"Thank you, buddy. This is so beautiful!" Ed gently put the cross down and said, "I have something for you too." He shuffled to his belongings and returned with a bag of small wooden crosses he'd had a friend make for him. "I want you to pick out the cross that you want."

"Okay." Nathan looked through the collection and selected his favorite.

"Now, I am going to pick out one for you that I want you to keep for your girlfriend when you get older."

Ed selected a cross with a lighter wood grain and handed it to Nathan. Nathan blushed and his eyes sparkled through his wire-framed glasses as he accepted.

"Thanks. I like these a lot."

"You're so welcome, buddy," Ed responded and patted Nathan's crown of short blonde hair.

As much as Ed enjoyed communicating with Nathan, he didn't always feel the same about other visitors to the exhibit. Most of the time, he would sit down and have a conversation with absolutely anyone. He would have all of the time in the world for those visitors. But every once in a while, he would look at someone and say, "I don't want to talk to this person," or "I don't want anything to do with that person." It was as if God were giving him an instant read on someone. Sometimes the person was considered upstanding and respectable to everyone else, but Ed could see something that others could not. He could see what their motives were and maybe even something much darker.

Whatever the explanation was, it worried the Evansville group. They didn't want anyone to be offended. Ed did this one evening when volunteer Kitty Williams was there, and she thought, *I am going to go talk to that same person and see if I get a feel.* But it didn't work. She wanted to know what Ed knew, but she couldn't figure it out. As a result, the docents kept aware and tried to intervene as quickly as possible when it did happen.

During Ed's stay in Evansville, different people took on different roles to keep him as comfortable as possible. Kay's role was much like Paul's role in Michigan. Her priority was to make sure all of Ed's needs were met. Steve was in charge of locking up the gallery every evening. He knew how to work the security system, and he felt that he should be the one to take on that role. Even if Steve was in the middle of something, he would drop everything to run to the gallery to close it up. If there was a reason that he could not carry out his duties, he could count on volunteer John Welcher to fill his shoes. Ed trusted Steve and Kay, and he knew how much they cared.

Steve and Kay also had to take Ed to the dentist. Ed started having trouble with his dentures. He had been losing weight because of his limited eating, so they became loose and started moving around in his mouth. This created painful sores. Kay convinced Ed to go to the dentist, which would not normally be an easy task, but the pain was excruciating, and Ed would do anything to make it stop. Kay contacted her local dentist and told him the situation. Kay's dentist was known as a giving Christian man in the community and often helped patients who couldn't afford dental work. He said, "Bring him in." When the work was complete, Kay pulled out her wallet to pay. He pushed the money away and said, "Oh no, that is okay."

Barbara Headlee and her daughter, Jana Kastle, would sit and talk with Ed when it was their turn to volunteer, and as a result, both women felt their faith grow. Their faith also grew each time they gave a tour of the panels. Jana explained that she gained faith just being a docent. Being able to talk about the panels and talking to strangers about her faith gave her faith a boost. When the docents explained the symbolism, for example, relating to how each disciple died in *The Last Supper*, it was like a master's course, and it was very clear to everyone how much Ed had studied.

Johnny Kincaid's wife, Jill, also played a large part in taking care of Ed. She was a caretaker of the exhibit and she became another of Ed's buddies. Jill was the person Ed would tell what he did or didn't need. She realized early on that he didn't need much, even when he had it. When Ed was in the hotel, he had a television with cable, probably for the first time in his life. But instead of channel surfing and watching TV for hours like most people would in his situation, he had it tuned to the Weather Channel. That was it. Rather than watch TV, he sat in the hotel window and people-watched, just like he did in the gallery. Life was his TV.

Ed was more interested in life than in taking care of himself. He wore the same clothes every day: his blue pinstriped suit and white dress shirt. He even slept in his clothes and didn't want to take them off. Jill would come in and say, "Ed why don't you change and I will take those to the cleaners for you." He'd refuse. Jill would say, "All right, Spanky, you're dirty, take them off." Ed didn't want anyone doing his laundry because of his deteriorating physical condition. The Evansville group had money set aside for things that Ed might need, so instead, Jill finally convinced Ed to go shopping for some underclothing.

One day at the mall, while Jill and Ed were joking around and racing with his walker and her shopping cart, Ed teased, "I must have flannel sheets," as they barreled down an aisle and past the sheet section.

"Sure," Jill responded, hoping that she could get him to buy something.

"Can I get two pair so I can have one at home and one at my hotel?"

"Of course you can."

"Really?" Ed said as he stopped. "Is it asking too much to get two sets so I have one for each place?"

"I will get you whatever you want. I'm your sugar momma!" Jill said as Ed roared with laughter.

Ed's time in Evansville was thoroughly enjoyable for him, and every time I talked to him on the phone, he expressed that. After a few weeks, however, he flew back to Petoskey. He came home to attend a concert by the Little Traverse Choral Society. The LTCS commissioned a nationally known jazz musician and composer, Wendel Werner, to compose six songs based on six of Ed's panels that would be grouped together and entitled "My Father's Love." When Ed was told months before about this, he was moved to tears. When the first song was ready, it was to be included in a fall concert, and Ed was invited to be there. A private pilot and acquaintance of Kay's volunteered his plane and time to fly Ed home. When Ed left, we were all unsure when and if he planned to go back to Evansville, so we decided to be prepared either way. After a week, Ed called Paul and said, "I need to go back now." He was missing his children and a week away was enough.

44

"Christians never say goodbye."

*C.S. Lewis, C.S. Lewis to Sheldon Vanauken
in A Severe Mercy*

When Ed returned, the Evansville group noticed a grave change in him. He seemed much weaker than before. Prior to his trip back to Michigan, Ed had given tours and talked with most of the visitors. Now, he barely talked to anyone and did not have enough energy to continue the tours. Even his visits with Nathan were less animated. After he arrived at the gallery each day, the docents noticed that he would fall asleep as soon as he sat in his chair. He was also eating less than before. When the volunteers took turns picking him up and taking him to breakfast, they observed that he was consuming even less, if that was at all possible. Another concern was that he was having trouble walking, so they dropped him off as close to the restaurant as they could, maybe ten steps from the door. Even so, it took Ed five minutes to get there.

Steve and Kay were alarmed and made a couple of phone calls, one to Paul and one to Dale. They shared their concerns and asked that they schedule a doctor's appointment for Ed before the holidays, when he was to return home. Ed wanted to stay with his panels until the exhibit ended on December 23rd, but everyone involved worried whether it would be better for his health if he stayed in Petoskey. Leaving the panels was not an option for him, so the Evansville group continued to do their best to keep him comfortable.

Even though Kay and the volunteers noticed a change in him, Ed never complained about how he was feeling, ever. Did he sense that his health was declining but didn't want to leave the panels? That is very possible, but when I talked to him, he would never say a word about his health.

Towards the end of November 2009, I called to check on Ed. He answered on the third ring.

"Hello, kid," he said.

"Hi, Mr. Ed. What are you up to?" I asked.

"I'm just sitting in the window at the gallery watching the walkers go by."

"How are you doing?"

"I'm doing fine," he said. I didn't believe him. From the tone of his voice, he seemed down.

"Kay told me that we've had over nine thousand visitors so far. They put a counter in the doorway after the first week and it keeps track for us."

"That's incredible, Mr. Ed! Nine thousand people?"

"Yep." There was silence for a few seconds and then Ed said, "Dale said the owner of the Petoskey gallery needs us to move out so he can lease it."

I then understood the sadness in his voice.

"Yes, it is time," I said. "I think we have overstayed our welcome. He has been so generous to give us the building for so long. Way longer than we agreed on."

"I know. He has been wonderful. I am going to miss it, though," he said. "I miss a lot of things. I really miss my Monday morning breakfasts with Dale and the farmers."

"I am sure they will be happy to see you when you get back."

"Me too," Ed chuckled. "You know, I was thinking about singing lately. I miss that too. I try to sing in my room when I am alone sometimes, but I just don't have as much energy as I used to."

"What songs do you sing?"

"Oh, songs from *The Phantom of the Opera* and *Fiddler on the Roof.* Maybe I will wait until I get home and listen to them on tape. I have a cassette of *Phantom of the Opera.*"

"What about *Fiddler on the Roof*? Do you have that one?"

"No."

"Have you ever watched that movie?"

"Oh yes. It's my all-time favorite."

"Well, maybe when you get home, we can rent it and watch it together."

"Oh, I would love that."

"Okay, it's a date."

As Christmas neared, more people came to view the murals. Christmas music danced around the panels and faces seemed brighter and cheerier, like they often do during that magical time of year. The number on the people counter on the door seemed to grow exponentially each day. The *My Father's Love* exhibit was alive and so was the mall. It was more alive in the Washington Square Mall than it had been in so many years. Since Ed and his panels had arrived in mid-October, business in the mall had more than doubled for Ed's favorite store, Just Cookies, as well as many others. Ed watched group after group take a tour of his life's work.

One night as Barbara Headlee was talking to visitors after a tour, Ed observed the viewers' expressions. He noticed the look of astonishment and admiration on their faces. He then sent a message upward. *Father, I just cannot believe this. You have granted me the most precious gift. Thank you for showing this to me. Thank you for sparing my life long enough to see that look on their faces. Every second that I have spent working has been worth it. Thank you for choosing me, Father. Thank you."*

Barbara told me later that she had noticed a man walking towards her. The man just stood there for a moment with tears in his eyes. Barbara did not recognize him and wasn't sure if she should have. Then he said, "I am the trooper who came to your door to tell you about your son." Barbara was shocked, and her eyes filled with emotion. The officer had been compelled to come to the exhibit after he'd read that the Daniel Headlee Foundation had given it a grant. In that full-circle moment, Barbara reached over and hugged him. "Thank you for coming. This means so much to me," she said.

As the December 23rd deadline and the end of the *My Father's Love* exhibit in Evansville neared, so did Ed's time there. Ed was ready to take his children home, and he felt that when he returned to Petoskey, it was time to start his last panel. He had had several ideas for new panels over the years, but he decided that *The Resurrection* would be his last child. He had only another week in Evansville, and it was time to start making his plans. Ed shared his ideas with the Evansville group for the last panel, and each member was excited and encouraging.

On December 17, 2009, Ed had the biggest surprise of his life. Johnny Kincaid felt that the impact Ed had had on so many lives in Evansville in such a short amount of time was beyond belief and understanding. How could an elderly man, once homeless, once considered crazy and treated like an outcast in society, make this kind of impression? Johnny made a phone call to the mayor of Evansville to share Ed's story. That call led to one of the most important events in Ed's life. It was the day that finally gave him closure, a day that put a period on the end of his long turbulent life and story. December 17, 2009 became Ed Lantzer Day in Evansville, Indiana. After all that Ed had gone through during his lifetime, he now had a day named after him.

When the mayor of Evansville, Jonathan Weinzapfel, first arrived at the gallery, he was introduced to Ed. The mayor had generously taken time out of his busy schedule to read the proclamation. There was only a short time before he had to leave for his next appointment, so as he and Ed talked, he looked at his watch every few seconds trying to keep track of his timetable. But it didn't take long before the mayor was drawn in and Ed asked his usual question, "Would you like a tour?" The mayor looked at his watch again and said, "Okay."

Ed escorted Mayor Weinzapfel to each panel and explained the symbolism. As the mayor inspected the panels, it was evident to everyone that he was truly amazed. The look on his face said, "I am trying to figure out how Ed did this." As Ed explained more, the mayor's look said, *No, really, how did you do this?* He was dumbfounded, just like everyone else who viewed the panels for the first time.

As the tour went on, Ed and the mayor started to joke back and forth. They were both having a good time, and Ed was honored and tickled to give a tour to such a prestigious man. After about forty-five minutes, it was time to officially start the event. Mayor Weinzapfel appeared in front of *The Last Supper*, the first seven of Ed's children, to declare the day Ed Lantzer Day in the city of Evansville. In his blue pinstripe suit and white dress shirt, Ed stood next to the mayor with pride. Then the mayor said, "Since I saw the article in the newspaper—what, a couple of months ago already?—detailing Mr. Lantzer and his work and how it is displayed here in Evansville, I have been wanting to come out and see for myself." Ed nervously scratched his head as he listened. The mayor looked at Ed and continued.

"Obviously it is a labor of love and a labor of faith. It is an inspiration to a lot of people in this community." He then started reading the proclamation to Ed as a roomful of people watched and listened.

"This is a Proclamation from the city of Evansville. Whereas, Ed Lantzer is an artist from Kalkaska Michigan..." The mayor looked up and asked, "Which is up near Traverse City?" Ed nodded. He continued as Ed stared at the paper in the mayor's hand. "Whose 30-panel work of art entitled 'My Father's Love' is on display at Washington Square Mall in Evansville from October 17 through December 23, and Whereas, this is the first time 'My Father's Love' has been displayed outside of Michigan; and Whereas, each four foot panel of 'My Father's Love' depicts a scene from the life of Christ and is comprised of thousands of small wooden diamond-shaped blocks cut either on a 30 or 60 degree angle; and Whereas, this technique, called Marquetry, was passed down in Ed Lantzer's family for eight generations; and Whereas, Ed Lantzer devoted more than 30 years of his life to create 'My Father's Love,' and much of the work was done while he was homeless; and Whereas, approximately more than 15,000 Evansville residents have viewed 'My Father's Love' at Washington Square Mall; and Whereas, the display has remained open to the public free of charge because Ed Lantzer feels strongly that everyone should have the opportunity to experience his work regardless of their financial means; and Whereas, Ed Lantzer's wish is that somehow his work may benefit unloved children whether it be spiritually, financially or artistically . . ."

Ed fought back tears when he heard the words "unloved children" and sniffled. He rubbed his nose hoping to stop the flow, but he couldn't. This moment was too emotional. He then looked up from the proclamation and directly into the audience while the mayor read on.

"Whereas, the culture of Evansville is enriched by the artwork of Ed Lantzer and many lives have been touched by viewing the awe-inspiring scenes from the Bible. Therefore, be it resolved that I, Jonathan Weinzapfel, Mayor of the great city of Evansville, do hereby proclaim December 17, 2009 as Ed Lantzer Day in the city of Evansville, Indiana."

"Thank you very much," Ed said with a tremor in his voice. The crowd erupted with cheer as flashbulbs bounced around the room like fireflies on a summer night.

"Let me remind you, this does not serve as a get out of jail free card," the mayor said. The crowd laughed as Mayor Weinzapfel handed the proclamation to Ed.

"Oh, right," Ed said as that familiar mischievous look came over his face. "Well, I would be the first taker on that." The mayor laughed, and the crowd erupted again as Ed said very modestly, "Thank you."

"My pleasure. Thank you," said the mayor.

Over the next few days, Ed beamed. He had been recognized in a way he had never expected or really needed. But knowing that his work was appreciated like that meant so much to him. He hoped this meant his children would continue to make an impression, even long after he was gone.

When Steve and Kay picked Ed up a day or two later, Ed said, "You know, when I go back to Petoskey, if anyone gives me any trouble, I will say that I know the mayor of Evansville."

Four days after Ed Lantzer Day was declared, Ed went home for the final time. Plans were being made by the Evansville group and the My Father's Love board members to keep the panels in Evansville longer. Since the storefront in Petoskey needed to be cleared out, the only alternative was for the panels to be stored in the garage in Elk Rapids again, or in the cube truck. Kay was working on getting more time in the Washington Square Mall so that Ed's panels would not have to be homeless again. But everyone involved felt that Ed needed to go home. He was still weak, and it was time for him to recuperate in his own apartment, where he had nurses to watch over him.

On the morning of December 21st, Ed went to check on his children one last time before he left. He spent time with each one, and then employees from the mall who had been touched by Ed and his work came down to have their picture taken with him. Many of the Evansville group and volunteers also came to say their final goodbyes. Ed had his suitcase with him ready to go. Inside was a special gift he had received from a group of prisoners who were residents of the Wabash Valley Correctional Facility.

Wabash had started a program in which inmates quilted. The prisoners made the quilts by hand, cutting each piece of fabric with safety scissors. They donated them to people or families in need. For example, they created a quilt for the family of every service man or woman from Indiana who had died in the Gulf War.

When Johnny Kincaid, who was part of a ministry group that served the facility, shared Ed's story with the prisoners, they decided to make Ed a quilt. At the time the inmates made Ed's quilt, they had been doing a huge number of quilts for homeless shelters around the state. Johnny told them about Ed's years of homelessness, and many of the prisoners could relate because they had been homeless too. They were so intrigued by his story that they felt compelled to make one for Ed.

The quilt was securely placed inside Ed's suitcase as he prepared to leave for the airport. Jill Kincaid asked him, "Can I see your quilt?"

"You're not getting into my suitcase," Ed responded in their usual joking manner.

"Come on, let me see it," Jill joked back.

"Nope."

"Listen, Spanky, I just want to see it. I won't let anything happen to it."

"I'm sorry. I can't. This quilt is just too precious, and I don't want anything to happen to it."

Ed was more than touched by the kindness of the inmates who'd created his quilt. It reminded him of his own battles with the law. He knew that each one of those men had a story, and each one also had a heart, just like he did.

As Ed left for the airport, each member of the group thought about the impact he had had on Evansville and their individual lives. It had been tremendous and unexpected. Ed had touched the lives of many of the homeless population in their area as well. After the opening night, which the homeless attended, many of them came back multiple times, and many of them brought guests.

As for the Evansville group, they had all come away changed in some way. Each person had learned that sometimes things are not as they appear. At first glance, Ed did not look like a person who would create a masterpiece for the Lord. Although, who is to say what someone like that should look like? Ed was often unkempt and expressionless. Sometimes he wore a scowl between his amber eyes. Some might even say that he looked scary. But in the end, he proved that appearance means nothing. It is what you do with this life that means everything.

Evansville saw that Ed had done something meaningful with his life, and he did it on such a grand scale with so little, yet many of us have so much and do so little. We often go through our days and think that the things we do are insignificant. Ed taught Evansville not to ignore or take for granted some of the things that seem insignificant. Instead, they now had hope that at the end of their days, when they recognized the period at the end of their sentence, that each one of them would have done what the Lord called them to do.

Ed was inspiring to them because the Holy Spirit was so evident in him. When they looked at those panels, they understood there was no way just one man could have created them, except through the Holy Spirit. Even when Ed was expressionless, he and his panels still burned with the Holy Spirit continuously, and that was what moved each and every person who walked through the gallery doors. Some members of the group felt that they were in the presence of a saint, and others believed that Ed was the equivalent of Michelangelo or Da Vinci. This was a long way from a man who had been treated like he was worthless for so many years.

Jill Kincaid said so powerfully, "My book that I am never going to write would be called *Face Value*. Some people saw Ed as a homeless loser with no value. They just took one look at him and labeled him. On the other hand, some people viewed him as Sir Edgar Lantzer, the artist, and they revered him at face value just based on his work. He was neither. He was neither worthless nor a saint. He was just Ed, a simple man. I saw him as the person, Ed. Others revered him, but he didn't want to be revered. He was human and he was flattered, but he didn't want to be worshipped. His love was for the Lord only. That was his heart, and part of him probably didn't feel like he deserved it anyway. Both views were wrong. He wasn't a worthless homeless person and he wasn't a revered saint. He was just Ed. Just a guy. That is how I saw him, my friend."

Jill walked away from this experience realizing that nothing could be taken at face value. "I would have been that person who would say, 'I am not rolling down my car window and handing him five dollars.' He taught me a lot about respecting people, and he taught me a lot about seeing homeless people in a completely different light," she said.

The one thing everyone agreed on was that Ed and his children represented hope and encouragement. They were grateful that Ed was willing to share his gift with strangers because in the beginning, that is what they were to him, just strangers. Over 15,000 people came through the gallery before Ed left, and by the time the panels traveled home months later, the number would grow to over 25,000. The beautiful part is that those 25,000 people went on to touch many, many more. Visitors came from all walks of life and a wide variety of geographical locations, which included seven different nations: the United States, Canada, Haiti, Kenya, Uganda, Germany, and France. There were thirty-two states, including Alaska, and over 250 cities were represented, and those were only the ones that were documented. The mural coming to Evansville, often known as the city of refuge, was for Ed, but it was also for Evansville. The mural came and did the job it was intended to do, and in the end, it made a deposit on their land that would forever leave a footprint.

When Kay said her final goodbyes to Ed, both were emotional. It was hard to believe all that had transpired since her first visit to the Petoskey gallery in the summer of 2008. When she first laid her eyes on the panels, she knew that she had no choice. This was her purpose at that time in her life, to bring the mural to her community to make a change in many lives, no matter the cost. And that they did. It was more than Kay and Ed could have imagined.

As Ed walked out of the Evansville exhibit for the last time, he said, "Well, it is time for me to go home and get back to work." Kay knew for certain that she would never be the same, and no matter what twists and turns her life would take in the future, she would take with her the biggest message of all that she had received from Ed: "Don't worry about it. The Father will provide."

Ed traveled to the airport with Terry and Linda Yunker for his final flight back to Petoskey. Another acquaintance of Kay's volunteered his piloting services and plane to fly Ed home in style. As Ed waited in the terminal for his departure, Nathan sat by his side as he did in the gallery every day after school. Both knew that saying goodbye was not going to be easy. Nathan leaned against Ed's arm and rubbed it. When it was time, they looked at each other and Nathan began to sob. He sobbed and sobbed, and Ed cried with him.

"Ed?" Nathan asked. "When will I see you again?"

Nathan's bottom lip quivered as he waited for an answer. Ed knew that he was going home for the last time, but he didn't want to worry his new friend. Tears rolled down both of their faces and Ed replied, "Buddy, you're going to have to come and see me next time."

Ed bent down and wrapped Nathan in his arms and squeezed as Nathan continued to sob. The little boy who had spent his young years struggling to express his feelings was now feeling so strongly, and Ed knew what that was all about. He too had spent his life struggling to show love. His fear of hurting the ones he loved was always in the forefront of his mind, and he had walked away because of it, but with this little boy, he didn't care. He decided to open his heart for the first time in a long time. As a result, Nathan was able to open his too. Nathan put his face up to the terminal window and watched Ed push his walker over the asphalt towards the small aircraft. He watched a man assist Ed into the plane, and he watched as the twin-engine plane rolled down the runway and lifted into the air and gradually disappeared.

45

"If you love deeply, you're going to get hurt badly. But it's still worth it."

C.S. Lewis, Shadowlands

One of the My Father's Love board members, Harold "Woody" Woodruff, watched Ed's plane land at the private pavilion at the Pellston Regional Airport near Petoskey. There were two people on board, the pilot and Ed. The plane could easily hold twelve passengers, but Ed was sitting all the way in the back row as if he were riding in a stretch limousine. Everyone involved felt that Ed deserved to travel home in style like a celebrity for his final flight.

When the plane stopped, the pilot came around and lowered the ladder. He helped Ed down and then escorted him and his walker into the pavilion. Ed was so grateful to the pilot for donating his time and his plane that he thanked him over and over before they parted ways.

"How was the flight?" Woody asked as he walked into view.

"It was just great!" Ed said. "But I think I need to rest for a minute before we leave."

He sat down on the seat of his walker to catch his breath after the long walk from the airplane. When he was ready, Woody gripped his suitcase and headed for the car.

"Are you hungry?" Woody asked.

"Yeah, I'm a little hungry."

"How about if we stop at Northwoods and grab a snack for lunch before I take you home?"

"That sounds nice."

While Woody made his way to the restaurant, Ed dialed Kay's cell phone.

"Hello?" Kay answered.

"It's Ed. I'm here. I just landed safely."

"Oh good. I am so glad you made it okay. How was the flight?"

"It was very good."

"Well, you take care of yourself, Ed, and make sure you get to the doctor for a checkup tomorrow, okay? Then you can get yourself settled back in."

"I will do that first thing. Oh, and Kay?"

"Yes?"

"If you are real quiet, you will hear the humming of my saw."

My phone rang as I was pulling into Glen's Market. I saw Mr. Ed's name on the caller ID, and I parked the car and quickly answered.

"Hi, Mr. Ed."

"I'm home, kid."

"You are? Yay!"

"Yep. Woody just dropped me off at the apartment. He took me to lunch, and we had such a wonderful talk. I tell you what. That Woody is such a nice man. It sure meant a lot to me that he took time out for me today."

"I am sure he enjoyed spending time with you too, Ed."

"He is going to pick me up in the morning to take me to my doctor's appointment."

"Oh good. I will be relieved when they give you another clean bill of health."

"Me too," Ed said hesitantly. "How are the kids doing?"

"They're doing good. Kaleigh moved to Florida, though, and I am really worried about her safety."

"You know what, kid? You just have to let her go and trust that the Lord will watch over her. She is an adult now, and that is all that you can do."

"You are right. Thank you for the advice. It always helps. How was the flight?"

Ed told me how much he had enjoyed the flight and how he couldn't believe that he was riding in a private plane with his own pilot. Then he said, "You know what, kid? I was doing a lot of thinking on my way home and I realized something. Petoskey and Evansville have been such an important part of my life. They both took me in like one of their own. I truly felt like they cared for me."

"They sure did, Mr. Ed."

"I will never forget that."

"And I know how much they appreciate the fact that you shared your life's work with them."

"Well, sharing is important to me, whether I am alive or dead. I also realized something else."

"What's that?"

"That Kalkaska is the only place that is truly my home."

"I feel the same way. It doesn't matter where you go in your life or how far you travel away, the place that raised you will always be home."

"Yep. I have also been thinking about where I want to be buried when I die."

"Don't talk like that, Mr. Ed."

"Well, I have to start thinking about these things at my age."

"I know, but you are so bullheaded, you will be around for a very long time." We both laughed.

"Yeah. I know I will be buried near my dad and grandmother in his plot, but you know what scares me?"

"What?"

"Not seeing someone that I recognize when I die. The Lord will be there, but will that be enough?"

"Mr. Ed, I know that your family will be there. And I especially know that your dad will be there."

"I hope so," Ed cried. "I sure do miss him sometimes." He became quiet for what seemed like infinity, and I knew he was in deep thought. I waited. Then he said, "Do you think my kids will forgive me someday?"

I was surprised by his question. This was the one topic that was difficult for him to talk about with me. It was actually the only topic he struggled with. Every time he had tried in the past, it was painful and he became emotional.

"Of course, Ed."

"I wasn't the dad that they needed or deserved. And I wasn't the husband that Jean needed or deserved either. I wish I could have been. That is my one and only regret. I wish I could have showed them how much I truly loved them. I felt it, but I didn't know how to express it."

"Ed, if they don't know that now, they will someday. I promise you."

When our conversation ended, I thought about all the times he had told me how proud he was of his kids. Actually, that was the very first thing he told me during our first talk. He explained how each one of his children had done something positive with their difficult lives. They had become pastors, missionaries, deacons, and professors. Most important to Ed, his children went on to be the parents to their children that he couldn't be for them. Ed knew how strong they were. He was so proud of all they had accomplished on their own. But he also knew that they had achieved all of this without him.

46

"But you must feel yourself that there is
something stifling about the idea of finality."

C.S. Lewis, *The Great Divorce*

Three days later was Christmas Eve. Ken and I were scurrying around trying to prepare for our first Christmas together. Ken's two sons, Justin and Josh, were coming to town, and my son, Ty, would be there. Kaleigh was the only one who would be missing. With our hectic schedules, we had little time to prepare, and we still had gifts to buy for the next morning.

All of a sudden, I stopped and looked at Ken and said, "We have to go."

"What?" Ken asked, puzzled.

"We have to go see Mr. Ed." Ken looked at me like he thought I was crazy. We had so much to do, and I knew that taking time out for anything else would almost be impossible. "I don't want Ed to be alone for Christmas Eve, and I just have this overwhelming feeling that we have to go today. Now."

"Okay. I know better than to argue when you get those feelings. Let's do it."

I picked up my cell phone and immediately called Ed. "Hello?" Ed answered.

"Hi, Mr. Ed. How are you?"

"Okay," he said. He sounded groggy.

"Are you okay?"

"Yes, I was just sleeping."

I was surprised that he was still sleeping at 10 A.M. "Would you like it if Ken and I came to visit you today?"

"Oh, yes!" Ed perked up.

"Would you like to get coffee or something to eat?"

"Yes. How about if we go to this new restaurant that I found in Petoskey? It's very, very nice, and they have this chicken that I found I could eat. Last time I ate there, I just devoured it."

"That sounds great. What is it called?"

"Oh, I can't remember the name."

"Where is it?" As Ed tried to explain the directions, I was curious about this new fine dining restaurant in Petoskey. Ken and I enjoyed fine dining, and we thought we had been to every nice restaurant in Petoskey. I couldn't imagine what it was. "How about if you just show us when we get there?" I said.

When we arrived at noon, I saw Ed waiting through the window, like he always did. As soon as he appeared at the door, I noticed his gaunt, pale look. This alarmed me. He seemed very tired and almost lethargic as he shuffled to the Suburban with his walker. Ken opened the door as Ed announced, "I think my stomach problems are back."

"Oh no, they are? I am so sorry to hear that," I said.

Ed then started directing us to this new fine dining restaurant. "Turn right and then turn left," he said. He continued on until we neared a stoplight. "Okay, turn left at the light and it's on the right-hand side." Ken and I eagerly looked in the direction that Ed was pointing, excited to see where he was taking us, and then he said, "There."

We looked, and to our surprise, we made a right-hand turn into a Wendy's parking lot. Ken and I glanced at each other and smiled. *Of course, Wendy's,* we both thought. It was the cutest thing I had seen in the longest time, and it reminded me of how simple Ed was. To him, Wendy's was fine dining.

When we entered, we escorted Ed to a table in a corner. He and I sat down while Ken went to order Ed's nuggets, French fries, and a Coke. I decided to order nuggets too.

"Mr. Ed, I have something for you." I showed him the previous week's edition of *The Leader and Kalkaskian* newspaper. "Look, they wrote an article about my new art studio. Can you believe that?"

"Home is Where the Art is," Ed said as he read the title aloud. "That is wonderful, kid!"

"I want to read part of it for you." I opened the newspaper and found a passage of one of my quotes and then began to read. "'I believed that if I could make a difference in the lives of my young students, maybe I could also make a difference in the lives of our community. Also, I have spent the last five years working with local artist Edgar Lantzer. He encouraged me to begin working towards my dreams as an artist, and he consistently told me that I could be successful as an artist, instructor, and gallery owner.'" I folded the paper back up and handed it to Ed. "I want you to have this."

"Wow," Ed said as he began to cry.

"Mr. Ed, I wanted you and every person who reads that article to know that it was you who inspired me. It was you who taught me to be strong, and it was you who taught me to believe. I don't think I can ever thank you enough. Thank you, Mr. Ed."

"You're welcome, kid. I have to thank you too for being my friend. You know more about me than anyone else. Through good and bad, you didn't run away from me, like so many others did throughout my life. I know that I sabotaged most of my relationships, and I know it wasn't always easy to be my friend. You showed me what a true friend is, and for that I will always be thankful."

Ed and I cried together as Ken made his way to the table with a tray full of nuggets.

Ed took his first bite and swallowed. "Well, I didn't find my soul mate in Evansville. I guess it wasn't meant for me."

"I'm sorry, Ed."

"That's okay. Maybe God is saving her for me in Heaven."

"I am sure you are right."

Ed picked up another nugget and devoured it. I was surprised, especially since he didn't look well, and I was thrilled when he ate every bit of his meal. This was the first time he had eaten all of his food in a long time.

Ken asked, "Mr. Ed, would you like me to get you some nuggets to take home?"

"Oh, that would be wonderful."

Ken took the tray of wrappers and cups to discard and got back into the long line. After Ken disappeared, Ed made eye contact with me. He had a look of seriousness, yet he seemed peaceful. Then he said, "You have changed."

"What do you mean I have changed?" I asked with alarm. Ed paused for a second or two.

"You are more responsible now. More mature." His amber eyes twinkled and he smiled.

"Thank you, Mr. Ed."

"And, I know that you are going to be okay now because you have Ken."

I couldn't believe what I was hearing. I hoped that Ed approved of Ken. I felt that Ken was God-sent. There was no other explanation for his entry into my children's lives and mine. But to have my dear friend say those words, those simple words, I was overjoyed.

Then I froze and stared at Ed. He stared back. There were no words, just silence and his message. I knew what he was saying. He didn't have to speak. *I can let you go now. It's time to release you to Ken.*

Just then, Ken returned to the table with a large Wendy's bag in his hand. "Here you go, Mr. Ed," he said.

"Thanks, Ken. I appreciate that."

I tried to regain my composure, and then pulled a present that I had wrapped for Ed out of my bag and handed it to him. "Here you go. Merry Christmas, Mr. Ed."

"What is this? You already gave me a gift." He carefully unfastened each piece of tape and then removed the wrapping to reveal a new DVD movie case. He looked at the cover and then at me. With his half laugh and half cry he said, "*Fiddler on the Roof!* Oh my, thank you so much." He wiped away another stray tear.

"Well, we have a date, don't we?"

"Yep. We do."

Before Ken and I took Ed home, I asked him if he needed anything from the store. This was something I asked him on every visit, but he always said no. I was surprised when he actually said yes. Not only did he say yes, but he also recited a long list of items that he wanted: ham, cheese, milk, bread, a twelve-pack of Coke, and so on. I was so excited that Ed wanted this food. It meant he wanted to eat and that he was going to be okay. Ken and Ed waited in the Suburban while I ran through Glen's Market to pick up everything on Ed's list. A short time later, I returned with a full bag of groceries.

We pulled around the back of Ed's apartment and right up to the door. Ken helped Ed out of the Suburban again and put his walker in place.

"Let us help you carry up your bag of groceries, okay?" Ken asked.

"Oh no, I got it. Just set it on the seat of my walker."

"Are you sure we can't take it up for you?"

"Nope. I got it," Ed insisted.

"What are you going to do tomorrow for Christmas?" I asked.

"There is going to be a Christmas meal in the apartment complex. I am going to go to that."

"You better be careful with the ladies. I know how much they fight over you there."

"I'll just focus on their pimples."

We laughed and I gave him a hug. "See you soon, Mr. Ed, and take care of yourself."

"See you soon, kid, and thank you for coming over. I really appreciate it."

"Anytime."

Ken and I got back into the Suburban. I didn't move as I watched Ed shuffle to the door. I couldn't take my eyes off him and I didn't know why. I tried to record every second in my memory: the way he moved, his few strands of gray hair, his blue pinstriped suit and white dress shirt. A large lump formed in my throat and I started to bawl.

Ken looked at me in alarm and asked, "What's wrong?"

"I don't know. I just have a bad feeling. Something is wrong."

I continued to sob, almost uncontrollably. This was not like me. It had been a long time since I had cried so hard, but I knew that he wasn't going to be okay. I just knew. Somehow, I knew that Ed and I had just had our last talk.

47

*"God whispers to us in our pleasures,
speaks to us in our conscience, but shouts in
our pains."*

C.S. Lewis, The Problem of Pain

Three days later I received a call from Paul.

"LaShelle, Ed is at the hospital. He wasn't feeling well, and his nurse came in and found that he had been throwing up. She called for help and they rushed him to Northern Michigan Hospital by ambulance."

My heart fell to the floor as I listened to Paul's words. "I knew something was wrong! Oh no, Paul. What is it?"

"They are going to take him in for exploratory surgery soon. Just stay put until we know more. I will call you as soon as I get word."

Paul sat by Ed's bedside as nurses and doctors prepared for the operation. Another board member, John Myers, arrived and sat in a chair across from Ed. Paul and John stared at their friend and sent silent prayers upwards. Ed appeared to be sleeping and his hands were placed next to him, palm-side down. It was so quiet in the room that they could hear Ed's every breath. Then suddenly, while he was still in a sleeping state, Ed's hands raised palm-side up into the air. It was as if he were praising the Lord. Ed's face glowed. *Was it the Father? Was it his father? Were they there?* they wondered.

Paul and John froze and their eyes widened as they watched. After about two minutes, Ed tenderly lowered his hands back down next to him, palm-side down. Just as his hands hit the bed, the nurse entered the room and said, "It's time to take him to the operating room." She unlocked Ed's hospital bed and pushed him out into the hall. Paul and John were feeling very emotional as they followed.

"Did you see that?" John asked.

"You mean the hand thing?" Paul said.

"Yes."

"Yes, I did too."

They looked at each other in amazement and turned just as the double doors closed behind Ed.

A short time later, my cell phone rang and I picked it up before the end of the first ring.

"What did they find?" I asked as my heart raced.

"It isn't good. His cancer is back," Paul said.

"What?"

"Not only that, it has spread all over his body. They closed him back up and said there is nothing they can do."

"Oh no, Paul!" I cried.

"I know," Paul cried back.

"How are we supposed to go on without him? This is just too much."

"I don't know. What we can do is be there for him now."

"How long does he have?"

"His doctor said one to four months. They decided to wait until all of the board members are here to tell Ed so he isn't alone when he hears. It's late and he needs to rest, so let's all meet here at 8:00 A.M."

"I will be there," I said.

Ken and I rushed to the hospital the next morning. I couldn't sleep at all the night before. All of my talks with Ed over the years flooded my memory and there was no turning off the stream. Paul and Woody were already there when we entered Ed's hospital room, and Lon walked in behind us. Ed was awake, and he had an oxygen mask over his nose. I immediately went to him. He grasped the front of the mask and pulled it away from his face.

"Did you talk to the doctor yet?" he asked. I noticed the fear in his eyes. I wished that I could take this away. I would have done anything to change the news the doctor was going to reveal.

"No, Mr. Ed. He will be in soon."

I tried to contain my emotion, but it was not an easy task. A few minutes later, John and Dale entered. All of Ed's board members surrounded him. We were not only his board members, though. We were also his friends and most important, his family. Then, I spotted the white coat and ink pens protruding out of the doctor's front pocket as he walked into the room with a clipboard in his hand.

"Hi, Ed. How are you feeling today?" he said.

Ed pulled the mask away from his face again and answered, "I'm doing okay."

"Well, Ed, I have some news for you."

"Okay," Ed said.

"You know how you had stomach cancer before?" Ed nodded. "Well, Ed, it's back. And this time there is nothing we can do." I watched as Ed's so-familiar amber eyes widened. "Do you understand what I am saying?" the doctor asked.

"Yes."

Ed took a deep breath, and I saw a look of acceptance expand across his face. When the doctor left, I went back to Ed's side and rubbed his arm.

"Ed, I love you."

Our eyes connected one last time, and then with a tear in the corner of his eye, he looked at Ken sitting in a nearby chair. He then looked back at me and whispered, "I love you too, kid."

The doctor told the board that we would need to call in hospice. He explained that there was a facility right in Petoskey, and before we left for the day, we should go look at it and see if there were any available rooms. The My Father's Love board members drove to the hospice house called Hiland Cottage.

When we entered the colonial yellow and brick building, we felt warmth all around. The facility was beautiful, and each patient had a private room. After the tour and talking to the staff, we concluded that this was the perfect place for Ed. We even decided that there was enough space to put one of his panels in the room with him. They told us that they had one available room and that they would hold it for Ed.

A few hours later, Ken and I walked back into Ed's hospital room. He wasn't there. In a panic, I darted to the nurses station.

"Where is Mr. Lantzer?" I asked.

"They moved him to another room," said the nurse on duty.

She scribbled down the room number and handed it to me. As we entered, I saw Lon leaning over Ed, crying. Lon had been Ed's friend for so many years, the longest of any of us. They had a bond that was strong, and the one thing Ed knew was that Lon would protect him, no matter what. I heard Lon say, "I love you, bud." There was no response. I was shocked when I realized that Ed was unconscious and his breathing seemed labored. I looked at Lon with fright. Lon then moved away to give me time alone with Ed.

I couldn't believe the change in Ed in just a few hours. When I had talked to him earlier, he had been awake and alert. Now the only thing I saw was death. I rubbed his arm again as I whimpered, "Ed, I'm here. Please don't forget how much I love you. Okay?"

Hours passed as Lon, Ken, and I sat by Ed's side watching every breath. I stared at Ed's pronounced nose and the pockets embedded in his face as his cheeks sunk in and out. I covered his big toe, which peeked out from under his blanket. I couldn't imagine how that toe might never move again. I wanted to ingrain him into my memory so that I would never forget him. I then looked at Ed's hands, those strong hands. I noticed every scar on his fingers that he had earned and wore like a badge of honor. Those two hands were his most precious tools. God had formed them perfectly so that Ed could create His story of life. Now, I was watching them die.

Then I heard Ken whisper in my ear. "Honey, it is time to go. They are going to kick us out of here in a minute."

"But I can't leave him."

The doctors said that Ed had one to four months, but I knew better, just like I had known when I drove away after our last talk a few days before. I stood up and held Ed's left hand.

"I will never forget you, my friend, my unlikely friend." I patted it one last time and my lips trembled as I said, "Goodbye, Mr. Ed."

At midnight, I placed my cell phone next to the bed and slid under the covers. I observed the phone for a moment knowing that when I woke, there would be a voicemail. I put my hands together and closed my eyes. "Father, please wrap your loving arms around Mr. Ed and make his transition smooth as he comes to you. And please, Father, let him hear the words 'Well done.'"

48

"I have come home at last! This is my real country! I belong here. This is the land I have been looking for all my life."

C.S. Lewis, The Last Battle, Chronicles of Narnia

The next morning I woke to the sun streaming in through the bedroom window. This was rare on a December morning in Northern Michigan. I bolted straight up and held my breath. Then I looked at my cell phone. It was still sitting near the bed. *I didn't hear it ring. Maybe I was wrong. Please let me be wrong!* I reached over and grasped it tightly between my fingers and stared at the button. I breathed in deep again and then I pushed it. There, on my screen, were the words, "Paul Hresko missed call and voicemail." I quickly went into my voicemail to find the message.

"LaShelle, it's Paul. Ed passed away this morning around 3:00 A.M. I talked to his nurse and she said that he passed very peacefully. This is so tough. I can't believe he is gone. Give me a call when you get this."

"No!" I screamed as what felt like Niagara Falls rushed down my face. I knew, but it was still unreal. I fell backwards onto the mattress and cried and cried and cried. I just could not imagine that I would never see Ed alive again. No more visits and no more talks. Just memories would be left. This loss felt like it was more than I could bear.

Then I realized that I was being selfish. Ed was with God. After all of the times he had told me that he was ready to go fishing, ready to be with the Father, he was finally there. I wiped my flannel sleeve across my face and calmed myself down. I set the phone down and walked into the dining room. I stood in front of the bay window. White snow sparkled like diamonds on the trees as far as the eye could see. I scanned from left to right, looking at how deep blue the water appeared on Grand Traverse Bay that morning. Then I looked towards the sky, almost feeling Ed all around. I wondered what he was doing now. Was he singing "How Great Thou Art"? Was he talking shop with God? *I bet he's starting his last panel,* I thought. I smiled as I imagined what his version of The Resurrection would look like.

"I am sure it will be beautiful, Mr. Ed. I can't wait to see it," I said.

A sense of contentment swept through me. It was not the feeling I was expecting. I knew that he was finally going to be okay. It was Ed's year, his perfect year. At seventy-seven years old, he had gotten to meet the Lord face to face for the first time. I could envision him walking towards the Lord as He opened up His arms to welcome Ed with a tender embrace. Now *that* is double perfection.

As I turned back towards the bedroom, I imagined the sound of Ed's saw humming in my head. I picked up my cell phone and started dialing Paul's number.

There were three memorial services planned for Ed: one in his hometown of Kalkaska, a "Celebration of Life" in Petoskey, and one titled "The Last Panel" in Evansville. In the end, Ed had three communities to call home. The man who had walked away from his life to answer his call was no longer homeless.

The Christmas tree lights were still blinking in the corner of the dining room as I stared at Ed's white dress shirt on the chair next to me. I rubbed the two diamond pieces of wood in my hand and thought about how Ed and his wood pieces had changed my life. He had taught me so many things during our talks, but most important, he showed me the path to my purpose. Ed taught me to have faith and trust in God. "Don't worry about it, the Father will take care of it," he would say. When I learned to do that, I found a sense of peace and contentment that I had been looking for my entire life. With trust and faith in the Lord and peace and contentment on my side, I had a new perspective regarding my life and the world around me. These new perspectives led me to my purpose.

God brought Ed into my life to help me recognize that I am on this Earth for a reason. I am here to do something He planned for me in advance. I am here to use my unique gifts, the unique gifts that each one of us has been given, to change the world, even if it is for only one person at a time.

Ed believed that this was the key to life and so do I. Ed told me that God doesn't promise that we will not have trials and tribulations, but He does promise that He will hold our hand and never leave our side. "Don't forget kid, pain is our teacher. You need it to feel alive, you need it to pay attention, and you need it to know good," Ed would say. I have felt so much pain during my lifetime and I still do. Thanks to Ed, I finally know what it means.

Ed never claimed to be perfect. He knew he was a sinner. He knew he made terrible mistakes. But he also knew that God loved him anyway, flaws and all. If you look back in history, you can see that God has often selected a misfit to be his soldier. He selected Ed, 6-22-34, to be his witness. Ed was lucky. He was reviled, abandoned, mistreated, and misunderstood, but he had a gift that few of us have: faith. Because of this, he knew what his purpose was. We all get that knock on our door that signals our purpose, but we don't always hear it. We often ask, "What is my life about? Why am I here? Do I have a purpose?" I now know what my purpose is. Do you?

Our purpose on Earth is to love: to love our family, to love our friends, to love our co-workers, and to love our neighbors. After all, the only thing we leave this Earth with is love. We are also here to love the homeless man under the cardboard box whom we repeatedly pass by.

Thinking about this reminded me of a question that Paul once asked: "Have you ever thought about what marvelous things that man might have done in the world?" After meeting Ed, I will never look at people the same way again. Imagine that the person who was thrown off his bike, spit on, the target of stones, homeless, would inspire and change so many lives through the work that God chose for him! Wouldn't it be wonderful if everyone had the courage and the stamina to do the work that God has set for him or her? Mr. Ed was a man who lived, he was a man who dreamed, and most important, he was a man who LOVED!

During one of our heartfelt conversations, Mr. Ed told me that when someone you love and admire dies, when you speak their name out loud, the person will continue to live, not as a mortal, but within the heart of the person saying the name. So if you happen by me at some point and you hear me speak Mr. Ed's name out loud, you will know that it's because he will never be forgotten in my life and in my heart. So, would everyone who has grown to love and admire Mr. Edgar Frederick Lantzer, please join me in speaking his name out loud so he will live in all of our hearts and not be forgotten. MR. EDGAR FREDERICK LANTZER, 6-22-34!

On the day before the funeral, I picked Ed's perfectly pressed white dress shirt up off my chair and carefully covered it in plastic as I prepared to take it to the funeral home. I then placed his two wood pieces in my front pocket. I would carry them with me throughout my days as a reminder of my purpose and of God's unconditional love.

I thought about all of the people on Ed's relay team that God had sent to him at just the right time. I was one of them. As I walked out the door, I recalled something that Ed had told me one day: "No matter who you are or what you have done, you are worthy and you are loved. Most importantly, don't forget the joy, kid!"

"I won't, Mr. Ed."

I smiled as I thought about his repeated request: "Find a synonym for your name. How do you want to be remembered and how do you want to sign your name?" I now knew the answer. I want to be remembered as one of God's soldiers, just like Ed. And I want to be remembered as Ed's friend, his unlikely friend.

Ed often wondered if it was all worth it to walk away from his life. He wondered if he had done enough. Through his mural, had he shown enough love? In the end, he knew that he did, and he knew that he would not have changed a thing. I believe that Ed made both of his fathers proud—his biological father and his Heavenly Father. That was all he needed.

I opened the door and headed to my car. I cradled Ed's shirt like a newborn infant and carefully placed it on a hook in my backseat. As I slid into the driver's seat, I could feel the wood pieces in my pocket pinch me. I looked upward. "I love you too!" I said.

Those two little pieces of wood changed my life. I hope they will change yours too.

Thank you, Mr. Ed. Well done, good and faithful servant! Well done!

The Evansville group.

Grand opening night dinner.

TV interview in Evansville.

At last Ed smiles!

(Clockwise from back left) Paul, Lon, LaShelle, Rich the
roadie, Ed.

(Clockwise from back left) Terry Haynie, Steve Sander, Kay
Sander, Ed.

Ed on his way to the cookie store.

Yummy!

Ed with his Hebrew/Latin bible.

Ed giving a tour.

6-22-34 in Ed's bible.

Paul, Ed, and Rich with matching shirts.

Ed at the Evansville gallery.

Ed Lantzer Day!

Ed and his friend Nathan.

Ed and Nathan at the gallery.

Nathan giving Ed a wooden cross.

Nathan's gift to Ed.

Ed's gifts to Nathan.

Ed and Nathan.

At the mall at Christmas.

Ed with Nathan and his grandfather.

Ed and Nathan say goodbye.

Ed's final plane ride home.

Ed with Nathan's grandparents, Linda and Terry Yunker.

Ed sitting in the window.

LaShelle and Ken.

Ed and LaShelle.

Ken helps Ed into the Suburban.

Ed's last photo.

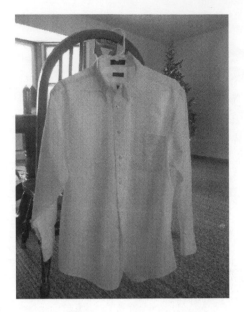

The last shirt Ed would ever wear.

Well done, good and faithful servant.

Epilogue

Since Ed's death, his relay team has continued to grow. Many people have worked hard to ensure that his panels have the opportunity to continue their job.

Kay and Steve Sander and the Evansville group graciously kept the My Father's Love exhibit open until the end of spring 2010. Instead of a two-month exhibit, it turned into eight months.

When the panels returned to Petoskey, they were reinstalled in the Petoskey gallery while the My Father's Love board members found their next location. After several months passed and no location was found, the panels went into storage.

Finally, in 2012, Deb Swanson from Ed's schoolhouse days made contact with the board to see if it was possible to bring the panels to Marquette, Michigan. After Deb was married she moved to Marquette. She felt called to bring the panels to her town for an exhibit, but she had no idea how she would finance the project. She remembered how Ed always said, "Don't worry about it; the Father will take care of it." This eased her mind and with faith, she put together a team of people to help her. Two members of the team were Lance and Diane Gauthier.

The exhibit opened in September of 2012. After I went to the grand opening, I met Diane and Lance and found out that the role they played in bringing the panels to Marquette was actually set up by Ed years ago. This is how the story goes.

In 2006, while Ed was working in the warehouse (this is when my students and I were working with Ed), he called Deb Swanson out of the blue and said that he needed her to come to Kalkaska to pick him up. Deb was surprised because this was unlike Ed. He had never done that before and he hated to leave his panels. She asked, "Ed, are you sure?" He said, "Yes, come and get me."

It was a five-hour drive. Deb got Ed to Marquette and put him up in a hotel. Shortly after Ed arrived, he was invited to a meeting to design a hospice room. He went to the event and he had some of his tabletops and hope chests with him, so he set them next to where he was sitting.

Diane happened to be at the same meeting. She went up to talk to Ed and was amazed by his artwork. She had an instant connection with him, which was unusual for her. She said that she wanted her husband, Lance, to meet Ed because he was a carpenter. She asked Ed to go to dinner with them the next night and Ed agreed.

Before she left, Ed gave her one of his tabletops. She refused it, but he insisted. He had given one of his masterpieces to a complete stranger and this was something that Ed did not do unless that person was special. On her way home, she began bawling uncontrollably, again very much out of character. The next night, they picked Ed up at his hotel and took him to dinner. They spent five hours talking about every topic imaginable. They all felt a real connection. They offered Ed the use of their cabin on a river for a couple of days and he accepted. Diane and Lance couldn't understand this connection with Ed, but felt so strongly that it was for an important reason. The next day, they called Ed at the hotel and he was gone.

When he returned to the hotel, he called Deb and said, "Okay, I am ready to go back home now." Deb said, "Ed, you just got here." He said, "I know, but I need to go home now." He was insistent, so Deb picked him up and took him the five hours back home. On the way, he talked about this couple he had just met and their deep conversation, how they took him to a beautiful place for dinner and that they spoke for hours. He then looked at Deb and said, "This conversation was meant to be." At the time, Deb thought that Ed meant he was there to guide them personally in some way. It was apparent that he was very happy to meet them. He was emotional describing them to Deb. Ed also mentioned to Deb during the conversation that Diane's career was in insurance in a little nearby town.

In the meantime, Diane and Lance were very sad that Ed was gone. They had hoped they would have the opportunity to talk to him again and get to know more about him. The only thing they knew was that he lived in a warehouse in Kalkaska. Over six years, they talked about trying to find him, but never did. They never forgot him, though.

Three years after Ed's death, Deb was making the arrangements to have the panels tour Marquette. She needed to get insurance on them while they were there and she didn't know who to get it from. One day, while she was driving, she said out loud, "Okay, Ed, help me out here." She then had a flash memory of the conversation six years earlier when Ed mentioned the couple and that Diane was in insurance. Deb only had a first name and a town where Diane lived. She googled what she had and found an insurance company with a person with the name Diane. She emailed her.

When Diane saw the email and that it regarded Ed, she started crying. She thought she had finally found him and that they would finally reconnect with him. She was heartbroken when she found out that Ed had passed. Diane agreed to meet Deb at a local restaurant in Marquette to talk about insuring the panels. Deb patiently waited in a booth for Diane to walk through the door. Since Deb had never met Diane before, the only way she would know her is from her picture on her insurance company Web site.

When Diane entered, Deb waved her over. She wasn't sure how to begin to explain the panels; they are impossible to explain to someone. She had brought two little pieces of wood with her. All she knew was that Ed had met Diane. Ed had talked about meeting them, but he never mentioned giving Diane a table, so as far as Deb knew, she had no knowledge of Ed's marquetry. Not knowing how to ask a stranger how to insure something priceless—something they have never seen or known about—Deb pushed the two tiny pieces of wood across the table to Diane and said, "I would like to start with these." Diane took one look at the wood and said, "I have some of those." Deb was shocked. Diane and Lance had heard about "the panels" from Ed, but they had never seen a picture of them or knew of their majesty. Diane said, "I have one of his tables." Deb almost fell on the floor and her heart practically stopped. Right then and there she knew this was in God's plan.

Diane and Lance ended up financing the entire exhibit. They financially supported Ed's panels on blind faith. They had no idea of their massiveness until they were loaded off the truck in Marquette. When the panels arrived at the gallery, Deb saw for the first time the overwhelming emotional impact meeting Ed had had on Diane. She could barely catch her breath as she cried uncontrollably, just like she had when she first met Ed six years before. It was as if Ed knew that he needed to go to Marquette to meet this couple. Once he met them, he knew his panels would be okay and he could go home. People from as far as Russia came to see Ed's panels while they were in Marquette. Many people came dozens of times and brought others. In the end, over three thousand people were touched by Ed's work.

When the panels returned from Marquette, they went into storage again until Todd and Brad Reed of Ludington, Michigan set up an exhibit in their hometown. Todd and Brad own a photography studio and are both well-known photographers and have authored many books on their work. When they heard about the panels they knew that they had to bring them to Ludington. This is how Brad Reed described their involvement before the panels traveled to Ludington:

The way Team Reed at Todd and Brad Reed Photography got involved is that a My Father's Love Foundation contact saw our 365 eyeball mosaic down at ArtPrize in 2011 and thought it would be a great fit to team up together with us somehow for the ArtPrize competition in Grand Rapids, Michigan. It is all still in the works, but we are hoping to join forces with My Father's Love for Artprize in 2014. The day Paul Hresko called me in the fall of 2012, I was immediately drawn in and felt an overwhelming calling to get involved and help tell Ed's story and show off his work. I have not even personally seen any of Ed's pieces with my own eyes, just photographs and videos of them, but for some unknown powerful reason, I know I am supposed to be helping to promote Ed's message of love and understanding for all human kind, no matter their appearance, social status, IQ, race, gender, or age. I strongly believe that Ed's work can help bring our local communities even closer together and have a unified voice of love and acceptance for all.

The panels spent the summer of 2013 in Ludington. This was the first time that they were split up among three locations: the Ludington Area Center for the Arts, the

Ludington Library, and Todd and Brad Reed's studio. The panels had an emotional impact on the town of Ludington and many volunteers came off the streets to help unload and load the exhibit, just like years before in Petoskey. The panels once again returned home in September 2013 and are in storage again as I write this. The My Father's Love Foundation's goal is to find a permanent home for Ed's panels, his children. Ed left them to us to care for, and each board member will spend the rest of his or her life doing just that. My hope is that through this book, Ed's children will never be homeless again.

My life has also changed since Ed's death. My brother, Larry, was right when he continuously told me that he had met my future husband. I married Ken a year after Larry introduced him to me. My brother was ordained and he performed our ceremony. On that day, there was only one person missing: Ed. But I knew he was with me. Ken and I decided to design our wedding rings in remembrance of Ed. Both of our rings have Ed's diamond shape engraved around the bands.

My children are both doing very well. I am writing this on Ty's eighteenth birthday. He has grown to be an amazing musician and man. His dream is to pursue music as his career.

My daughter, Kaleigh, has never been better. After fighting for her life time and time again, she has won her bipolar battle. We finally recognized that she had been overmedicated for years. When we made this discovery, she gained control of her emotions and her life. Kaleigh is now an amazing mother. Her daughter, Ellianna Renee, is the most beautiful gift God has ever given her. When she decided on a name during her pregnancy, she wanted it to have meaning. She decided to give her my middle name, which was so emotional for me. Then one day she told me that she was thinking of selecting Ellianna for her first name. I told her that according to Ed, "El" is the female name for God. That sealed the deal. Kaleigh spent years praying and pleading with God to help her, to take away her pain, to give her life. With Ellianna, she finally found life.

I remember her desperately asking me many times throughout her life when she was so sick, "Why hasn't God answered my prayers?" I felt so helpless and I wished that I had the perfect answer, but none seemed to help. The other day, she sent me an email that said, "You won't believe it, but I researched Ellianna's name to see what it means, and this is what I found. Her name means 'My God has answered me.'" I cried and looked above. "Thank you, Father! Thank you!!!" Yes, God answers our prayers, and sometimes He does it in a way that we don't even realize it's happened.

It has been marvelous to witness the lives that have been touched and changed by the panels since Ed's death, including my own. It has also been miraculous to watch how God has continued to add to Ed's relay team so that his children can do their work. One day Ed told me that he hoped his panels would be used for at least five hundred years. I believe they will, and I can see that baton being handed off for generations to come.

30260282R00238

Made in the USA
Lexington, KY
25 February 2014